THE JEWISH ELEMENT
IN FRENCH LITERATURE

THE JEWISH ELEMENT
IN FRENCH LITERATURE

Charles C. Lehrmann

Translated from the French
by *George Klin*

Rutherford • Madison • Teaneck
Fairleigh Dickinson University Press

Library of Congress Catalogue Card Number: 75-120998

Associated University Presses, Inc.
Cranbury, New Jersey 08512

To the memory of my brilliant brother
Naftali-Natalio,
victim of a tortured world

ISBN: 0-8386-7725-8
Printed in the United States of America

Contents

Foreword

What has always struck me the most in the history of the Jews since the Middle Ages is the absurdity and the implausibility of the legends which so many baseless hatreds have used to persecute them. In the last 800 years everything has changed in Western civilization. Barbaric and ignorant periods have been succeeded by cultured and civilized periods. The anti-Jewish legend has also changed, without, however, getting closer to the truth. It can even be said that with the progress of intellectual culture its extravagance and absurdity have increased instead of diminishing.

This book brings another proof of this incredible paradox. It studies the Jew as he was seen by popular literature in the Middle Ages, and as he was seen either by the literature of the nineteenth century or by the first anti-Semitic movements of the end of the last century, from which the modern persecutions are the outgrowth. Those who have some knowledge of the Jewish *milieux* of Europe and America will be fully convinced that the legends on which present-day anti-Semitism feeds are even more absurd and unreal than those that attempted to justify medieval anti-Semitism. Some have gone as far as to accuse the Jews of being a formidable secret establishment that tries to dominate the world through the power of gold and that unleashed the two world wars to achieve its end. Merely that. It is impossible to surpass this fantastic exploitation of human credulity.

This monstrous practice seems inexplicable to all those, and they are many, who believe that the nineteenth century was a critical and rationalistic time, enlightened and free of the terrors and the injustices of the past. It was nothing of the kind. The terrors have changed, and with them the superstitions. But within its own sphere of superstitions the nineteenth century was as much the victim of its imagination, its cowardliness, and its cruelty as the Middle Ages. It even falsified the universe more than the preceding periods by combining its imaginary fears with a certain number of whimsical hopes, inspired by its vanity and its success. The result was a romantic century in which everything was false, chimerical, at odds with reality: literature, philosophy, history, politics.

This visionary era has been wasting its strength since the French Revolution in bloody, cruel, atrocious struggles against unreal dangers, sinister shadows created by hatred and fear. Anti-Semitism is one of those numerous struggles that are exhausting our times. Who can count the number of innocent victims of this fight against shadows created during the last fifty years? And the violence of the struggle increases instead of abating—a seeming paradox, but an explicable one because in this struggle man is tackling shadows created by a delirious imagination.

The increasingly threatening difficulties with which the Western world has been confronted during the last fifty years—all the catastrophes that have befallen it, that are befalling it, and that will befall it—are, after all, the revenge of the profound and eternal realities of life against the unbridled Romanticism of the nineteenth century, which attempted to submerge them under a deluge of feverish visions. In the long run, a civilization cannot navigate in a great fog of romantic hallucinations like the one through which the nineteenth century set sail, without foundering on shoals and sandbanks. However,

when the human mind, carried away by the delirium of
its imagination, and made a victim of pride and fear,
clashes with reality, it is always seized by a sudden
frenzy and sinks even further into its madness. This is
its supreme reaction before surrendering and admitting
defeat in its struggle between the fantasies of its mind
and the eternal realities of life.

For thirty years we have been the spectators and the
victims of this terrible phenomenon of life that is ravag-
ing the whole world. But ultimately the eternal realities
will overcome the errors of previous generations in the
life of the Western world. The world is in process of
cleansing itself from the Romanticism of the nineteenth
century, that incoherent, contradictory combination, delirious with hatreds and whimsical attachments, unfair
resentments and Utopian hopes. A more accurate vision
of life would also be a fairer and more humane vision.
The Jews who have suffered so greatly from all these
hate-filled fantasies will one day benefit from the return
to sanity that is stirring in the Western mind. Investiga-
tions such as those in this book will help to hasten this
purification of the imagination and feelings which events
are inflicting upon us with the merciless punishment of
truth and justice. They prove by a case as characteristic
as France to what extent these alleged candidates for
world domination through force and gold have contributed to the enrichment of the national cultures of the
West with precious and original elements in the whole
spiritual life of the modern world. This is reality. The
rest is romantic delusion.

Geneva 1941   Guglielmo Ferrero

Introduction to the First American Edition

The question of the Jewish contribution to French literature deserves to be studied on the same basis as the influence of Italian, Spanish, English, and German cultural elements, but it is more difficult to determine and circumscribe. In this instance, the inspiration does not come from without, but from the heart of France, so that French culture and Jewish culture often meet in the same man and blend almost inseparably.

If we look over the long history of French literature, we discover throughout subjects inspired by Jewish life, Jewish thought, and Jewish personalities.

On the one hand, the influence is passive: the mere presence of Jewish communities in France creates problems that find an echo in literary works, problems that change with the evolution of history. In the Middle Ages they assume a religious aspect; in modern times they take on a social, financial, political and racial character. In the controversy surrounding the Jewish question, celebrated writers commit their personalities and their genius —witness such names as Montesquieu, Voltaire, Saint-Simon, Zola, Anatole France, Romain Rolland, Georges Duhamel, Sartre.

In addition to this passive role, the Jewish element has exercised an active influence on French letters. First, indirectly: the ancient Jewish writings, especially the Bible, acted on French writers through the medium of the Christian religion and culture, and sometimes inspired their works. This is the case with a Pascal, a Bossuet, a Racine, a Chateaubriand, a Lamartine, a Victor Hugo, and a Claudel.

More directly, the contact of Judaism and French literature was brought about by Jewish writers or writers of Jewish origin—first, by the rabbis of the Middle Ages who played a remarkable role as intermediaries between the Oriental cultural world and the West, then by contemporary poets and writers such as Edmond Fleg, Gustave Kahn, André Spire, Albert Cohen, Emmanuel Eydoux, Roger Ikor, André Schwarzbart, and so on.

In this category of writers, we find those whom one of them has called the "unconscious Jews." They hardly remember their origins; they feel almost entirely, exclusively French, such as, for instance, Maurois, Benda, Bernstein, Tristan Bernard; they are more than half integrated (often even biologically, like Montaigne and Proust), and yet their works, their ideas, their methods of treating psychological, social, philosophical, or religious questions reveal in them echoes of the thinking of their ancestors.

What is the origin of this ineradicable mark that we find even among Jews farthest removed from their ancestral tradition? This leads us to raise the much-discussed question of the Jewish spirit. While it is relatively easy to take an inventory of Jewish activities in the modern world, it is less easy to define what has been called "the Jewish spirit." It is possible to quote with Roback[1] figures on the percentage of Jews who have won the Nobel prize, and note that they constitute a ratio of 11 to 12%.[2] It is possible simply to give, like J. Jacobs,[3] a list of eminent Jews who for one hundred years (1785-

---

1. A. A. Roback, *Jewish Influence in Modern Thought* (Cambridge, Mass., 1929).
2. These statistics do not take into consideration the situation after the Second World War.
3. J. Jacobs, *Jewish Contributions to Civilization* (Philadelphia, 1919).

1885) have contributed to every aspect of human activity and include 385 names like Disraeli, Heine, Lassalle, Mendelssohn-Bartholdy, and Meyerbeer. This enumeration can be extended into the present, where we meet men such as Einstein and Oppenheimer, Freud and Husserl, Ehrlich and Metchnikof, Brandes and Gundolf, and a great number of musical performers.[4] But what is the common characteristic of these men who have thought and worked as Englishmen, as Frenchmen, as Germans, as Russians?[5]

The problem becomes even more complex when we consider the diversity of Jewish activities. In philosophy we encounter the realism of Bergson and of Husserl side by side with the idealism of Spinoza and Léon Brunschwicg, the duality of the theories of Lévy-Bruhl and Meyerson on the logical structure of the mind, and all the forms of thought, from rational deduction to mystical intuition. Thus, for some, the Jewish genius is characterized by logic and intellectual honesty, qualities which the German Nietzsche values in them: "Wherever the Jews have had influence, they have taught to distinguish with greater subtlety, to draw conclusions more rigorously, to write with more finesse and clarity; their mission has always been to bring reason to nations."[6] Sartre also, without considering the Jews more intelligent than the Christians, attributes to them a proclivity for "pure intelligence." The Frenchman Brunetière, on the other hand, singles out irrational mysticism as the salient trait of the Jewish genius, if we are to judge from this passage: "If we were to suppose that the sources of Hebrew inspiration had dried up, the Germans would not have

4. The great contemporary violinists, whether living in the U. S. or in Russia, are practically all Jewish, if we are to judge by those who are known in the West.

5. At the presentation of the Nobel Prize in 1906–1907, for instance, Ehrlich, Lippmann, Michelson, and Metchnikof were respectively the German, Franco-Luxemburgian, American, and Russian prize winners.

6. *Gai savoir,* p. 348.

Luther, nor the English *Paradise Lost,* nor the French Bossuet, Pascal, Hugo, and the poets of the obscure and the inaccessible."[7] (Let us note in passing that in the land of romanticism it is their rational side that is noticed in the Jews, and in the land of reason it is their irrational aspect; a phenomenon that suggests the "double identity" by which Emile Touati defines the dialectical character of Jewish history.)

Others would contest all trace of unity in the Jewish spirit, since Jewish history presents breaks that seem to interrupt its continuity, and since Judaism manifests itself successively under totally different aspects: the Judaism of Moses is different from that of the Judges, and the latter has nothing in common with the Judaism of the Prophets, just as Maimonides bears no resemblance to Hassidism. But have not other nations produced similar phenomena? Have they not known a classicism and a romanticism, a Stendhal and a Hugo, a Newman and a Huxley? Yet the existence of a French or English spirit has never been questioned. Thus, one can assume, as Julien Benda does in his contributions to twentieth-century French literature, that a Montaigne summarizes the rational pole of Judaism, while a Proust, by his psychoanalytical style, and a Bergson, by his idealistic drive, are an echo of the nonrealism that led from the Prophets of Israel to the mystical outpourings of Hassidism. For, to quote Proust, "the unifying element is not the community of opinions, but the consanguinity of the spirit."

The cultural history of a nation, in spite of its contradictory manifestations, forms a unified whole, and that is similarly the case with Judaism, whose various aspects are only the organic branches of the same trunk; and although present-day Israel is not the Israel of two

---

7. *Nouveaux essais sur la littérature contemporaine* (Paris, 1897), p. 232.

or three thousand years ago, it is as naturally related to it as the Catholic Church of today to the Church of Innocent III. The unity resides in the consciousness of the unity of person that links the old man to his childhood, in spite of the changes that have occurred in his physical and mental life. The transformation has taken place slowly and gradually by a natural evolution, a biological growth, where the new forms are conditioned by the preceding states. The past relives in the present and is renewed in the "real duration" that Bergson described. Thus, in spite of statements to the contrary, there has never been a break in the continuity of Judaism, even though it has taken various forms through the ages.

It has also been objected that Israel's case is not the same as that of other nations: these have grown under normal circumstances, the French genius being the product of the French soil, the English genius having developed in England, while the Jews, long deprived of a homeland and scattered in various national civilizations, could not form a clearly determined spiritual community. "They do not have the same country, they have no history!" exclaims Sartre. They have only an "identity of situation": what is called the Jewish character is only a collection of atavistic reminiscences acquired in similar social conditions. The fact remains that the "personality" of Israel continued to exist even outside of its historical homeland, having been formed during fifteen centuries of national existence; the two thousand years of dispersion that followed have not succeeded in destroying its fundamental traits. It is just as it is in a family, where brothers and sisters brought up on the same paternal principles retain a similar manner of thinking and seeing even though they may subsequently be dispersed and be confronted with different ways of life. The years of separation do not erase the spiritual kinship acquired at home.

Thus we see that the absence of the three classical unities, action, time, and place, in the life of Israel, does not exclude the existence of a homogeneous spiritual unity, manifesting itself in various climes and in various fields of activity. But is there no concrete formula to define the spiritual or biological community of Israel?

The sociologist Ruppin[8] points out that the specific characteristic of Jews of all languages is "quick thinking." It is especially important for success in economic life and in commerce, but it has equal value in other fields: scientific research, discovery, and even politics.

But this author adds that the quick-wittedness of the Jews is not at all a peculiarity of the race, but is simply because of their age, two thousand years greater than that of modern nations. "The mental qualities that are considered at the present time particularly Jewish, rapidity of thought, logical thinking, repression of instincts, can become those of other people; it merely means that the Jews have been precursors in the common development."

Defining the Jewish spirit as "quick wit" corresponds to the conception that attributes to the Jews the role of "leavening," of a dynamic force in Western civilization. But rapidity and agility of mind, acquired, according to Ruppin, in the course of thousands of years, do not explain completely the dynamism that already characterized Israel in its youth. Biblical prophetism, culminating in Messianism, testifies to that. We believe rather that this "ferment" that constitutes the Jewish contribution in the most diverse fields of modern civilization is, in the last analysis, the product of a certain temperament, of a disposition, acquired at the beginning of time, developed and emphasized under ways of life simultaneously varied and identical, of the post-Biblical existence of the Jews. In ancient times, this disposition gave

8. *Les Juifs dans le monde moderne* (Paris, 1934).

birth to the Messianic doctrine of the Prophets; transposed to scientific fields, it gave rise to a great many
pioneering theories; on the moral plane, these acquired
and inherited qualities led the Jews to become champions
of justice and reason, according to Sartre "the best part
of the message that they deliver to us and the true sign
of their greatness."[9] In this common disposition, and not
in a diabolic plot, lies the invisible link among Jews, who
think, feel, and act in all languages and on all planes of
human activity.

These summary thoughts on the distinctive traits of
the Jewish genius in general apply also to the character
of the Jewish element within the French framework. Is
this a foreign element in French literature because it
came from the outside? But what has not, at one time
or another, come from the outside? The Comtesse de
Noailles said that France grows in the realm of the mind
through the devotion of those who choose and serve her.
More than any nation, France has been able to gather
the heterogeneous elements it has found on its path, to
feed on all cultures, and to assimilate all influences. Far
from rejecting what was not the product of its own historical origins, it has gladly accepted and taken as its
own whatever it found in other nations that conformed
to its own genius.

Throughout its history French literature has experienced several periods of foreign influence. Each of these
phases has enriched her by making her conscious of a
new aspect of her own individuality. Thus, to the Italian
influence she owes that aesthetic harmony, that equilibrium of power that was to be so well understood by a
people whose genius consists in great part of measure,
equilibrium, and harmony. This contact, with its introduction of the Hellenic heritage, led to the French Renais-

---

9. J. P. Sartre, *Reflexions sur la question juive* (Paris, 1947).

sance and to Classicism. Then came a period of Spanish influence that gave French writers a liking for chivalrous adventures; then a period of German and English influence that developed in the French the love of philosophy and romantic reverie.

French genius was able to gather from the outside elements which it integrated and from which it drew a new impetus, giving back generously the wealth it had borrowed. Various foreign influences have prevailed in accordance with the political and social constellations in Europe; they were often followed by violent reactions against Germanism, against Italianism, against Judaism. However, after these crises French culture always managed to regain its equilibrium, understanding that human families must enrich one another with the values of their genius.

Among all these spiritual influences, the Jewish contribution also has its place. French civilization, anxious to draw what might be useful to its development, has found something in the Jewish spirit that was in harmony with its own being and was capable of adding an offshoot to its trunk.

Let us remember that the French language, that exquisite instrument of the human genius, was formed on the model of the Bible, through the medium of Latin. No book has been translated into French so often as the Scriptures, which, consequently, have greatly contributed to the evolution of the language. By literal borrowings, by the imitation of Biblical language, by the development of its imagery in religious and lay literature, French has been profoundly influenced by the Bible, if not in its vocabulary, at least in its spiritual character.

Let us remember that the most French of literary genres, born from the genius of the most genuinely French poet, La Fontaine, matured on French soil only after having been imported from the distant East, and that the Jews Pierre Alphonse in the eleventh century and Rabbi Berachia in the twelfth were the precursors and the elaborators of the *fabliaux* in France.

Consider all that the University of Montpellier, ranking first in the medical science of the Middle Ages, owes to the contributions of Jewish doctors, who had learned their art in the flourishing Judeo-Arab academies. More generally, let us think about the role of intermediary played by the Jews between the admirable Semitic civilization and the primitive world of the Middle Ages. A very prosperous Jewish colony developed in the South of France, from which the Jews, thanks to their intellectual and commercial relations, directed toward the interior the intellectual baggage imported from the Orient. Its spiritual level was so high that the compilers of the literary history of France, working under the direction of Ernest Renan, have devoted several chapters to the literature of the French rabbis of the Middle Ages, even though they wrote in Hebrew.

The spiritual influence of Judaism did not always operate on first encounter, nor did it always have the same characteristics. Instead of an organic evolution, there were, on the contrary, violent reactions on several occasions to a new penetration of Jewish influence. Spiritual resistance long originated with the Church, anxious to keep absolute mastery over minds and looking suspiciously at the presence in the Christian world of heretical centers. The rivalry between the two enemy sisters gave rise to a whole special literature of theological disputes, which were gradually replaced by discussions that did not focus on spiritual preoccupations.

In the fourteenth century, period of decline of medieval culture, Europe fell into darkest barbarism, into intolerance and persecution of all who did not agree with self-interest disguised by religious dogmas. France, too, paid tribute to this state of mind, which culminated in the expulsion of the Jews, who were stripped of all their possessions. The few centers that survived here and there in the South of France vegetated, their inhabitants imprisoned in their ghettos, too preoccupied with material cares to be capable of developing a culture, too wretched to inspire in their neighbors anything but contempt.

And yet, even at times like these, the legacy of Israel to France has been most positive. Montaigne, Jewish on his mother's side, and probably in part on his father's side, strongly contributed to the mental attitude that is called the French genius; furthermore, the Reformation and the Renaissance contributed the discovery, following that of Greco-Roman antiquity, of Judaic civilization.

The Reformation and the Renaissance—one a religious, the other a secular movement—have in common their desire to go back to original sources. The Renaissance is the discovery of the sources of Greek civilization; the Reformation is a return to the Bible, whose text had been forgotten under the commentaries and supercommentaries amassed for fifteen centuries. Those who reacted against the absolutism of Rome claimed the right to read the Bible; it inspired the poets, the scientists, and the men of action, also the apostles and the martyrs of Protestantism; Coligny, Agrippa d'Aubigné, and the Huguenots spoke the language of the Prophets of Israel and evoked their memory by their virile spirit and their enthusiasm. It was a kind of rehabilitation for the descendants of the Jewish martyrs to see the book for which they had sacrificed their lives inspire the Protestants in their controversy with the Catholics and support a whole generation of Christians whose fathers had perhaps been among those who had subjected the Jews to auto-da-fés.

But the ideas of the Bible were also appreciably revived in profane literature: French tragedy drew its

inspiration not only from the spirit of Greece, but also
from Judea. Poets Robert Garnier and Jean de la Taille,
who laid the groundwork for French Classicism, drew
the subjects of their dramas from the Old Testament as
well as from Greek mythology. And when the Classical
era reached its apogee with Racine, the latter produced
his masterpiece *Athalie* from an episode of Jewish history. In this play, Judaism and Hellenism meet: the
Biblical spirit of the content adopts the dramatic form
of Greek tragedy. The idea of Providence, drawn from
the Bible, wins over that of Fatality, the essential element of the Hellenic vision of the world. The Old Testament was to remain a major source of inspiration, not
only for the Romantic School but even in the twentieth
century, with Paul Claudel as the main protagonist in a
line of writers imbued in various degrees with the morality of the Holy Scriptures.

The propagation of the Biblical spirit among nations,
the secularization of the ideas of the Bible, may be partially responsible for the movement which tended to re-
construct human society on the basis of the "rights of
man," an idea that came from England when the Puri-
tans had formulated it under the inspiration of the Bible.

> Even the atheistic philosophers of the eighteenth century were
> inspired by the social doctrine of this Bible against which they
> were fighting; they were opposing rather its false priests, those
> who had distorted its spirit. The social doctrine of Moses has
> thus contributed to preparing this spirit of tolerance which was
> to lead to the emancipation of the Jews.
> It was the Jewish people itself that had prepared it by its
> whole past and by its prophets, the great religious creators of
> Israel, who had called for the future unity of mankind in faith
> and in law.[10]

The Great Revolution destroyed the walls of the

10. E. Renan, "Judaisme et Christianisme," in *Discours et conférences*
(Paris, 1887), p. 335.

ghetto; all fields of activity became accessible to the Jews in the century of liberalism. Happy and grateful, they fervently espoused the French cause; so fervently, that to demonstrate their patriotism they did not always behave kindly toward their coreligionists in other countries.

One might have expected that liberty of thought and action would produce a flowering of Jewish spiritual life, inspiring French culture and in turn receiving inspiration from it, just as an Ibn Gabirol or a Maimonides had established the juncture of Jewish and Arab thought during the golden age of Judeo-Arabic civilization in Spain. In fact, the spiritual contribution of Judaism during the nineteenth century was insignificant. Of course, some Jews individually played a brilliant role in the scientific, artistic, and political life of France. But how much energy was wasted by the sterile efforts of French Judaism to eradicate its origins and to repudiate its heritage! Under the influence of Clermont-Tonnerre's watchword "to the Jews as individuals everything; to the Jews as a nation nothing," the French Jews were haunted by a real complex, by the fear of not seeming sufficiently patriotic. Insofar as Jewish thought existed, it tended to reduce the sense of Judaism merely to the humanitarian doctrine that found full satisfaction in the republican constitution's guarantee of the "rights of man."

If French Judaism seemed to surrender, it did not, on the other hand, dry up the anti-Jewish current that had flowed since the Middle Ages, carrying old prejudices on its waves in strange contrast with the political ideal of that epoch. The literature of the nineteenth century reflects the most opposing tendencies; Jewish subjects and Jewish figures are as abundant as they are contradictory and, all things considered, sterile.

It is toward the end of the century that a series of extraordinary events occurred which transfigured the moral and social aspect of France and gave a blow to

French Judaism, intoxicated by too many individual successes to the detriment of the Jewish tradition. The Dreyfus Affair, a reactionary as well as revolutionary crisis, occurring exactly one hundred years after the other crisis of European society known as the Great Revolution, had the effect on the best elements in France, Jewish as well as non-Jewish, of an awakening of conscience. Péguy, with the moving voice of a seer, speaks of a "chosen issue" that became "an eminent crisis in the history of Israel, in the history of France, and in the history of Christianity." This crisis had as a consequence the creation of a Jewish literature in French that was not solely the work of Jewish writers. No more to be found is Balzac's cliché of the Jewish usurer or the Jewish parvenu, but instead the real sociological position of the modern Jew, drawn by the pen of Lacretelle, Duhamel, and Roger Martin du Gard. This spiritual movement is among the happiest phases of Judeo-French contacts, a phase again limited, in this life whose law is change. For the political convulsions that followed the Second World War have had some repercussions in the relations between France and Israel.

The present introduction will have made clear the triple aspect of the expression "Jewish element," encompassing three subjects for study:
1. The influence of the Bible and of Jewish themes and works on Christian authors
2. The works of Jewish authors (or partially Jewish) if their works bear a Jewish accent
3. The political, religious, and social problem, through the centuries, that the presence of Jews among Christians raises, and the attitude of non-Jewish authors toward this problem

THE JEWISH ELEMENT
IN FRENCH LITERATURE

Part I

IN THE SHADOW OF THE CROSS

Whatever we might have thought of Hebrew books and the philosophy of the Jews, we should not have forgotten the enormous claim to universal gratitude that they earned during the Middle Ages. They were for a long time the only link between the East and the West that maintained a permanent contact of trade and light between the two worlds in the impious divorce of humanity, thus frustrating the two fanaticisms, both Christian and Moslem.

—J. Michelet
History of France

1

Between the Orient and the Occident

To explain the personality of a man, biographers describe certain traits of his childhood, explore certain influences that have contributed to his development. The same is true with the soul of a people, as expressed in its works of art and in its thought. To understand the character of French literature—so homogeneous and at the same time so varied—one must go back to its origins. We note that in order subsequently to become a powerful stream, French literature had accepted tributaries on all sides. Judaism has also fed this stream, either by direct collaboration, or as intermediary between the East and the West. In certain countries, there has been a tendency to trace all positive elements to Nordic sources. Long before recent political trends, a horde of philosophers and literary critics was laboring to discover these Nordic sources, often as nebulous as the songs of Ossian. French criticism is not guilty of this exclusivism, and consequently oriental influences are mentioned as naturally as autochthonous elements—Gallic and Breton.

Literary history has established the fact that it is through the Crusades that France became acquainted with the literature of the Orient. No doubt, the Crusades awakened the interest of the masses in the Orient but the deeper influences followed paths other than the main highways taken by the Crusaders. In the heart of

France there already existed an element that constituted a mixture of East and West, with a predominance of the East.

The first Oriental stimulus had appeared long before the wars organized under the sign of the Cross. In 787 Charlemagne brought in the Zakan family, and in 801, from Bagdad, the learned Rabbi Makhir the Babylonian. These two men, settling respectively at Mayence and at Narbonne, introduced Hebrew literature in the North and South of France. Under Louis le Debonnaire and Charles le Chauves, other cultured Jews came to France and prepared for the establishment of the great Talmudic schools in Lothaire's kingdom.

In the South, under Arab influence, Hebrew literature took a poetic turn. Talmudic studies and Hebrew poetry come from a common religious origin, but it was the poetry that came into contact with French literature, stimulating an essentially Oriental genre that subsequently adapted itself completely to France: the fable. The Talmud contains a great number of didactic tales, scattered among juridical discussions. These fables were meant to illustrate and interpret the austere religious and moral meaning of prescriptions. The oldest known fables were invented for that purpose. In this light, Jesus of Nazareth, if we disregard his personality as religious founder, appears as a master in the art of popularizing the moral teachings of the Bible by means of parables.

According to the Talmud, Rabbi Meir, second-century scholar, knew three hundred of these fables. After him, other scholars cultivated this art, drawing on a wide assortment of subjects and adapting them to the occasion. Thus all the Hindu and Arab fables have passed through Hebrew into European literature. The major authors of Hebrew collections lived in southern France, crossroad of the Christian and Arab worlds. In the compilations

of Berachya ben Natronay (ca. 1200) and Isaac de
Corbeil, Hindu tales, Aesop's fables and Talmudic parables are serenely gathered together; other Jews, who
had gone over to the Christian camp (Pierre Alphonse,
Jean de Capoue) translated these collections into Latin,
and henceforth the way was clear for adaptations into
all the European languages. But it is in France that the
fable was to find its true homeland.

Rabbi Berachya and his colleagues compiled Aesop's
fables, drawn from Arab sources; and the Talmudic
"Tales of Reynard the Fox" (Mishle Shualim), with
the sole aim of instructing their coreligionists; the oral
transmission of the tales to the Christian population had
not been planned and occurred only accidentally. On the
other hand, Pierre Alphonse and Jean de Capoue specifically undertook the task of giving the Christian world
the benefit of the treasures amassed by Hebrew literature. Both of them, belonging by birth to Judaism and
by choice to Christianity, attempted to utilize this duality
to mediate between the two cultures.

The first is the most interesting one, this Rabbi Moses
who was baptized in his native city of Huesca in 1106
on Saint Peter's Day; his godfather was Alphonse VI,
king of Castille, whose doctor he became. This conversion provoked an intense indignation among his coreligionists, who accused him of having changed his religion
for practical reasons, with the sole purpose of escaping
the fate of his people and to build a career at the royal
court.

Moïse-Pierre Alphonse defended himself by composing
a series of dialogues between the Jew Moses and the
Christian Peter, in which the latter refutes decisively the
attacks of the Jew. It is an early example of these religious disputes that we shall encounter later on.

The major work of this author (who accomplished
a fusion of the two religions without achieving a synthe-

sis) is the *Disciplina Clericalis,* translated into French
under the title *Discipline de Clergie,* of which a twelfth-
century translation bears the title: *Chastiement d'un père
à son fils (Admonition from a Father to his Son).*

This book, which enjoyed great popularity, is a treatise
on education in the style of *Chastiement des dames* by
Robert de Blois, which is a manual on how to behave
in life; for instance: no swearing, moderate drinking,
moderate eating, no stealing. In Pierre Alphonse's work,
a father undertakes the education of his son by means
of practical examples chosen in Oriental, especially Arabic, tales. By this entertaining moral treatise in the style
of his former colleagues, the rabbis, the Judeo-Christian
author scored a big success with his new coreligionists.

His work provides one of many channels through
which Oriental wisdom infiltrated Europe. The moral
tales of Oriental inspiration, largely Jewish, took the
name of *fabliaux* when they became thoroughly Galli-
cized. Gaston Paris notes in this respect:

> Just as in certain Oceanian islands, plants imported from
> Europe, stronger and hardier than the indigenous vegetation,
> wage a relentless struggle against it and finally destroy it, or
> relegate it to some inaccessible valley, the guests that old French
> literature welcomed, not only became as solidly rooted as its
> own children, but also deprived them of their original vitality
> and took absolute possession, so that national works, at first
> disfigured by foreign influences, then more and more neglected,
> died almost without posterity, and have remained confined to
> some old manuscript where chance had preserved them until
> the investigations of modern erudition. We have here an ex-
> tremely curious and important phenomenon for the history of
> modern literature and civilization, and that's what gives these
> borrowings made by our old poetry from sources of foreign
> inspiration a special interest.[1]

It is true that Joseph Bédier refuses to recognize these

---

1. G. Paris, *La Poésie du moyen âge,* II (1903), 77.

sources as the most essential in the *fabliaux* genre. But
A. de Montaiglon, the author of *Recueil des fabliaux,*
whose work is the basis for all research in this field, is
of another opinion. He says:

> The real intermediary is the cosmopolitan nation *par excellence*
> and the only one in the Middle Ages, that is to say the Jews,
> Oriental themselves in spirit and tradition, who alone knew
> Arabic and who also were able to translate it into Latin. . . .
> A very curious and very positive clue are the *Disciplina Cleri-*
> *calis* of Pierre Alphonse and the framework as well as the
> stories of the Seven Wise Men must have been passed on by the
> Jews even more than by the Greeks who had so little influence
> on our real Middle Ages. . . . The solution of the question,
> that is to say the real passage of Oriental tales into Europe
> is perhaps entirely in the Talmud. If it is to be found in the
> Talmud and in India, it's the Talmud that preserved them
> among the Jews, and it's they who, by writing them in Latin,
> gave Europe its themes and subject matter.[2]

The translations (from Arabic to Hebrew, and from
Hebrew to Latin) made by Jewish scholars were probably not the only means by which the spiritual baggage
of the Orient passed into Western literature. A great
many of these fables must have taken, in addition to the
royal road of learned translation, popular byways, thanks
to the intimate contacts that existed up to a certain time
between Jews and Arabs on the one hand, and Jews and
Christians on the other, the Jews always speaking the
language of the population in the midst of which they
lived and with which they were in touch by everyday
dealings. For French, we have proofs that go far back
and are among the first documents of Old French. The
rabbis in France and particularly Rachi (1040-1104)
have inserted in their commentaries on the Bible a number of French glosses that are extremely valuable for
the study of that language. Since these glosses were writ-

---

2. A. de Montaiglon, *Recueil des fabliaux,* I (1872), Avant-propos.

ten in Hebrew letters, modern philologists use them to determine the pronunciation and the vocabulary of the eleventh and twelfth centuries. After an early study by E. Bohmer,[3] the works of Arsène Darmsteter and of Blondheim are of supreme importance in this branch of French philology. The glosses and Hebrew-French glossaries are the first attempts at a dictionary of the French language of the eleventh century. Darmsteter relies on the French glosses that are found in the commentaries on the Bible. He owes three thousand words to Rachi's texts alone. The library of the University of Basel owns the manuscript (A III 39) of a Hebrew-French glossary commenting on several texts of the Prophets. This document, dating from the twelfth century, gives the translation of several thousand Hebrew terms. The manuscript, which has not yet been analyzed from a philological viewpoint, promises to furnish precious findings for the history of the French language.

In the beginning, these bilingual glosses contained only certain words inserted in the Hebrew text, since French was not recognized as a literary language. Hebrew played this role among the Jews, just as Latin remained for a long time the literary language of the French during the Middle Ages. Later, in many popular writings the process is inverted; the text is in Old French. Theological locutions drawn from Hebrew are scattered throughout. This Franco-Hebrew alternation corresponds to the Franco-Latin writings. Finally, the Jews wrote an almost pure French, giving it a familiar aspect by using Hebrew letters.

Two documents from the end of the thirteenth century, recently brought to light, give us precious information on that point. One is the manuscript of a "mahzor,"[4]

---

3. *De Vocabulis Francogallicis Iudaice Transcriptis,* Romanische Studien (Halle, 1872).

4. *Fragment de Heidelberg,* ed. H. Pflaum, *Romania,* LIX.

prayer book for the holy days, written in the standard style of official prayer books, composed entirely in the French of the thirteenth century, written in Hebrew letters. The other is the famous *Complainte de Troyes,*[5] the most impressive literary document of Franco-Jewish literature of the Middle Ages. From a comparison with a Hebrew *Selicha* (elegy) dealing with the same subject, Arsène Darmsteter has concluded that the anonymous author of the "complainte" is the same as the one of the Hebrew elegy: Jacob, son of Juda de Lotra (Lorraine). The work deals with the fate of thirteen martyrs burned at Troyes, two weeks before Pentecost 5048 (1288). Here is a stanza of this poem, transcribed from Hebrew letters.

Préchors vinrent R. Ichak rekerir:
K'i se tornat ver lor creace o il li kevanret périr.
Il dit: Ke avès tant? Je vol por Gé morir;
Je suis Cohen, e offrande de mon cors vos ofrir.

Preachers came to invite R. Isaac
To adopt their faith or be forced to die.
He said: Why are you so wrought? I want to die for God.
I am Cohen (priest) and I want to make an offering of
                                        my body.

The quotation refers to a mass execution, carried out by the Inquisition. Even though it caused great indignation in France, it is an indication of the night that was to darken the European sky for several hundred years. Here is the concrete story of the tragic event of Troyes: On Good Friday, March 26, 1288, Christians "who wanted to avenge the death of their Lord," invaded the house of a rich Jew, Isaac Châtelain. While they probably accused him of some crime or other, they pillaged his house and handed him over, with his whole family

---

5. Vatican Library; fragment edited by Arsène Darmsteter, *Romania,* III (1874).

and eight other notables, to the Dominicans. The Inquisition condemned them all to torture by fire. Their lives were to be spared only if they abjured their faith. They refused and a month later they were burned at the stake; Isaac Châtelain, his pregnant wife, his two sons, his daughter-in-law, "qui tant était belle" (who was so beautiful), Baruch d'Avirey who "s'enhardit de blâmer le bourreau" (had the courage to defy the executioner), Simon the cantor, who "si bien savait orer" (who could pray so well), Isaac the priest, and the like. They encouraged each other, jeered at their executioners, and died reciting the Shema, the Jewish credo.

The *Complainte de Troyes* is a moving and instructive document. Darmsteter considers the French version superior to the Hebrew elegy; the author, in spite of his flawless command of Hebrew, expresses himself more spontaneously and more naturally in French, his mother tongue. This integration in speech did not correspond to a reconciliation of minds and hearts. Just as in the philological field, Franco-Hebrew texts of the Middle Ages acquire importance only in the light of modern research, for the general contributions of the Jews were not recognized and appreciated when they were taking place. Even in ancient times, nations had adopted the Holy Book of Israel while rejecting its people. During the Middle Ages Christian civilization, while accepting the many ideas and leads of Jewish philosophers, doctors, translators, and scholars, vented their hatred against those whose role as intermediaries was of necessity more visible in trade and financial transaction than in the field of spiritual mediation.

But these social grievances appeared only later. At the time, what prevailed was the stubborn religious resentment. In France, eldest daughter of the Church, champion since Charles Martel of the winning struggle against the Saracens, there must have existed in clerical circles a real malaise at seeing the continuing existence, in the heart of the country, of a religious community that defied the sword and the word of a church victorious on the outside. This attempt to reduce the nucleus of resistance is reflected in literature on a vast scale. The theme of the conversion of the Jews recurs on the most unexpected occasions, without mentioning the official controversies between Jewish and Christian theologians. Jewish influence makes itself felt in important parts of French literature during the Middle Ages in the sense that the stubborn resistance of Judaism haunts writers who strive to break down this unyielding obstacle, either by the example, often fictional, of successful conversations, or by persuasion, the latter running the gamut from the subtlest dialectics to the coarsest insults. The dialectical arguments are predominant until the thirteenth century and often reach a remarkable level, because of the necessity of answering the Jews, not the least bit at a loss for counterarguments, while during the decline of the Middle Ages the Christian arguments bear a cruder character, since the opposition had been reduced to silence.

In the following chapters we shall examine all the above-mentioned forms under which the Jewish theme appears in French literature before the Renaissance.

2

Religiously Inspired Literature

Under the southern portal of the cathedral of Strasbourg, two fourteenth-century statues of pink sandstone, representing two women, face each other; they symbolize, in the eloquent language of the Middle Ages, the Church and the Synagogue. The Church, erect, crowned, proud, looks at the uncrowned Synagogue, head bent, blindfolded, sad-faced, holding in one hand her broken lance, in the other trying to hold onto the Tablets of the Law that are escaping her. The young Law victorious, triumphant, faces the old Law vanquished, defeated, but filled with grace and nobility. Thus the pious artist has engraved in stone the major problem that haunted the Christian conscience for many centuries. Israel defeated, losing its authority to the triumphant Church, reduced to the sad fate of all losers, yet refusing to recognize what seemed to be an unquestionable reality. It took refuge in a pride that scoffed at its victors and that seemed to them stubbornness and blindness. To overcome this blindness was the goal of all sincere Christians. At the beginning, persuasion, the conversion of miscreants, was reserved to the clergy; its efforts were expended in religious controversies between priests and rabbis, staged like knightly jousts. Later, lay writers also dedicated themselves to the wretched task of saving Jewish souls, a task that became the *ceterum censeo* of numerous literary productions. One often has the impression that this literary proselytism is meant to relax the censorship of the clergy so that it will close its eyes to the vulgar scenes written to appeal to the lower classes. This is the case, for instance of the *Pèlerinage de Charlemagne,* burlesque story, bastard offspring of the noble *chanson de geste.* The emperor, who feels that his wife has offended him by claiming that King Huon of Constantinople was a head taller than he was, sets out for that city. The story is full of the most vulgar "gabs" (boasts), but it redeems itself by having the Christian cause triumph through the conversion of Jews and pagans met on the way, which occurs with bewildering rapidity. Thus, in Jerusalem, a Jew struck by Charlemagne's majestic appearance has himself baptized on the spot.

> Un Jueus i entrat, qui bien l'out esguardet;
> Com il vi le rei Charle, comença a trembler;
> Tant out fier le visage, ne l'osat esguarder;
> A poi que il ne chiet, fuiant s'en est tornez.
> Et si montet l'eslais toz les marbrins degrez.
> Et vint al patriarche, prist a aparler:
> Alez, sire, al mostier, por les fonz aprester;
> Orendreit me ferai batizier et lever.
> Doze contes vi ore en cet mortier entrer,
> Avoec els le trezime, onc ne vi si formet.
> Par le miens escientre, co est meismes Deus!
> Il est le doze apostle vos vienent visiter.

> A Jew entered, and looked at him carefully
> As he saw King Charles, he began to tremble;
> Such a proud face had he, that he dared not
>   gaze at him;
> He nearly fell, and ran away.
> Springing forward, he ascended the marble steps.
> And came to the patriarch, and began to speak:
> Go to the monastery, O Lord, to prepare the
>   baptismal fonts;
> I want to be baptized and christened immediately.
> I just saw twelve counts enter this monastery.

With them the thirteenth, never did I see such a
        handsome figure.
To my knowledge, that is God himself!
He and the twelve Apostles have come to visit you.[1]

In reality, the success of the Church with the Jews
was rather discouraging; even stronger weapons than an
emperor's majestic aspect did not produce any appre-
ciable result. That is because, in the religious controversies initiated by the Christians, they had chosen precisely
the battlefield in which their opponents were past masters:
dialectics. It was the only weapon that the Jews possessed, having been put on the defensive without means
of counterattacking. They were reduced to defending
themselves by displaying a maximum of ingenuity and
cleverness: a famous example is the following tale,[2] which
must be the source of the fable of the three rings:

King Peter of Aragon (1094-1104) one day asked
an intelligent Jew, intimate of the royal court, the embarrassing question of the comparative value of religions.
After three days of meditation, the Jew appeared before
the king in a very troubled state. The king asked him
what had happened to him. "Lord, I ask your support
against those who have mistreated me. A month ago,
my neighbor left for a distant journey and he left each
of his two sons a precious stone. This morning, the two
brothers came to see me and asked me to let them know
the qualities of their jewels and their differences. I
pointed out to them that nobody knew it better than their
father, who, being a jeweler, knew to perfection the
nature and the value of precious stones, and that they
should direct their questions to him. Thereupon, they
insulted me and hit me." "They were wrong," said the

---

1. *Le Pèlerinage de Charlemagne*, vs. 129-40.
2. This tale is told in the chronicle *Shébet Yéhouda*, in which the
Rabbi Aben Verga, a compiler of the fifteenth century, has corrupted
old and authentic Jewish traditions.

king, "and they will be punished." "Well," replied the Jew, "let your ears listen to what your mouth has spoken, O King. Look: Esau and Jacob are also brothers; each of them has received a precious stone, and you want to know which is best. Send, O King, a messenger to Our Father who is in Heaven. He is the great jeweler, and He will be able to tell you the differences between the stones."

This parable must not be considered a plea for tolerance, the role that it plays in Boccaccio's version. Tolerance implies the possibility of being intolerant, which the Jews certainly did not possess at the time, except among themselves in the ghetto. Rather, it is a way of eluding a question and a supplication addressed to the Christians to be tolerant. In Italy, the development of peaceful relations between Italian and Moslem merchants contributed to a mutual forbearance, which explains the lesson of tolerance, not to say skepticism that is expressed in Boccaccio's tale. In France, however, the appeal implicit in the fable told the king of Aragon did not produce the expected impression. As proof we cite the version in which it appears in France.

The *Dit du vrai aniel* [The Story of the True Ring] is by an unknown author of the thirteenth century. It tells the story of an Egyptian who owns a magic ring, an infallible remedy against all ills. Of his three sons, the eldest is a bad seed, "bougre et mécréant, hai de Dieu et du monde" [lout and miscreant, hated by God and the world]. The second is not any better, while in the third all the virtues are gathered. Before he dies, the father has a jeweler make two rings similar to the miraculous ring, which he entrusts to his youngest son, warning him of the trick he played on his brothers. The latter, when they discover the subterfuge, manhandle the youngest brother and mutilate the priceless jewel. But God sends three princes to rescue it. The ring recovers

its power after it has been repaired. Here is the moral
of the tale:

The beloved child, Christianity, is in great distress,
because its evil brothers have robbed it and chased it
from its inheritance. Christ's tomb is in the hands of the
infidels because of the Pope and the great lords, who,
concerned with their worldly goods, are not willing to
endanger them for the sake of the authentic ring. Cardi-
nals, bishops, and priests think only of their well-being.
They are not going to repair the broken ring and the
unfortunate child would be lost if God did not inspire
three valiant princes, the King of France and the counts
of Artois and Flanders, with the desire to avenge him.

This whole tale has thus only one purpose, to arouse
the interest of the French in the Crusades, probably
during the time of Philippe le Bel. We are far from the
lesson that the poet M. J. Chénier will draw later on
from this fable at the time of the Revolution.

If the anonymous author of the *Dit du vrai aniel* had
given this interpretation to the fable, not only the fabulist,
but the fable too would have remained unknown; it
would have been condemned by the censor.

By its general tendency, by its intransigence, the *Dit
du vrai aniel* is an interesting example of apologetic literature in the service of the Church. It belongs to the
genre of religious controversies, a more vulgar example
of which is *La Disputation de la Synagogue et de la
Sainte Eglise* by Clopin,[3] a "jongleur" [minstrel] of the
thirteenth century. The tone as well as the language of
this *dit* tells us that we are dealing with a pale reflection
of the serious and scientific controversies that were taking
place in Latin.

---

3. A. Jubinal, *Mystères inédits du XVe siècle* (Paris, 1837). A historical
study of this subject was made by Hiram Pflaum, Jerusalem: *Der alle-
gorische Streit zwischen Synagoge und Kirche in der europaeischen
Dichtung des Mittelalters,* Arch. rom. (1934).

The two religions are symbolized in the same manner as the statues on the southern portal of the cathedral of Strasbourg.

The author in a dream witnesses a dispute between two ladies, "Holy Church" radiantly beautiful and "Synagogue" a faded beauty ("Her banner is broken, her tablets are shattered"). The dialogue that is begun resembles in tone that of two gossips, although the substance of the discussion contains some defensible arguments. The Synagogue calls the Church "une garce et une chétive folle" (a slut and wretched madwoman) and the latter regards her spiritual mother as a "vieille ribaude folle" (old, foolish wench). After these introductory Homeric insults, the conversation turns gradually to the subject of their disagreement, interrupted at intervals by familiar remarks. The Synagogue does not feel much respect for the god of its rival: "le tiens dieux ne vaut pas plein basse d'eve chaude" [your god is not worth a basin of hot water] and demands obedience of the Church because "tu issis de m'escole" [you are the product of my school]. But the Church silences her: "tais-toi, vieille folle froncie" (be quiet, mad, wrinkled old woman) and she invokes Isaiah's prophecy, where it is said that from the root of Jesse a stick was to be born, and from the stick a flower—a prophecy that applies to the Virgin and to Jesus. The stubborn Synagogue is hard to convince and declares that this prophecy refers to Jesse's immediate posterity: David and Salomon. Then it enumerates the sufferings of Jesus and the ignominious death that he suffered, from which it concludes that, if he had been God, he would not have subjected himself to such a fate. "Onc si fole creance ne vi comme la toe" [I have never seen a faith as mad as yours]. Thereupon the Church triumphs: these sufferings and this death are the price for redeeming the children of Adam from sin and death. The Church undertakes one last attack by means of a stream of insults. She accuses the Synagogue of misleading and deceiving the Jews by spurious words and of making them "querre les moules aux rissoles," that is, look for something in the wrong place.[4]

The Synagogue, however, claims that the "Messie est à venir" [the Messiah is yet to come]; but it was said that "quand le Messie viendra, vous autres Juifs perdrez votre onction" [when the Messiah does come, you Jews will stop being the chosen people]. Well, your privileged position has been lost, you are forever enslaved; therefore, the Messiah has come, and in waiting for him even though you are no longer the chosen people, you make the mistake of "querre les moules aux rissoles." The Synagogue does not have the chance to show the effect of this tight line of reasoning because the poet wakes up. He does not even dare think that the Synagogue, stubborn as ever, might become reasonable.

The same arguments, which testify to a remarkable dialectical temperament in the opponents, reappear in the *Debate Between a Jew and a Christian.* They are similar with regard to Isaiah's prophecy and the loss of the anointed position which up to then belonged to the Jews. But, while Lady Synagogue does not admit defeat, here the Jew recognizes the superiority of the Christian law and requests baptism.

The fictional dialogue that we have just examined embraces all the arguments used by Christian apologetics. Above all, they are the evidences of the Old Testament in favor of the Trinity, divine unity, the Messiahship of Christ and his Davidic genealogy; we perpetually encounter the same attempt to demonstrate that according to Christian tradition the Law had been transmitted to the Christians, that the Jews were condemned to reproba-

---

4. As H. Pflaum explains it: look for oysters in a meat pâté.

tion, but that the survivors of Israel would nevertheless be saved one day by conversion.

La Disputation de la Synagogue et de la Sainte Eglise is perhaps a direct echo of the great controversy that had taken place at the Royal Court in Paris in 1240, where the superiority of the Church triumphed, if not by authentic eloquence, at least by the conclusive result that the Talmud was condemned to the stake. This *auto da fé* was a mortal blow to the intellectual life of French Judaism, flourishing up to then. The destructive action was to extend also to the material life of the Jews, social grievances replacing religious grievances.

3
Appearance of Social Grievances in Literature

The preceding analysis has given us the opportunity to know a custom of the Middle Ages that reflects a very naïve state of mind. It was believed that opponents could be convinced of the superiority of one's own religion by rational arguments.

Polemical literature had up to then an idealistic character in spite of the cruder tone that it gradually assumed. It was thesis literature, of complete integrity, and the thesis was developed with various degrees of sophistication, depending on the talent of the author. We may smile at this naïve zeal that attempted to win souls by literary arguments; the fact remains that it was inspired by a certain idealism. This attitude was to yield to a purely material attitude; the religious disputes became a pretext and a framework. This fact corresponds to the decline of Christian thought, which had been replaced in the masses by a barbarous and fanatical Christianity.

Social evolution was a decisive factor in the breakdown of the Christian world. This is the time when the bourgeoisie develops and the power of capitalism is born. Commerce is transformed, the value of gold increases, the passion for gold grows. Religion alone does not direct the destinies of nations anymore. A new god, gold, takes its place at its side. And if the old God of the Bible did not succeed in uniting his children, the new god will only succeed in dividing them further.

We encounter the first precise echo of the social grievances in the works of Abbé Gautier de Coincy (1177-1236), although he wrote exclusively religious poetry. He is a moralist who adds moral appendices, called tails, to the stories that he borrows from Latin sources. They are either wordy and trite religious effusions, or very curious descriptions of the customs of the times, especially of the vices, defects, and absurdities. He roundly denounces his era without sparing the members of the secular clergy, or even those of the cloisters. But above all, he violently hates the Jews. First, for the religious motives already mentioned; he accuses them of not having recognized the Messiah:

Plus bestial que bestes nues
Sont tuit Juif, ce n'est pas doute.
Aveugle sunt, ne voient goute.
Quar miracle, ne prophécie,
Ne raison nule com leur die,
Leur cuers ne purent amolier,
Ne veulent croire notrier.
Ce méesme qu'a leur yex voient
Ce que prophécie avoient,
Ne voudront croire, quand le virent.

More like animals than the animals themselves
Are all Jews, there is no doubt.
They are blind, they do not want to see anything
No miracle, nor any prophecy,
Nor any reason that one might give them
Succeeds in touching their hearts.
They refuse to believe anything
Even what they see with their own eyes
What the prophecies announce,
They would not believe them, even if they saw them.[1]

1. *Les Miracles de la Sainte Vierge,* ed. Abbé Poquet (Paris, 1857). *Miracle de Saint Hildefonse* (Helsingfors: Nouvelle Edition Langfors, 1937).

But in addition to these traditional religious accusations, he attacks them for immediate reasons. It is their wealth, their power, that arouses his indignation. And it is the fault of the powerful, "the prominent men."

> Certes hauz homs qui les endure,
> Ne doit mie onc temps durer.

> Any prominent man who tolerates this state of things
> Does not deserve to live long.

Through avarice, they have sold Christianity to the Jews, and they have betrayed Christ again, more treacherously than Judas. "Par les Juifs, le monde espuisent" [Through the Jews, they ruin the world]. The Christians languish in the chains of the Jewish usurer; counts and kings are unconcerned, as long as they share the booty. And Abbé Gautier exclaims, full of anger, that if he were king he would not leave a Jew in France:

> Vers eus sui dure si durement
> S'estoie roys pour toute roie
> Un seul durer je n'en lairoie

> I am so bitterly opposed to them
> That if I were king, not in one place
> Would I allow any to remain.

Gautier de Coincy's complaints were certainly motivated. From his point of view, which was that of the suffering people, he could only abhor the apparent causes of the misery of the masses: the Jews who, by the force of circumstances, as early as the thirteenth century, were primarily a tribe of money-changers and businessmen since they were forbidden the practice of a trade and the ownership of land. These professions seemed somewhat impure to Christians since the Church forbade interest loans. Economic anti-Semitism had then, at the beginning, a religious character. Soon religion was to be no more than a screen that disguised the resentment of Christian competitors.

Gautier de Coincy, even while berating the Jews, already expressed his indignation against the great Christian lords. But he did not yet recognize their full share of responsibility for the misery of the people. He did not know that the Jewish capitalists were often no more than front men, a "mental restriction" for certain Christian capitalists who provided them with funds and became wealthy through their agency while safeguarding appearances with regard to the Church. Thus the Jews were simultaneously deceived and deceivers. Later, the chronicler Geoffroi was forced to recognize that,

> Car Juifs furent deboneres
> Trop plus, en faisant tels afferes
> Que ne sont ore chrestien.[2]

> For the Jews were much more honest
> In handling that type of business
> Than the Christians are now.

---

2. Lavisse, *Histoire de France,* III, chap. V.

4
Jews on the Stage in the Middle Ages

In the work of Gautier, we have encountered another nuance of the Jewish theme in literature. The literature of the following centuries was to bear the mark of the double accusation, religious and social, against the Jews. The darkest period of the Middle Ages was about to begin. The literature of religious polemics, in spite of its crude and insulting tone, still expressed a conciliatory spirit. Its purpose was not to annihilate the opponent completely, but to humiliate and finally "save" him by converting him to Christianity. "I do not want the death of the sinner, but that he abandon his ways and that he live." This could logically be the thesis of these discussions, although the means employed were questionable. At any rate, the exaggerated zeal was, if not justified, at least excusable because of the religious motive that inspired it. If the Jews had been willing to yield to pressure, they would have been received warmly in the bosom of the Church. The twelfth and even the thirteenth centuries are thus characterized by the predominance of a crudely benevolent attitude towards Judaism. From the fourteenth century on, open hatred was to prevail. *Vengeance* is the title of a passion play: it could be the motto of anti-Semitic literature during the fourteenth and fifteenth centuries.

The literature of this period was to be not only the

mirror of the passions disturbing the masses, but it was
itself going to inspire these passions. The poet J. Chenier
said: "The mores of a nation first shape the spirit of
its poetical works; soon its poetical works shape the
spirit of its mores." This applies particularly to dramatic literature, which has been at all times and particularly at the beginning of its history in close contact
with the public.

For in modern Europe, as in ancient Greece, the
theater was born from the ritual of religion. It was a
teaching device to which the Church had been led to
resort because of the ignorance of the majority of the
faithful and their inability to learn in any other way.
Liturgy in pantomime, intended to instruct the people
in matters of religion while entertaining them, was in
usage in a great number of churches until the end of
the sixteenth century. The way it grew justifies the name
of liturgical drama given to it. Even when this liturgical
drama became a more independent genre and stopped
being an integral part of the service, it remained nevertheless under the influence of the Church.

The theater of the Middle Ages has been divided
into three distinct branches according to the nature of
its subjects: moralities, miracles, and mysteries. The
function of all three is edification. But it is in the *Grands
Mystères de la Passion* that the theater of the Middle
Ages reached its apogee. It dramatizes the life of Jesus;
this subject was treated by generations of poets, guided
by the common goal of glorifying Christ. Originality is
manifested only in certain details, in the personal interpretation of this or that passage or by the emphasis on
some minor episode. The absence of critical sense prevented the writers from distinguishing between ecclesiasti-
cal history and legend. Historical truth was subordinated
to the apologetic purpose, to the glorification of Christ,
and to religious propaganda.

It is obvious that in these plays an important role, in fact the key role, was reserved to the Jews, a stereotyped role that was repeated in numerous variants. The Jews had a specific place on the simultaneous stage of the theater,[1] "the Jews' place," from which they followed the action carefully, accompanying it by gestures that expressed their purported feelings towards the Christians. They wore the clothes of the Middle Ages, as was to be expected in view of the undeveloped historical sense of that period. Needless to say, the reactions of the spectators did not take into account historical truth either, and was directed against contemporary Jews whose caricature they saw on stage. We think it might be interesting to give here a brief summary of the *Mystery of the Passion,* based on the variants of its major authors.[2]

The scene presents the Jews greatly excited. John the Baptist has just announced the Messiah promised in the Holy Scriptures. The Jewish doctors, worried about their prestige and their role as religious leaders, smell danger and plan measures against the coming reformer. They act against the truth, even though they know it. Indeed, Caïphe confesses to his colleague, under the seal of secrecy:

> Il est escript pour vérité,
> Qu'il convient de nécessité
> Que uns homs muire pour la gent toute

---

1. The stage of the Middle Ages represented simultaneously all the places where the plot was to unfold; it was consequently divided into a great many "lieux" [locales] and all the characters, instead of appearing on stage according to the demands of their roles, were on the stage at the same time, each in his "lieu." For further details see G. Cohen, *Histoire de la mise en scène du théâtre religieux du moyen âge* (Paris, 1925).

2. Arnoul Gréban, *Mystère de la Passion,* ed. G. Paris & Raymond (Paris, 1878). Jean Michel, *Mystère de la Passion et Résurrection,* ed. Kruse (Greifswald, 1907). *Mystère de la Passion* joué à Arras, ed. J.-M. Richard (Arras, 1891).

Ja de ce ne soiez en doubte.
Mais parlons bas.

In truth, it is written
That it has been ordained
That one man should die for all mankind
Of this do not be in doubt.
But let us speak softly.

They must speak softly, so that the people will not learn the truth about the Bible's prophecies about Jesus. We encounter here the Middle Ages' naïve belief that educated Jews privately believed in Jesus and that they refused to recognize him openly through sheer stubbornness and meanness. This explains the accusations of having profaned the host often formulated against the Jews, which would be groundless without the assumption that the Jews secretly believed in the truth of Christianity.

The miracles performed by Christ did not make his adversaries more reasonable; rather, they are frightened by the series of miraculous cures that take place on stage, in accordance with the story of the Scriptures. When Jesus has cured the paralytic who leaves carrying his bed, the Pharisees criticize him:

Scès tu bien qu'il est huy sabbat?
Veuls tu metre en no loy debat?
Ton lit ne te loist pas porter
En sabbat, tu le dois fester.

Do you know that today is the Sabbath?
Do you want to fight against our law?
You do not have a right to carry your bed
You must honor the Sabbath.

But Jesus continues his reforms by accusing the Pharisees of practicing only the external ceremonies and of neglecting the spiritual substance of Judaism. Now the Pharisees not only realize that their moral authority is endangered, but they fear a reduction of their revenues as Jesus conquers the loyalty of the masses.

> Pis y a: notre revenu
> En diminue et notre avoir

> And there is worse; our income
> And our wealth diminish.

Thus, it is in order to defend their material interests that the Pharisees want to try him. They now have to find a pretext.

> Il nous faut songer la manière
> De la charger de quelque crime,
> Soit de blasphémie, soit de schisme.
> Ou d'autre grand cas, tel ou tel,
> Qui soit exécrable et mortel.

> We have to think about the manner
> Of accusing him of some crime
> Either of blasphemy, or of schism
> Or of some other great offense
> That is execrable and fatal.

They set traps for him to find a pretext to accuse him. One scene, for instance, shows us the devils deliberating on measures to take against Jesus: the Jews seem to them the appropriate instruments. This satanic alliance is strongly emphasized by the poet. Finally, the Jews go to find Judas to buy his betrayal. This scene allows the authors to give free rein to their imagination. Judas is skeptical of the honesty of his coreligionists and wants to be paid in advance. Another scene shows Judas examining the money, coin by coin, in the presence of the Jews. In a German mystery play the Jews find the price too high, which gives rise to a lively bargaining scene, probably highly enjoyed by the public.

It is understandable that the writers did not want to miss the chance to underline the role of usurers, for which the Jews were hated. Created for the stage, the type of Jewish usurer was to acquire great popularity. It survived the theater of the Middle Ages and passed into modern drama. From *The Jew of Malta* by Marlowe to V. Hugo's school and even in the contemporary theater, this type recurred even after the historical conditions of its existence had long disappeared. Shakespeare alone, while using the traditional and stereotyped figure, was able to animate it with his creative genius to make of him the tragic figure of Shylock.

Judas's betrayal hands Jesus over to the Jews. He is asked whether he is the son of God. When he answers affirmatively, Caïphe rends his clothes:

> Blasphémavit, blasphémavit;
> Qu'est-il besoing d'aller plus loin?
> Mon manteau désireray
> Du très grand deul qu'au coeur en ay.
> Il est digne de mort souffrir,
> Que vous en semble?

Les Juifs:

> Ostez, Ostez!
> Il est coupable de mort griefve.

> He blasphemed, he blasphemed;
> Why proceed further?
> I shall rend my cloak
> From the great grief that fills my heart.
> He deserves to die.
> What do you think?

The Jews:

> Away, away!
> He is guilty of serious death.

But the sentence depends upon confirmation by Pontius Pilate, who opposes it with all his powers. The authors of the mysteries show Pilate in the most favorable light to bring out more strongly the responsibility of the Jews. It is only the threat of being reported to the Emperor that induces him to pronounce the death sentence.

The crucifixion scene is the climax of the mystery and at the same time the one that exhibits the worst taste. The Jews compete in zeal with the Roman executioners to mock Christ, to mistreat him, to spit in his face. While he agonizes, they shout

> Le roy des juifs, Dieu te sault!
> Se tu es filz au Dieu d'amont,
> Qui est venu sauver le mond,
> Descend de la croix, par ma loy,
> Et nous croirons trestous en toy.

> King of the Jews, may God save you!
> If you are the Son of God,
> Who came to save the world,
> Descend from the cross, by my law,
> We shall all believe in you.

Anyone who knows the reactions of a naïve person to stage techniques will appreciate the fatal consequences for the Jews in that type of situation. What emotions must have arisen in the heart of the spectator against those who offended and mistreated their God in such an obvious way.

It should also be realized that the staging of a mystery play was an infinitely more important event than a modern performance. The whole city participated. Anyone who could walk crowded the parvis of the church where the play was given; the events were not acted out, they were lived. The masses made no distinction between the Jews of Jesus' time and their own contemporaries, just as we have seen that the clothes of the Jews on stage

did not differ from those of the Middle Ages. Religious
zeal often led the spectators to avenge on the spot the
insults inflicted on Jesus "in front of their eyes." Thus
the solemn theater days were for the Jews, in regions
where they had remained after repeated expulsions, days
of humiliation and even of danger.[3]

There is not a more faithful mirror of the spirit of
the Middle Ages than its theater, which concentrated all
the living forces of the people. In Petit de Julleville,
the theater of the Middle Ages is described in these
words: "The literary mediocrity of the mystery plays in
no way diminishes their literary importance, and it is
still true that the history of this imperfect theater reflects more completely and more faithfully the time in
which it was composed than it did in any other period."
It is therefore natural that we find, side by side, the two
basic reasons for the resentment against the Jews: the
religious and the economic.

The Jews are considered exclusively guilty of the
Passion of Christ. The Pharisees, represented as sordidly
mercenary hypocrites, rid themselves of the figure who
could disturb their absolute power over the conscience
and the purse of the faithful.

Caïphe and Anne are the spokesmen of a heretical
and fanatical Judaism. The consequences of the mentality of the Middle Ages are of necessity those described
by Vaublanc:

> The people dream up horrible mysteries: Christ is insulted,
> deicide is repeated, Christians are insulted, their blood is drunk,
> and the people call vociferously for the death of the Jews. . . .
> They forget that Christ was born a Jew, the Immaculate Virgin

---

3. In Toulouse, there was a custom of slapping a Jew publicly on the
days scheduled for the performances of the Passion play. The adminis-
tration of this slap was reserved for an important person. Once, Viscount
Chappelain d'Aymerie was honored with this "act of faith." The vigor
of its execution was so in keeping with the fervor of the faithful that
the Jew died.

was Jewish, the first apostles were Jewish: they only see in them the persecutor of their God, and in turn, they would like to crucify them.[4]

The Church is not without responsibility for this state of affairs, since it is under its auspices that the liturgical drama developed such magnitude. It is true that the theater freed itself gradually of the tutelage of the Church, and that it crudely vulgarized the theological apology that it used as a framework. But had not the clergy, the lower clergy especially, already planted the seed of intolerance in its religious controversies? And those who sow intolerance reap blood.

Let us remember, however, that in the period of the greatest development of the theater in France, anti-Semitic tendencies stemmed less from religious than from economic grievances. Certain plays make of usury their central theme (for instance the *Miracle of a Merchant and a Jew*). Soon the word "Jew" was to be used only in the sense of Jewish usurer. It is repeated in every possible way that "les juifs sont riches comme mer" [as rich as the sea] or that "les juifz n'ont point de povreté [Jews have no poverty]. Religious and economic griev-ances are mixed in such a naïve manner that one has the impression that spiritual reasons are advanced only to disguise more concrete and less noble grounds for resentment—a procedure that did not disappear after the Middle Ages.

A thesis, *Jews in the French literature of the Middle Ages*,[5] gives a list of defects attributed to Jews in the mystery plays. We read: disloyalty, thievery, meanness, duplicity, treachery, skepticism ("ils n'ont foi, ne fonde-ment" [they have neither faith nor religious foundation], anger, irritability ("irement, moult courroucié, au juif

---

4. *La France au temps des Croisades,* I (Paris, 1844), 280.
5. Manya Lipschuk, Golden ed., Publications of the Institute of French Studies, Columbia, 1935.

bouli touz li sans") [angrily, very irate, all the Jews'
blood boils]), contempt ("crestienté moult despisoit"
[they deeply hated Christianity]), hatred against Mary
("trop la héent durement" [they hate her very much]),
and so on. This somber list proves that the Jew had
become the personification of evil. Since the end of the
fourteenth century there were not any Jews left in the
greatest part of France. Thus, more than ever they lent
themselves to the role of bogeymen that the theater
always needs to impress primitive minds.

At the time of the Renaissance and of classicism, the
Jews were also out of France. But how different the role
of Judaism had already become during this period! The
spirit had changed; a new inspiration pervaded Europe
and then Judaism became a constructive element in the
various influences that contributed to the formation of
French classicism.

5
Contribution of the Bible to the French Language

The authors of the mystery plays used to ridicule the Jews' pseudo-Hebrew chants, which were really a sequence of nonsense syllables; for instance, this song in the Passion by Sémur:

> *Caïffas:* Je le chant meneroy.
> [I shall lead the singing]
> Gazaron gerron Manuel
> Rabom arnotte Aaron Mathusaly
> Groguostin tomvelle Samuel.

At that time, it was impossible to realize the importance that Hebrew, apparently an absurd gibberish, was going to have in the formation of the European languages.

The vocabulary of each language contains a varying number of foreign words, because every language in the course of its development has borrowed from neighboring languages. In spite of the efforts of certain purists to reduce the language to its autochthonous elements, there is no doubt that the richness of a language, such as English for instance, comes from its ability to incorporate borrowed elements. The German language, even though it resisted Romance elements, has been subjected to influences of capital importance in the development of its syntax, as, on the other hand, it was crystallized thanks to Luther's translation of the Bible.

The French language, in turn, before becoming a universal language, has come under a number of foreign influences. These, according to the political constellations of Europe, appeared suddenly and disappeared after having left their mark. This is the case with German, which, following its abrupt appearance in the fifth century, afterwards lost all noteworthy contact with the language to which it had contributed. One influence, however, has quietly and regularly continued to affect the usage of French during every phase of its formation: the Bible. Its work has been slow and discreet, but continuous and long-lasting.

Of course, the number of Hebrew words that passed into the language is very limited. Gammilscheg's etymological dictionary mentions only about twenty. But the indirect contribution to the formation of the language was quite important. This contribution consists in expressions and images faithfully adopted or developed by imitation. A language at the beginning is poor and rigid. This was the case with Old French, born of a mixture of Vulgar Latin and a few Gallic elements, to which was added the Germanic element. The vast Biblical universe found no room in this impoverished idiom, spoken by the lower classes and barely adequate to express the concrete facts of existence. The ideas that are the heart of the Bible did not yet have any equivalent in French. Hence, it was for a long time beyond the grasp of the people and long remained the "secret" book of the clergy. When the time finally came to translate it, it meant creating a new language with a limited vocabulary and a terminology applied until then to concrete reality. The mystics played an important part in this process of transposing the language into the spiritual realm, for it is the nature of mystical language to transform all things into images by the transfiguration of the concrete expression. Mystical allegories retained a vitality that went beyond the original religious intention.

Thus, a primitive language was invested with a new content. The French language was being formed in the image of the language of the Bible, by the intermediary of Latin. The first translations were literal, timid, respectful of the exact term. It was only by oral commentaries, frequent readings, and explanatory glosses that the Biblical sense of a term entered the original terms of the translation. Soon readers became familiar with the Biblical language; preachers often used its images, imitated them, transformed them, and gradually created a picturesque language in the Oriental style. The twelfth century is the golden age of this procedure; the clerics, masters at that time of all literary genres, transposed into French a whole terminology that they had mastered.

The major work of the thirteenth century is the translation of *The Complete Bible of the University of Paris* (1226-1250). Until the Reformation it remained the basis of all French translations, and indicated the extent of the influence of the Scriptures on a language in the making. In addition, the *Bible historiale* by Guiart Desmoulins (1295) also largely contributed to the introduction of Biblical terms and expressions. The reaction of later translators against Biblical neologisms remained ineffective, because these terms were already definitely incorporated into the language.

Dramatic works of religious inspiration, the mysteries of the Passion, enjoyed a great popularity and have therefore greatly contributed to acquainting the masses with Biblical language, even after the clergy lost control over this type of dramatic liturgy. Even secular literature of that period is filled with Biblical expressions, evocations, and allusions that indicate a knowledge of the

Scriptures as extensive among readers as in the poet himself. This evolution was to receive a new stimulus from the Reformation, Racine, and Romanticism.

Thus, at first by the direct road of translations, then by more or less free borrowings, by imitation of the Biblical language, by the development of images in lay and religious literature inspired by the Bible, the Bible strongly contributed to the enrichment of the French language, less in the vocabulary than in its spiritual character.

Let us illustrate these observations with a few examples. At the beginning, the speaker adopted Biblical turns of phrases, maxims and proverbs relating to concrete facts told in the Bible, and then the sense of the expression was amplified.

L'homme est fait à l'image de Dieu [Man was created in the image of God]

C'est la chair de ma chair [He is the flesh of my flesh]

Suis-je le gardien de mon frère? [Am I my brother's keeper?] (the latter in more or less witty variants).

Etre grand chasseur devant l'Éternel [To be a mighty hunter before the Lord]

Tu mangeras ton pain à la sueur de ton front [You will earn your bread by the sweat of your brow]

Aimer son prochain comme soi-même [Love thy neighbor as thyself]

Faire jaillir l'eau du rocher [To bring forth water from the rock]

Rien de nouveau sous le soleil [Nothing new under the sun]

Chaque chose à son temps [Everything in due time]

Savoir tout depuis le cèdre jusqu'à l'hysope [To know everything from the cedar to the hyssop.]

Vivre autant que Mathusalem [To live as long as Methuselah]

Enfanter dans la douleur [To bring forth children in sorrow.]

Adorer le veau d'or [Worship the golden calf]

Charger quelqu'un de tous les péchés d'Israël [Accuse somebody of all the sins of Israel]

Etre le bouc émissaire [To be the scapegoat]

Ne pas entrer dans la terre promise [Never to enter the Promised Land]

It is easy to see that these locutions and a great many others readily lent themselves to a symbolic use in daily conversation. This also applies to ellipses such as

Le veau d'or, la verge d'Aron, la force de Samson [The golden calf, Aaron's staff, Samson's strength]
La sagesse de Salomon [The wisdom of Solomon]
La vigne de Naboth [Naboth's vineyard]
Les amis de Job [Job's friends]

Parables drawn by Biblical preachers (the Prophets) in the pastoral existence of Israel in Biblical times have kept all their eloquence in the modern language of city people.

Etre une brebis égarée, une brebis sans pasteur [To be a lost sheep, a sheep without shepherd]
Comme la poussière qu'emporte le vent [Like the dust that is gone with the wind]
Sécher comme l'herbe [To dry like grass]
Comme la rosée du matin [Like the morning dew]
Comme l'oiseau échappé aux réseaux de l'oiseleur [Like the bird that escaped from the bird-catcher's net]
Aussi nombreux que les étoiles du ciel, que le sable de la mer [As numerous as the stars of heaven, as the sand of the sea]
S'appuyer sur un roseau [To lean on a reed]
Se prendre à son propre piège [To be caught in his own trap]
Celui qui sème le vent, moissonera la tempête [He who sows the wind, will reap the whirlwind]
Celui qui sème dans la douleur, moissonera dans la joie [He who sows in sorrow will reap in joy]

The Bible owes part of its popularity to the fact that it replaces abstract ideas by striking images that were successful in all languages. Thus the idea of justice is expressed by:

Oeil pour oeil, dent pour dent [An eye for an eye, a tooth for a tooth]
Les pères ont mangé du verjus, et les dents des enfants en ont été agacées [The fathers have tasted of verjuice, and the children's teeth have been set on edge]

The idea of piety by:

La bonne, la mauvaise route, la voie d'iniquité [The right, the wrong road, the path of iniquity]

The idea of death:

Dormir du sommeil éternel, retourner à la poussière [To sleep for eternity, to return to dust]

The origin of a thing is circumscribed by, for instance, the fountain, or the tree:

L'arbre de vie; la fontaine de la vie, de sapience [The tree of life; the fountain of life, of wisdom]

These images in turn created expressions such as:

Arbre d'orgueil; plante d'iniquité; fontaine de miséricorde, de droiture, de piété [Tree of pride; the plant of iniquity; fountain of mercy, integrity, piety]
Calice d'amertume, coupe de douleur [Cup of bitterness, cup of pain]

Certain Hebrew expressions were adopted in a poetic sense:

La rosée du ciel, la rose du Saron, le lis des vallées, le soleil de justice, la vallée des larmes, le lit des douleurs, le pain de misère [The heavenly dew, the rose of Sharon, the lily of the valley, the sun of justice, the vale of tears, the bed of pain, the bread of misery]

Other locutions, literally translated and readily accepted by usage, were instrumental in the creation in French of a certain number of expressions grammatically related to Hebrew, constituting real Hebraisms:

> Aimer Dieu *de* tout son coeur, *de* toute son âme.
> Dieu *de* vengeance; homme *de* sang; parole *de* vérité.
> Aller *en* paix; se fier *à* Dieu.
> *Dans* la simplicité de mon âme.
> Trouver grace *devant* quelqu'un.

In addition to these direct borrowings, there are innumerable expressions created in the image of the Biblical tongue. This system of imitation was renewed every century, and lasted as long as the Bible retained its influence, and it has not ended yet. Since language is the mirror of the spirit of a nation, it would be possible to judge from it the full contribution of the Bible to the formation of the Western mind. Even then, it would be difficult to recognize the scope of this deep and discreet influence. For, in addition to numerous expressions (and we have cited very few examples) whose Biblical origin is self-evident, others reworked and recast by usage, have, at first sight, lost all trace of their origin.

Long ago, the Biblical element, swept along by the vast tide of the language, had become immersed in it, had become lost in it, so to speak. . . . This is one of the elements of the alloy of which the solid metal of the French language is composed.[1]

---

1. J. Frénel, *L'Ancien Testament et la langue française du moyen âge;* thesis (Paris, 1904), p. 58.

Part II
SUNRISE

6

Toward the Formation of the Classical
Spirit: Montaigne

The contrast between the theater before and after 1550 is most amazing, and not only with regard to the role played by the Jews. Except in the comic theater, there is no organic transition between the theater of the Middle Ages and the modern stage. It is because of a completely new orientation that it was able to grow gloriously and rapidly, preceding by a hundred and fifty years the development of the German theater.

When in 1548 the Parlement of Paris made the decision to forbid the Passion plays, it was to oblige the Church, which had lost control over the theater that was born and had grown under its aegis. Created to become a center of religious education, the theater had turned into a worldly form of entertainment, adapting itself to the deteriorating taste of the masses, and reflecting the depravity of that period.[1] We noted this evolution from a special viewpoint; but the anti-Semitic hatred is a symptom of the ferocious instincts dominating the stage and the spectators. In *Le Mystère du Vieil Testament* appears this remark by the director: "We need blood!" Gustave Cohen makes the accurate observation that this

---

1. Cf. Le Roy, *Epoques de l'histoire de France en rapport avec le théâtre,* p. 453.

rule should be applied to all the mystery plays. The
words in which another director summarizes his play
were probably not exaggerated:

Vous avez vu vierges dépuceler
Et femmes mariées violer.

You have seen virgins seduced
And married women raped.

This was granting too many concessions to the lowest
appetites of the unrestrained masses. The worst instincts
of the populace were no longer content with the sop
represented by the Jews; they overflowed all bounds. It
was therefore high time to stop these exhibitions, which
were becoming a danger to the Church.

The Parlement's edict forbidding the Passion plays
found its justification in the eyes of the literary historian
when, in 1553, the first classical tragedy was performed.
Henceforth, the French theater, and French literature in
general, were to follow new directions. This renewal was
determined in part by the contributions of the Bible.

When the humanists turned their attention toward the
spiritual treasures of Antiquity, they discovered a Hebrew culture equal to the Greco-Latin. The total absence
of Jews in France facilitated, in a backward century, the
birth of monstrous legends; but for a generation of
scholars who had jettisoned the prejudices of the Middle
Ages, it was rather a favorable condition, creating toward
the Hebrew world the same neutral attitude that was
observed toward the Hellenic. The discovery of the
Bible by lay scholars has not been the least of the great
discoveries of the sixteenth century.

In 1530 King Francis I founded the institution which
was soon to give birth to the Collège de France. The
Collège was going to represent the modern trends in
teaching as opposed to the Sorbonne, center of medieval

knowledge. Around these two institutions were grouped
the parties of progress and reaction; the struggle was
soon going to turn in favor of progress. The two intellectual currents, the Reformation and the Renaissance, the
first of Nordic origin and the other from the South, meet
in France in the sixteenth century, and while they differ
as to their specific aims, they coincide in their attempt
to destroy the authoritarian spirit of the Middle Ages
and to go back to the original sources.

The Reformation was concerned with discovering the
sources of established doctrines, in order to remove the
veil in which the Bible had been shrouded for fifteen
hundred years. It wanted to rediscover its original sense,
altered and overburdened with too many commentaries.
The Catholic Church, distrusting the critical spirit that
free access to the original sources would have developed,
had succeeded in banishing it, at least among the laymen:
Innocent III had forbidden the reading of the Old Testament; the Council of Toulouse had ordered the burning
of the translations of the Bible into the vulgar tongues.
In the sixteenth century, on the other hand, the goal was
not to burn these books, but to print them in order to
further their circulation. Medieval exegesis saw in the
Old Testament only the expression of the preparation for
Christ's coming. According to this exegesis, the Old Testament's only justification was its character of prefiguration. This does not disappear completely. Even in *Athalie*
one can note the tendency to relate Biblical prophecies to
the advent of Christ, to interpret the Old Testament in
the light of the New. Still, as a whole, it was the spirit of
the Old Testament that was revived in its new disciples.
Calvin[2] wrote commentaries to the Pentateuch and to the
Prophets without taking into account Christian apologetics, in order "not to appear ridiculous in the eyes of

---

2. A. J. Baumgartner, *Calvin hébraïsant et interprète de l'Ancient Testament* (1889).

the Jews." A great number of Protestant sects looked toward Judaism. Anti-Trinity doctrines were preached by the Protestants who fought Catholicism with the weapons of the fearsome exegesis borrowed from the rabbis, past masters in that discipline. Nor was it only the scholars who took up the study of the Old Testament. The book of the Jewish people filled with its spirit the men of action, the apostles and the martyrs of Protestantism: Coligny, Agrippa d'Aubigné, the Huguenots. French Protestantism, like Judaism two centuries before, was sacrificed to national unity, but its spiritual influence has remained, and both have been rehabilitated by history.

As for the Renaissance, the tendency to go back to the original sources was motivated by purely scientific considerations. The study of Latin and Greek had opened up the spiritual treasures of Hellenism; the same spirit of discovery impelled humanists to seek access to Jewish wisdom. The secrets of the Cabala greatly preoccupied them; they hoped to find in it the formula of the mystic harmony between the individual and the universe. In Italy, especially, Jewish philosophers were held in high esteem. Elie del Medigo taught metaphysics in Padua and Juda Abrabanel, known as Leon Ebreo, delighted his contemporaries with his famous dialogues on love, in which he had created an admirable synthesis of Platonic ideas and Jewish thought. Hebrew is listed among the first courses given at the institution of Francis I. Pantagruel explains the new educational ideal in these terms: "I expect you and I want you to learn languages to perfection: first Greek, then Latin, then Hebrew for the Holy Scriptures." Furthermore, he recommends the study of medicine in Greek, Latin, and Hebrew books "without neglecting the Talmudists and the Cabalists."

During the century in which in Italy the works of Leon Ebreo exercised their contagious influence on the minds of the Renaissance, there lived in France a man who presented in his very person a Franco-Semitic alliance and whose influence was to go even further than that of the Judeo-Italian philosopher: Michel Eyquem de Montaigne. This man, in whom all the living forces of the Renaissance were to find their synthesis, the humanist *par excellence*—whose thinking has decisively stimulated the French mind composed of reason, measure, tolerance, moderation, and courage, in a word, of humanity—was of partially Jewish origin. Cecil Roth has concluded that "in the veins of the most exquisitely French of all French writers ran a non-Gallic blood; that this genius who blossomed into maturity on French soil was nourished and vivified by a foreign influence—Semitic—becoming therefore more powerful and nimble, without being any the less French."[3]

Although Montaigne did not draw any of his culture from Jewish sources, their influence is nevertheless quite visible on the formation of his mind. From the family of his mother, née Lopez de Villanuova, Portuguese Jewish converts whose ships carried merchandise on the seven seas, he had received a broad vision which made him a stubborn fighter against the prejudices and narrow viewpoints of his time.

> Montaigne probably learned from all these Pacagons, turned Lopez de Villanuova, to consider himself a citizen of the world and to look beyond the Garonne, or even France. His curiosity was drawn to the four corners of the earth by those relatives whose vessels carried merchandise to every sea, while he himself took root on his native soil.[4]

Some feel that he draws from the alliance of his Jewish background and his Latin education his extraordinary ability to combine gifts which usually destroy each other:

3. Cécil Roth, "L'Ascendance juive de Montaigne," *Revue des Cours et Conférences,* 30 XII 1937.
4. Fortunat Strowski, "La Jeunesse de Montaigne," *Revue des Cours et Conférences,* 30 III 1938.

his powerful spirit of synthesis allowed him to discover general laws in the description of particular facts.

> It is claimed that there is in his genius an element of instability, of anxiety, of skepticism, which reveals a specifically Jewish element. But isn't this element the lot of many men of all races? The human condition: instability, boredom, worry, said Pascal, Christian and descendant of a long line of Christians. Spinoza, on the other hand, with his magnificent constructive certainty was Jewish.[5]

Thibaudet, however, sees in Montaigne's intellectual mobility a Jewish attribute that brought a precious stimulus to French civilization, an attribute that he discovers even in the style of Jewish writers or writers of Jewish origin.

> I am thinking of this mobility, of this anxiety of Israel, of these tents that were for Bossuet the symbol of God's people: *Quam pulchram tabernacula tua, Israel!* Wandering cloth house that one of the great rhythms of history opposed to the stone house of Rome. . . . A Montaigne, a Proust, a Bergson introduce in our complex and rich literary universe what might be called the Franco-Semitic doublet, just as there are Franco-English literary doublets, Franco-German, Franco-Italian, just as France is a doublet—of the North and South.[6]

We believe that these observations sufficiently underline the value of the Jewish element in Montaigne, without overestimating or diminishing its importance. Even if the bold thesis according to which Montaigne is also Jewish on his father's side[7] were to be confirmed, it must not be forgotten that by his spiritual education he is above all a humanist and French. According to the subjects that attracted his attention, he was French; but he drew essentially the mode and the method of his thinking

---

5. *Ibid.*
6. *Nouvelle Revue Française*, January 1, 1923.
7. Henri Bertreux, *Revue hebdomadaire*, February 12, 1938.

from his Jewish background. By modifying one of
Charles Péguy's observations we might say that Montaigne's work presents "Jewish anxiety grafted on the
most vigorous trunk of French strength." And it is to
Montaigne essentially that we trace this attitude of constructive skepticism, kindly irony, and balance, in spite of
occasional excesses—an original attitude known as "the
French spirit."

7
Biblical Tragedies Before Racine

The Franco-Semitic synthesis determined Montaigne's genius; it is likewise the meeting of two spiritual trends that created the classical tragedy of the seventeenth century. It would be mistaken to assume that classical tragedy developed exclusively under the aegis of Eschylus and Sophocles. The prevalence of Greek form should not make us forget that the spiritual content was largely inspired by the Biblical world. Jean de la Taille says of his tragedy *Saül furieux* that "it is taken from the Bible, treated according to the art and the style of Ancient Greek tragic authors." This formula was elaborated from the precursors up to its climax in Racine. The latter produced masterpieces inspired by Greek tragedy, such as *Phèdre* and *Andromaque*. But his art found its most perfect expression in a play that is an incomparable fusion of Greek form and Biblical content: *Athalie*.

This union of the two currents of antiquity that Racine was able to effect was painfully pursued by the Romantics. "Of all books," writes Hugo in the preface to the Odes, "that circulate among men, I must study only two, Homer and the Bible." The author of *Le Génie du Christianisme* goes as far as to declare: "The Bible alone does not resemble anything else." It is rather interesting that the two great schools of French poetry, classicism and romanticism, so antithetical in their aesthetic doctrines,

should have the same veneration for the Bible; it is the
only point on which these two extremes agree. The
classical tragedy in which the Biblical spirit has found
its purest expression, *Athalie,* is at the same time a source
of inspiration and a model for romantic authors. The
central problem of classical drama is that of human destiny. This is precisely where the Jewish and Greek spirits
diverge. The leitmotiv of Sophocles and Aeschylus is a
melancholy complaint about the blind fatality that
crushes earthly creation. All human greatness is powerless before the omnipotence of the gods, whose jealousy
destroys whatever is sublime on earth. Greek literature
presents the great figures of its history or of its legend
either in a submissive attitude towards the gods, to win
their good graces, or in an attitude of defiance, of revolt
when their whims are opposed to mortal aspirations, or
in a state of fatalistic resignation; this powerless resignation of the vanquished before the proud victor is different from the humble and trusting self-effacement of
Biblical heroes before the divine will. Stoical resignation
or desperate revolt prevails where a blind fatality is
recognized as the supreme principle; Biblical obedience
has its roots in faith in Providence. This faith pervades
the Bible from the first to the last chapter. The description of creation implies that the evolution of the world
has a final end, planned by the creator. Abraham, Isaac,
Jacob, and Moses are conscious of being patriarchs: they
feel the responsibility of being the ancestors of a line led
toward a destiny according to a preestablished plan. To
serve that plan, they sacrifice their private happiness,
even where this plan seems capricious and unfathomable.
Abraham accepts the sacrifice of his child, surrenders his
personal and legitimate happiness, without rebelling
against the test which seems the will of his God. How
far removed is his attitude from the exasperation of a
Theseus against the gods who have destroyed his family

happiness! One can see here the wide gap between the Greek and Biblical conceptions.

Jean de la Taille, in his play *Saül furieux* (1572) introduces us into the thick of the struggle between the Greek and Biblical idea. Saul had been ordered by God to destroy in the city of Amalee not only the people but also the animals. However, he spared king Agag and the fattest cattle. From that day forward, the spirit of God had abandoned him; defeat and a wretched death were going to be the conclusion of a glorious reign. This is announced to him by the apparition of Samuel, conjured up by the Pythoness of Endor. How had Saul's mercy been an unforgivable crime? Why had God taken him from his obscure condition and raised him so high, to let him fall so low?

> Tu me tiras, ô Dieu envieux de mon être,
> Où je vivais content sans malédiction
> Mais pour me faire choir d'un saut plus misérable!

> You took me, O God, envious of my being,
> From where I lived happy and uncursed
> But to make me fall even more miserably.

This cry of anger that accuses the Biblical God of being envious of man's happiness, is similar to Orestes' uncontrolled rage against the gods in *Andromaque*, tragedy of Racine's first period:

> Grâce aux dieux! Mon malheur passe mon espérance.
> Oui, je te loue, ô ciel, de ta persévérance
> Appliquée sans relâche au soin de me punir,
> Au comble des douleurs tu m'as fait parvenir.
> Ta haine a pris plaisir à former ma misère;
> J'étais né pour servir d'exemple à ta colère,
> Pour être du malheur un modèle accompli.
> Hé bien! je meurs content, et mon sort est rempli.

God be blessed! My misfortune goes beyond my expectations.
Yes, I praise you, O Heavens, for your perseverance.
Relentlessly dedicated to the task of punishing me.
Your hatred has delighted in shaping my misery;
I was born to serve as an example of your hatred,
To be a perfect model of misfortune.
Well! I die happy, my fate has been fulfilled.

Exactly the same language in *Saül*:

Oh! la belle façon d'aller ainsi chercher
Les hommes, pour après les faire trébucher!
Tu m'alléchas d'honneur, tu m'élevas en gloire,
Tu me fis triomphant, tu me donnas victoire,
Afin de m'enfoncer en mil malheurs après!...
Tu élis donc tes rois de tes ennemis mêmes!
Hé bien, aime-les donc et favorise-les!
Mais je vais, puisqu' ainsi en mes maux tu te plais,
Finir au camp mes jours, mon malheur et ta haine.

O what a beautiful thing to seek out men
And then to trip them!
You whetted my appetite with honors, you covered me with
   glory,
You made me triumphant, you gave me victory,
Only to crush me with a thousand misfortunes afterwards!...
So, you pick your kings among your very enemies!
Well, love them and favor them!
But, since you enjoy my tribulations, I am going
To finish at camp my life, my misfortune and your hatred.

These are almost the same lines, because it is the eternal cry of the man crushed by too many tribulations,
abandoned to despair. If the play had ended at this point,
it would have been, in spite of its Biblical subject, a
tragedy in the Greek spirit. But here begins Saul's transfiguration. He does not resign himself to sink into the
night of despair, but he scrutinizes the meaning of the
events of which he is the victim. His grief purifies him,

and elevates him; he humbly submits to the impenetrable
will of the divinity:

Oh! que Sa providence est cachée aux humains!

Oh! How His providence is hidden from human beings!

We all are, he admits, in the hands of God, who leads
us to a destiny known to him alone. He uses us, but for
purposes far removed from the ones our intelligence
allows us to imagine.

According to a Jewish tradition reported by the Talmud, Aman, persecutor of the Jews in the Persian empire,
is a descendant of Agag. This tradition is meant to high-
light the inadequacy of reason for divining God's orders.
If Saul, imprisoned in the limited horizon of his ephemeral existence, does not understand why his mercy toward
Agag is so pitilessly punished, a distant future could teach
him that it is going to be fatal to the existence of his
people. The trusting faith of the believer makes up for
the limitations of individual understanding.

This idea is vigorously developed in the drama by
Robert Garnier: *Sédécie ou les Juives* (1580). The plot
is drawn entirely from the Bible and summarized in the
preface by the author: Sédécie, king of Judea, disobeying
the prophet Jeremiah, forms an alliance with the king of
Egypt against Nabuchodonosor. The latter hastens to
Jerusalem which falls after a heroic defense of eighteen
months. The temple is pillaged and burned, the city ravaged. Sédécie is taken into slavery, with a great part of
his people, among whom is found his high priest. Nabuchodonosor "after having angrily reproached Sédécie for
his ingratitude and his disloyalty, has his children slaughtered in his presence and the high pontiff decapitated
with the most important lords, then he has his eyes put
out."

The central action of this tragedy is the punishment of Sédécie through Nabuchodonosor. However, it is not an individual tragedy, but the tragedy of a whole nation. The characters, while they retain their individuality, are at the same time symbolic figures. When Amital and the queens vainly implore the barbarian Nabuchodonosor to spare the captives, it is defeated Zion that is weeping, it is the Jewish people at the hands of its enemy. On the other hand, it is the unfortunate fate of Sédécie himself that touches us, when his eyes, before being blinded, are offered as a last spectacle the massacre of his children.

> Astres, qui sur nos chefs éternels flamboyez
> Regardez mes tourments, mes angoisses voyez.
> Mes yeux ne verront plus votre lumière, belle,
> Et vous verrez un roy privé de liberté,
> De royaume, d'amis, d'enfants et de clairté.
> Qui vit si misérable? Autour de cette masse
> Voyez-vous un malheur, qui mon malheur surpasse?

> Heavenly bodies, that burn above our heads,
> Look on my torments, see my anxiety.
> Never again will my eyes see your beautiful light,
> And you will see a king deprived of his freedom,
> Of his kingdom, of his friends, children, and light.
> Who lives as wretchedly? Among these masses
> Do you see a misfortune that surpasses my misfortune?

Up to here the scene resembles the one where Oedipus King surrenders to despair. But then the hero of the Greek tragedy bitterly berates the gods, blind fate that cruelly toys with man. Sédécie, in his misfortune, rises to a moral greatness that he did not possess when he was happy. When the prophet exhorts him:

> Il en faut louer Dieu tout ainsi que d'un bien

> You must praise God, as if it were a blessing,

he bows before this God who has struck him so harshly:

> Toujours soit-il bénit, et que par trop d'angoisse
> Jamais désespéré je ne le déconnoisse.
> Je scay bien que l'ai mille fois irrité,
> Que j'ay son ire esmüe, et que par mon seul crime
> J'ai incité au mal toute Jérosolyme.
> Je suis cause de tout, je le scay. . . .

> May he ever be blessed, and may I never deny him,
> Through the despair of exceeding misery.
> I know I have irritated him a thousand times,
> That I have stirred his anger, and that by my crime alone
> I have incited to evil all Jerusalem.
> I am responsible for everything, I know.

He accepts his punishment, and he accepts the punishment of his people, exile, for he understands its redeeming virtue for the Jewish nation. The complaint against fatality, blind and destructive, that appears occasionally in *Saül furieux* has been replaced by the humble confidence in an almighty God who punishes his creatures, not with the aim of crushing them, but of elevating them and leading them to a better fate. It is the triumph of the idea of Providence. The precept "Il en faut louer Dieu, tout ainsi que d'un bien" (which, incidentally is still a force in Judaism today) summarizes the central idea of this classical drama, an idea that transcends the stoical attitude that consists in not resisting evil.

We are thus far from Greek tragedy, in spite of the carefully respected framework. It is the spirit of the Old Testament, in all its purity. The poet says in his preface: "C'est un discours chrétien et religieux." (It is a Christian and religious discourse). Christian, of course: but that part of Christianity (whose other elements are borrowed from Stoicism and Platonicism) which comes from Judaism. It is first of all a discourse in the spirit of the great Prophets of Israel, whose style and lyricism are

often deliberately imitated. There are passages filled with
the inspiration of the lamentations of Jeremiah: i.e., the
choir in Act II:

> Nous te pleurons, lamentable cité
> Qui eus jadis tant de prosperité
> Et maintenant, pleine d'adversité
> Gis abattue
>
> Las! au besoing tu avais eu toujours
> La main de Dieu levée à ton secours,
> Qui maintenant de remparts et de tours
> T'as dévestue.
>
> Il t'a laissée au milieu du danger,
> Pour estre esclave du soudart étranger
> Qui d'Assyrie est venu saccager
> Ta riche terre

> We weep for you, pitiful city
> That was once so prosperous
> And now, overwhelmed by adversity
> Lies defeated
>
> Alas! in your hour of need, God's hand
> Was always raised to help you
> Now he has stripped you of walls and towers
>
> He has abandoned you in the midst of danger,
> To be the slave of the foreign mercenary
> Who came from Assyria to devastate
> Your rich land

This chorus, element of the Greek theater but whose
content is inspired by the Bible, forecast the synthesis
which was to give the French theater its masterpiece.
"A day will come when, like Garnier, a great dramatic
poet will choose a Biblical subject, will be inspired by
the poetry of the sacred books, will have choruses inti-

mately integrated with the plot, a stage always filled, vivid and varied supernumeraries; like Garnier, he will conceive of a great religious idea and will make of it the moral unity of his play; he will introduce in the theater sacred eloquence, and he will dare carry it to the terrible and ardent disorder of prophetic delirium; he will add genius to what Garnier has conceived and sketched out, and Athalie will be born."[1]

1. E. Faguet, *La Tragédie française du XVIe siècle* (Leipzig-Paris, 1897), p. 253.

8
Racine's Biblical Dramas

What has struck Racine's admirers above all, is the fact
that the most pagan of French playwrights is at the same
time the greatest Biblical poet. No other poet has been
able to rival him in fulfilling the principles that govern
classical tragedy; *Andromaque* or *Phèdre* inspire fear
and pity like a drama of Sophocles or Aeschylus, with
the only difference that Racine has replaced the superhuman forces, which in ancient tragedy toyed blindly with
human destiny, with man's innate passions, also blind,
crushing, triumphant over human will. The same man
was able to create in *Esther* and *Athalie* works filled with
the idealism of the true believer. The poet himself feels
this dualism of his being and expresses it in his *Cantiques
Spirituels:*

> Mon Dieu, quelle guerre cruelle!
> Je trouve deux hommes en moi:
> L'un veut que, plein d'amour pour toi
> Mon coeur te soit toujours fidèle:
> L'autre à tes volontés rebelle
> Se révolte contre ta loi.

> My God, what cruel strife!
> I find two men in me:
> One wants my heart, full of love for you,
> To be always faithful to you:
> The other, rebellious to your will
> Rises against your law.

In reality, there is no contradiction: the two tendencies of his heart have the same source: in *Phèdre* as well as in *Athalie* Racine is the poet of the irrational. Racine as a religious poet has not stopped being the poet of passion; passion is his religion, and he conceives religion itself as a passion. It is not, it is true, a destructive fury, annihilating human will, but a noble passion, exerting a beneficial influence on the moral aspirations through which divine will operates. The characters of *Athalie* are the shapers of their own destiny for good or evil, while they remain the instruments of the divinity; according to the words of the royal poet "the sinners fall in their own traps." Even though he reserves a place for divine intervention, Racine remains a realist. In this fashion, by humanizing supernatural forces, the poet of pagan fatality has become the perfect interpreter of Biblical Providence. A detailed analysis of his religious plays will clarify this point.

Athalie

The first act introduces Abner, who loyally heads the queen's army, but without love and without true devotion. The people, faithful to the house of David, are discouraged and helpless, because they believe that the whole Davidic dynasty has been exterminated.

> Dieu même, disent-ils, s'est retiré de nous:
> De l'honneur des Hebreux autrefois si jaloux,
> Il voit sans intérêt leur grandeur terrassée;
> Et sa miséricorde à la fin s'est lassée.
> On ne voit plus pour nous ses redoutables mains
> De merveilles sans nombre effrayer les humains:
> L'arche sainte est muette, et ne rend plux d'oracles.

> God himself has abandoned us:
> Once so preoccupied with the honor of the Hebrews,
> He now looks unconcerned upon their ruined greatness;
> And his mercy at last has grown weary.

No longer do we see his fearsome hands
Frighten mankind for our sake;
The sacred ark is silenced and does not pronounce any
   more oracles.

But the miracle is announced when Josabeth tells the
circumstances in which she saved the child Joas. She and
the high priest Joad are the only ones who know that he
is alive. Joad is convinced that God has chosen him to
restore the House of David and he waits for the appropriate moment to act. We have to act, and not merely
leave to God the task of realizing his will by a superhuman miracle; we encounter here one of the basic pos-
tulates of Judaism.

The act ends with a noble prayer by the high priest.

Grand Dieu, si tu prévois qu'indigne de sa race,
Il doive de David abandonner la trace,
Qu'il soit comme le fruit en naissant arraché,
Ou qu'un souffle ennemi dans sa fleur a séché.
Mais si ce même enfant, à tes ordres docile,
Doit être à tes desseins un instrument utile,
Fais qu'au juste héritier le sceptre soit remis;
Livre en mes faibles mains ses puissants ennemis;
Confonds dans ses conseils une reine cruelle.
Daigne, daigne, mon Dieu sur Mathan et sur elle
Répandre cet esprit d'imprudence et d'erreur
De la chute des rois funeste avant-coureur.

Good Lord, if you foresee that unworthy of his race,
He is to betray David's example,
Let him be like the fruit torn off at birth,
Or dried in its flower by a hostile wind.
But if this same child, obedient to your orders,
Is to be a useful instrument of your designs,
Ordain that the scepter be handed over to the legitimate heir.
Deliver unto my feeble hands his powerful enemies;
Confound in her counsels a cruel queen
Deign, deign, my Lord, to fill Mathan and her
With the spirit of carelessness and error,
Fatal forerunner of the downfall of kings.

We have thus in the very first act a complete picture of the kingdom of Judea under Athalie's domination. On one side we find the usurper; around her throne, still dripping with the blood of the royal family she had murdered, are grouped those who are attached to her by self-interest or fear. These are her Tyrian guard, the ministers of Baal to whom she has dedicated a temple in Jerusalem and whose cult has been made official; Jews like Mathan whose ambition has turned them into renegades; the people, who accept with resignation the accomplished fact. On the other side, defying the bloody queen, is the high priest Joad, his head unbowed, supported in his resistance solely by the true priests, the Levites, and by a small number of Jews who have remained faithful to God. Between these two parties ready to tangle, there is a child, the prize of the struggle, the descendant of the legitimate dynasty. Athalie's party seems the strongest. But a pillar of its power has been weakened: the army is commanded by Abner, who is torn between his loyalty to Queen Athalie and his devotion to the legitimate race of the House of David. Victory will depend on the army. These are of course, purely political considerations; what will be the spiritual motives, signs of the will of God, that will decide the attitude of the army?

Joad's prayer, with which the first act ends, seems answered. The queen, disturbed by a nightmare, goes to the Temple, where she sees the child that has appeared to her. She questions him and quickly suspects his real ancestry: a descendant of the legitimate dynasty who escaped the massacre. But her fierce energy was destroyed by a disturbing dream, and by the innocent and touching answers of the child.

In the third act, the decisive battle is being prepared in the two camps. Athalie sends Mathan, Baal's high priest, to ask Joad to give him the child as a hostage, because she wants to raise him at court. Joad chases the apostate priest from the temple. It is an open declaration of war. Now the time has come to act, without waiting for any further sign from Heaven.

> Dieu défend-il tout soin et toute prévoyance?
> Ne l'offense-t-on point par trop de confiance?

> Does God forbid all preparation and all foresight?
> Doesn't one offend him by too much trust?

The high priest's holy zeal exalts him to a prophetic vision that announces to him the destruction of the Temple and the resurrection of the House of David in a new Jerusalem. This splendid contemplative scene is completely inspired by the spirit of the great prophets of Israel; here and there are found textual borrowings. The lamentation over the destruction of the Temple is drawn from Jeremiah. The prophecies dealing with the Messianic period are taken from Isaiah. Racine, however, as a Christian poet, applies them to the coming of Christ; he interprets the prophecies in the light of the New Testament.

> Quelle Jérusalem nouvelle
> Sort du fond du désert brillant de clartés,
> Et porte sur le front une marque immortelle?
> Peuples de la terre, chantez:
> Jerusalem renaît plus brillante et plus belle.
> D'où lui viennent de tous côtés
> Ces enfants qu'en son sein elle n'a point portés?
> Lève, Jerusalem, lève la tête altière;
> Regarde tous ces rois de ta gloire étonnés;
> Les rois des nations, devant Toi prosternés,
> De tes pieds baisent la poussière;
> Les peuples à l'envi marchent à ta lumière.
> Heureux qui pour Sion d'une sainte ferveur
> Sentira son âme embrasée!
> Cieux, répandez votre rosée.
> Et que la terre enfante le Saveur!

What new Jerusalem
Emerges from the heart of the desert dazzling with lights,
And bears on its forehead an immortal sign?
People of the earth, sing out:
Jerusalem is reborn, more brilliant and more beautiful.
Whence come from all directions
These children she has not borne?
Raise, Jerusalem, your proud head;
Look at all these kings amazed at your glory;
The kings of all nations, bowing before you,
Kiss the dust of your feet,
The people are to walk behind your light
Blessed be he whose soul will be consumed
With a holy fervor!
Heavens, shed your dew
And may the earth give birth to the Savior!

The next act shows us even better that the seer, the Biblical Prophet, is not just a contemplative. In him, rather, contemplation leads to action. After crowning the child Joas, the high priest, with the coolness of a general, gives the strategic orders for the defense of the Temple against the Tyrian guard. His courage is communicated to the Levites, whose hands, accustomed to carrying the harp and the psalter, seize the sword. They are about to carry out the words of the psalm that they have sung: "I praise God with all my limbs." They are ready to praise him by offering him their bodies.

To serve the cause of his God, Joad sets aside all qualms as to the choice of means. He entices the Queen into the Temple. As soon as she has entered with Abner and some of the soldiers, he orders the doors closed and shows them the young King, wearing the crown. At the same time, he spreads in the city the news of the miraculous survival of David's descendant. The psychological effect is just as Joad had expected. Abner kneels in front of the young King, the Jewish soldiers follow his example, the Tyrian guard flees, Athalie is led outside the walls of the temple to be put to death. The legitimate party has carried the day against the usurpers.

What we have here, basically, is nothing but a dynastic quarrel like those that make up the subject of so many plays by Shakespeare, Corneille, Racine. There is no *deus ex machina*, no superhuman intervention; everything unfolds according to the psychological laws that govern politics. The action and the dénouement are produced by the confrontation of characters, just as in Racine's nonreligious plays.

And yet, another atmosphere pervades *Athalie*. The "God of the Jews, who prevails," nowhere visible, is present in every scene. He imposes his terrible presence on his friends and enemies. His is the motive force that activates the whole machinery; only after the first disturbance occasioned by a mysterious force does the action unfold according to what is known as psychological laws. A dream is the catalyst of the action. But this dream can be explained naturally by the dread in which Athalie constantly lives; her power is based neither on the trust nor on the love of her people; it is supported by the swords of mercenaries. The people bow to tyranny because they believe that God has abandoned them; after the apparent extermination of David's race, the people, discouraged, do not have the strength to react. But Athalie knows the nature of this people, weak when hope leaves them, but terrible and invincible when the spirit of God is revealed. And the survival of a descendant of the House of David is the sign that will awaken the people from their lethargy. That is why she has been haunted for years by the fear that a scion of the dynasty of David has survived the massacre. Her dream is thus explained psychologically and very naturally, and Athalie herself could rationalize it. Yet from this moment on, her energy is paralyzed.

She makes mistakes. Mathan has to take her to task:

> Grande reine, est-ce ici votre place?
> Quel trouble vous agite, et quel effroi vous glace?
> Parmi vos ennemis que venez-vous chercher?

> Great Queen, is this your place?
> What worry disturbs you, what terror paralyzes you?
> What are you seeking among your enemies?

Therefore the queen's uneasiness, caused by the dream, is for Joad the opportunity to act. It is for him the sign awaited from God. He is convinced of Racine's idea: the sinners are caught in their own traps, and God blinds those he wants to punish. But he does not leave to God the task of carrying out his work. God has given him a sign; it is now up to him to do Heaven's bidding by every means at his disposal, by duplicity or by force. He is a fervent believer, but he is very practical; he has a realistic concept of miracles; he is the prototype of this robust religion that does not want to offend God by too much reliance on him. Joad personifies the Jewish belief that forbids man to wait passively for divine assistance through a miracle.

Even the scene of the third act, where the high priest announces the coming of the Redeemer, does not lend to this play a particularly Christian character. It gives rather, the impression of a brilliant tour de force, through which the poet, as a practicing Christian and taking Christian tradition into account, attempts to attribute to the story the meaning of the prefiguration of Christ. He does it unobtrusively. The spirit of this tragedy is hardly changed, and bears, on the whole, the Jewish rather than the Christian imprint. This conclusion is corroborated by Racine's other Biblical tragedy: *Esther.*

Esther

The Christian touch is completely lacking in this play.
We again encounter this synthesis of realism and idealism,
this faith in Providence expressed by human activity, that
we have already discovered in *Athalie*. Mordecai, like
Joad, does not carry his trust in God to the point of waiting for a miracle in favor of his threatened people, but
expends every ounce of energy to ward off the danger.
The maxim that guides Joad's activities, "Doesn't one
offend God by too much trust?" is also Mordecai's and
Esther's, and it finds its counterpart in the line that an
Israelite of the chorus utters in speaking of Esther:

> Elle a parlé, Dieu a fait le reste.

> She has spoken, God has done the rest.

Esther has acted, and with God's help, her enterprise was
crowned with success. The providential role of the dream,
which in *Athalie* sparks the action, and which, without
deviating from the order of cause and effect, is used by
Providence as an instrument to carry out its design, has
its corollary in the circumstances that allow Mordecai to
save the king's life. The chain of events that leads to
Mordecai's elevation, and, through him, to that of the
Jewish people, never transcends the framework of political and psychological action, but the believer recognizes,
with the author, the hand of Providence, which "has done
the rest." Racine was able to draw the spiritual substance
from this Biblical tale, which to this day owes its popularity among the Jews to the fact that it presents the
main characteristic of Judaism: active faith. Neither
Mordecai nor Esther expects a miracle from Heaven,
but they act and God does the rest. Joad and Mordecai
symbolize the realistic character of the Jewish faith that
distinguishes it from the religions born from it.

Judaism, whose roots are in Heaven, in faith in a providential justice, exhibits at the same time a vitality and a practical energy directed toward all the activities of this world. There is not, in this religion, a gulf between the spiritual and temporal world, which are, on the contrary, intimately bound. Racine understood this synthesis peculiar to Judaism, and he symbolized it in figures such as Joad, Mordecai, and Esther, as well as in every event of his Biblical tragedies.

Corneille had written a religious tragedy where divine intervention leads the action. Polyeucte, convinced of his vocation to sanctify the name of the Lord, thinks that he can fulfill it only by a martyr's death. He does not "lower" himself by carrying out this divine mission by human means. He is above material contingencies and must succumb to political intrigues. Felix's conversion to Christianity is not a natural event, psychologically prepared; it is a miracle, it is divine grace bestowed on him. *Polyeucte* is a Christian tragedy. Racine has created political tragedies and tragedies of passion lacking in superior idealism and governed only by human forces. These were pagan tragedies. In *Esther* and *Athalie* Christian idealism and pagan realism meet to give birth to a new concept, and we have tragedies inspired more by the Jewish than the Christian spirit.

Racine did not intend to write a Jewish tragedy. No doubt, as a good Christian he wanted to interpret a Biblical subject for the glorification of the Christian religion. But, as he pored over the Biblical texts, helped by the powerful intuition of his poetic genius, he became gradually imbued with the Jewish spirit and filled his plays with it, abandoning the project of injecting it with the traditional spirit of Christian plays. The reader might remember that a similar evolution took place in the mind of the author of the *Merchant of Venice*. Trying, at the outset, to draw in the figure of Shylock a traditional monster, familiar to popular imagination since the medieval theater, the poet, as he lived his character, was overwhelmed by the tragic conditions of the Jewish merchant's existence. The gay and charming comedy that he intended to write became a drama, poignant in spots, and it is only with a deliberate effort that the poet, remembering his primary intention, imposed on his play a dénouement in accordance with his original plan. It was by a similar psychological process that Racine, turned Christian poet but having remained a poet first of all, wrote in *Athalie* and *Esther* masterpieces strongly imbued with the best Jewish spirit. Racine put all the religious passion and poetry of Israel into French words of immortal beauty.

A Plea in Favor of Tolerance

Racine was able to grasp intuitively not only the religious character of Judaism but also its national and social aspects as it existed throughout history. When he has the chorus of young girls at Esther's court express nostalgia for Zion and attachment to Jerusalem, that is a trait not reserved to the Jews or to Biblical times. The plot of this play, the anti-Jewish persecutions ordered by Aman and Esther's intervention with the King, gives the poet the chance to enter more resolutely the arena of discussions over the historical as well as the contemporary Jewish question. This scene as a whole bears the character of a full-dress plea in favor of tolerance in general and the emancipation of the Jews in particular.

The queen begins by admitting to her husband that she is a member of the Jewish race. The dismay of the king is not without its comic side, but it was natural in Racine's time:

> Ah! de quel coup me percez-vous le coeur?
> Vous la fille d'un juif? Hé quoi, tout ce que j'aime,
> Cette Esther, l'innocence et la sagesse même,

Que je croyais du ciel les plus chères amours,
Dans cette source impure aurait passé ses jours?
Malheureux!

Ah! with what a blow are you piercing my heart?
You, the daughter of a Jew? All that I love,
This Esther, innocence and wisdom itself,
Whom I thought dearly beloved of Heaven,
Has spent her days in this contaminated source?
How wretched I am!

Racine shows the full horror that the term "Jew" produces on those who know this word only through a screen of legends. Esther patiently tells her husband the origin and the real nature of her people.

Ces juifs, dont vous voulez délivrer la nature,
Que vous croyez, Seigneur, le rebut des humains,
D'une riche contrée autrefois souverains,
Pendant qu'ils n'adoraient que le Dieu de leurs pères,
Ont vu bénir le cours de leurs destins prospères . . .

These Jews from which you wish to deliver nature,
That you consider the dregs of mankind,
Were once the rulers of a wealthy country,
And while they worshipped only the God of their fathers,
Their prosperous destiny was blessed. . . .

She presents a defense of the Jewish people, valid even today. She refutes the accusation that the Jews are the eternal cause of war (or, depending on the situation, of peace); she reaffirms the loyalty of her coreligionists toward the state in general and toward its head in particular. She points out the services that certain Jews have performed for the king, for the state, and the like:

Et que reproche aux juifs sa haine envenimée?
Quelle guerre intestine avons-nous allumée?
Les a-t-on vus marcher parmi vos ennemis?
Fut-il jamais au joug esclaves plus soumis?

Adorant dans leurs fers le Dieu qui les châtie,
Pendant que votre main sur eux appesantie,
A leurs persécuteurs les livrait sans recours,
Ils conjuraient ce Dieu de veiller sur vos jours,
De rompre des méchants les trames criminelles
De mettre votre trône à l'ombre de ses ailes.
N'en doutez point, Seigneur, il fut votre soutien,
Lui seul mit à vos pieds le Parthe et l'Indien,
Dissipa devant vous d'innombrables Scythes,
Et renferma les mers dans vos vastes limites,
Lui seul aux yeux d'un juif découvrit un dessein
De deux traîtres tout prêts à vous percer le sein.

And what does his venomous hatred reproach the Jews?
What domestic wars have we kindled?
Have they ever walked among your enemies?
Were there ever slaves more resigned to the yoke?
Worshipping in irons the God who punishes them,
While your hand weighed down upon them,
And delivered them helpless to their persecutors.
They implored this God to watch over your life,
To crush the criminal plots of evil men,
To put your throne under his wing.
Never doubt it, O Lord, he was your protector,
He alone put Partha and India in your power
Scattered before you the Scythian hords,
And placed the seas within your vast possessions.
He alone uncovered to the eyes of a Jew the plot
Of two traitors to stab you in the heart.

These lines, we repeat, plead substantially the cause of
Esther's contemporaries, but also of the Jews of Racine's
time (and those of every period, scattered in every land).
The historical accuracy of Racine's plays has been exten-
sively discussed. It has been stated that, in spite of a
certain local color with which Racine endows the event
of his dramas, the portraits he draws are those of his
time and environment. Classical art paints human emotions and the events they cause in a way applicable to any
period. The framework and local or historical color play

only a secondary role. By changing a few details in the speech of Aman, the symbolic persecutor, and a few details in Esther's refutation, we can grasp the perfect resemblance between these distant events and the actual situation of the Jews. Furthermore, the poet, the philosopher, even if he deals only with the most general problems, sees them always from a certain angle, through the mirror of his time. Every man, even the most independently minded, absorbs more or less the influence of his period. Racine could know the psychological situation of the Jews in the Persian Empire only by studying their condition in Europe. Thus the dialogue between Assuerus and Esther reflects more or less the atmosphere of the Jews of Racine's time. And Esther's speech shows clearly enough which side Racine took, one hundred years before the Emancipation by the French Revolution.

It would not be improper to attribute to the events in Racine's plays a similar feeling of actuality. Louis XIV's courtesans always detected certain allusions to some contemporary person or event. This tendency even went too far by claiming to recognize Mme de Maintenon in Esther, a comparison which pleased the great lady considerably. The young Israelites, reared in a corner of Assuerus's palace, near whom Esther forgets her greatness, supposedly represented the young girls of Saint-Cyr; Assuerus was Louis XIV; the haughty Vasthi was Mme de Montespan. Aman seemed to represent Louvois, who was losing favor. The edict of the proscription of the Jews meant the revocation of the Edict of Nantes. That type of interpretation does not take into account the author's statement in his preface that he does not want "to change any circumstance of any importance in the Holy Scriptures."

We should not seek actuality in Esther's tragedy by a strained comparison between Assuerus's court and Louis XIVth's, but in the depiction of the Jews in the Persian empire and in Europe. It is not without warmth that this Christian poet celebrates on the stage the defeat of anti-Semitism, the triumph of Mordecai's loyalty over Aman's perfidy, the victory of Esther's virtue over the daughters of Persia. Perhaps Racine had no conscious intention of pleading the cause of the Jews; he chose the subject because of the charm of the tale in order to satisfy Mme de Maintenon's wish for a play for her girls' school. But, as a true poet, he found in his subject matter more than he had looked for; he found truth under the veneer of convention, and the true poet is akin to the prophet in the fact that he can express only the truth. Similarly, the great British poet, when treating the stock character of the Jewish usurer, developed it until it reached tragic and deeply human proportions. Shakespeare and Racine are like Saul, who went in search of his she-asses and found a kingdom instead.

9
Bossuet and Pascal

The ideas expressed in *Esther* show that tolerance is not a creation of the Enlightenment; the seventeenth century is not only the great century from a literary standpoint, but also the great century of the development of new humanitarian ideas. The political results of the Great Revolution can be traced in a straight line to the men of the sixteenth century who broke with the Middle Ages, which meant for Judaism a revision of the attitude toward it. This about-face became increasingly more general and the Church itself took a hand in the emancipation of the mind through the words of representatives as authoritative as Fénélon, Pascal, and Bossuet, "the last Father of the Church."

Bossuet

In a way, Bossuet[1] carries on the humanistic trend that consisted in assigning the Jewish people its rightful place in the concert of ancient peoples. The humanists had worked on the philological and philosophical plane; Bossuet worked on a historical plane. In his *Discourse on Universal History*, while basing himself on the theological tradition of the Church, he develops with a great deal of vigor and originality a philosophy of history, in which Israel plays a role of prime importance. The purpose of

1. F. Brunetière, *La Philosophie de Bossuet*, critical studies, 5th series.

his philosophy is to show the many links that connect
Biblical history to general history; the life of a nation
is of interest only in so far as it plays a part in the progress of humanity. It seems to him that from that point
of view the people of Israel is a more decisive factor
than the great nations mentioned in secular history, and
that the election of this people is explained by its influence on the spiritual advancement of humanity. "As each
people was following its own path and was forgetting its
creator, this great God, to prevent the spread of so
great an evil, in the midst of corruption, began to set
apart a chosen people. Abraham was selected to be the
stem and the father of all believers. God called him to
the land of Canaan, where he wanted to found his cult."
Using Providence as his guideline to distinguish among
the infinitely varied aspects of ancient history, Bossuet
passes from the Patriarchs to the kingdom of Argos, to
continue with the story of the combat between Jacob and
the Angel; he speaks of Moses and the Deluge, of Deu-
calion, of Deborah and Ninus, of Saul and Medon, son
of Codrus; all that precisely for the purpose of estab-
lishing the relationship between Israel and the rest of the
world, to demonstrate "that there are no human powers
that do not serve in spite of themselves other purposes
than their own," that the Jewish people has been entrusted with a particular mission by Providence. Bossuet
shows us the errors, the punishment, even the dispersion
of that people, as many striking signs of its divine vocation; the foreign conquerors are the instruments that God
has used, either to punish his people or to protect it from
destruction.

But the watchful eye of Providence favored the Jews
only as long as they were the keepers of the true religion.
Since Jesus Christ, their legacy has been passed on to
other hands. Bossuet dedicates a whole chapter to the
"errors" of the Jews in the explanation of the prophecies.

"The Jews," he claims, "blind to the sign of the time,
interpreted erroneously the sermons of their prophets
and saw the Messiah in the person of Herod, Vespasian,
St. John the Baptist and Bar Cochebas. Disillusioned,
they claimed later that they had no more Messiah to
wait for. The rabbis came to write: 'Every period marked
for the coming of the Messiah is over. A curse on those
who will calculate the time of the arrival of the Messiah.'
They were not afraid to destroy the tradition of their
fathers, as long as they could deprive the Christians of
these admirable prophecies." So the Jews, for so long
the legitimate guardians of divine truth, had supposedly
lost it because they had not recognized Christ. The
nations that believed in the coming of Christ replaced
the one waiting for him. Bossuet criticizes the Jews for
not seeing the direct chain that leads from Adam to
Innocent III; their humiliating and miserable lot is God's
punishment for the stubbornness with which they maintain
their error. "Judea is nothing to God anymore, nor to
religion, nor are the Jews: and it is just that as a punishment of their callousness, their ruins be scattered over
the whole earth."

But even though Bossuet condemns the attitude of the
Jews toward Jesus, he tries to understand it: under the
hard yoke of Herod and the Romans, they forgot "so
many of the prophecies that spoke to them so specifically
of humiliations, that neither their eyes nor their ears
were attuned to those that announced triumphs, although
very different from the ones they wanted." In spite of
his indignation against the "blindness" of the Jews, Bossuet proclaims that God has not rejected his people forever, but that he will welcome it to his bosom as soon as
it abjures its errors: "Since they must come back some
day to this Messiah they have ignored, and since the God
of Abraham has not exhausted his mercy for the race of
this patriarch, in spite of its unfaithfulness, he has found

a means unique in the world to perpetuate the Jews outside their country and in their ruined state longer than
the people who have vanquished them."

The Last Father of the Church adopts toward Judaism the attitude of the Church in its merciful mood, forgotten during the night of the Middle Ages. One hundred
years before him, the great Genevan reformer had already declared that the rejection of Israel was only
temporary, that God had singled out that people, however small, from among the powerful nations that sur-
rounded it, and that it would recover its glory after
expiating its errors. But Calvin's influence did not spread
in France. Bossuet's authority contributed to the introduction of new criteria for the historic judgment of the
people of Antiquity and to the destruction of viewpoints
from which the history of human civilization had been
studied. What had been considered of major importance
turned out to be a little cog in the big machine, the mainspring of which appeared suddenly to be a small and
despised nation. The Jews, who had never been mentioned
in the same breath with the Romans and the Greeks, were
not only rehabilitated, but became suddenly the center of
world history. How daring it is to state: "God used the
Assyrians and the Babylonians to punish that people, the
Persians to restore them, Alexander and his first succes-
sors to try it, the Romans to support its freedom against
the kings of Syria bent on destroying it."

It is not surprising that this bold attempt to focus
world history on the Jewish people provoked lively pro-
tests. Voltaire and his disciples accused Bossuet of having
taken as the central point of his "so-called world history"
that "miserable little Jewish nation, that tribe whose
obscure existence in an isolated corner of the Orient occupies such a small place in the annals of the civilized
world." It is obvious that Voltaire's unfavorable bias
toward the people of Israel is as unfair as Bossuet's atti-

tude, too favorable in his eyes. The salient point in Bossuet's historical and remarkably modern conception is
the now commonplace idea: that the role of a people in
history is not measured only by the number of its citizens
or by its military exploits. Another historian, Renan, two
centuries later was to restore the history of Israel to its
rightful place. "For a philosophical mind," says Renan,
"that is to say to a mind interested in origins, there are
really only three histories of primary interest: Greek
history, the history of Israel, Roman history. These three
histories together constitute what might be called the
history of civilization, since civilization is the result of the
alternating collaboration of Greece, Judea and Rome."
Renan seems to confirm explicitly Bossuet's thesis when
he adds: "If Christianity was and remains up to now the
most important phenomenon of the history of the world,
it can only be explained and understood in the light of the
history of the people of God."

The merit of Bossuet's philosophy lies in having
recognized Israel's place in the history of the human
spirit, in spite of the exaggerations for which the devel-
oper of a new thesis is known. If his condemnation of
post-Biblical Judaism corresponds to the official Church
position, his evaluation of the civilization created by the
people of the Bible and surviving to the present day
clearly transcends the theological framework.

Pascal

If Bossuet avoided a moral conflict by respecting the
usual demarcation between post-Biblical and Biblical Judaism, his greater contemporary Pascal did not enjoy
the peace of mind resulting from the unquestioning acceptance of dogmas. His religious faith, to be sure, was
no less fervent than Bossuet's, but it was not a gift inherited and retained, once and for all, the way it had been
received; it was created and formed daily in his soul,

this creative soul composed of "instability, boredom, and anxiety."

This spiritual torment is also revealed in his discussion of the problems that the presence of an indestructible Judaism surviving every catastrophe presents to every sincere Christian. On the one hand, he cannot forgive the Jews their denial of Christ, and he condemns them for their stubbornness; on the other hand, he cannot resist a certain understanding, even a certain esteem for the Jewish genius whose outstanding trait is to be precisely a stiff-necked people, whether for good or for evil:

When I examine the unstable and bizarre variety of customs and beliefs in the various eras, I encounter in a corner of the world, a distinct people, separated from the other people of the earth, the oldest of them all and whose history precedes by several centuries the most ancient that we possess . . . I find that this nation is great and numerous . . . descending from a single man, adoring a single God and governed by a law that it claims to have received from His hands. They say that they are the only ones to whom God revealed his mysteries, that all men are corrupt and in God's disfavor, that they all have abandoned themselves to their senses and their minds, and that's the reason for their strange aberrations and the continual changes of religion and customs that occur among them, instead of their remaining unswerving in their behavior, but that God would not abandon forever the other people in the darkness, that a liberator would come for them, that they have been placed in the world to announce it to men, that they have been created specifically to be the forerunners and the heralds of this great event and to call upon all nations to join them in the expectation of this liberator. The encounter of that people surprises me, and seems worthy of attention. I examine that law that it claims to have received from God, and I find it admirable. . . . The Jewish people has received truth in trust. Circumstances have enabled it to fulfill to perfection its mission of guardian of truth. The Jewish people has a continuous existence, without interruption. . . . While the nations of Greece, Italy, Lacedemonia, Athens, Rome and the others that have come so much later have perished so long ago, they still survive, and in spite of the attempts of

so many powerful kings who have tried a hundred times to destroy them, as their historians testify . . . nevertheless, they
have not perished (and their survival has been predicted); and
stretching from the first days to the last, their history in its
length contains all our histories.[2]

How far removed is Pascal from the attitude that
considers Israel's longevity a curse afflicting the Wandering Jew; with friendly intuition, he grasps the three-
thousand-year unity of Jewish history. His point of view
diverges radically from orthodox tradition, according to
which Jewish history stops with the advent of Christ
and all the rest has no real justification. He recognizes
that continuity exists not from the Christian point of
view alone, according to which the truth was passed down
from the Ancient to the New Testament, and that it must
be admitted that the uninterrupted chain that connects
the Jewish generations is not without inherent logic.

The Jews' stubborn attachment to their past, which
the Church condemns as blindness, fills him with a surprise that borders on admiration. What distinguishes the
Jews from all the other people is their sincerity. For, he
notes, they had nothing to gain in preserving their Holy
Scriptures that testify not at all in their favor. The least
they could have done was to retouch certain prophecies
that criticize their ingratitude toward God, and announce
their dispersal as a form of heavenly punishment.[3] This
faithfulness of the Jews to their texts is for Pascal a sign
of their sincerity, and a fact that testifies greatly in their
favor. "Sincere against their honor, and dying for that,
there is no precedent for it in the world nor roots in

---

2. *Pensées,* section IX, 619-620. Léon Brunschvicg, ed. (Hachette,
1925).
3. *Ibid.,* p. 651. Ingenious observation that Voltaire should have kept
in mind during his intemperate attacks against the misdeeds, committed
according to him, by the heroes of the Old Testament. Would it not have
been handier for its author to arrange it in such a way that it might be
read unexpurgated in a girl's school?

nature." He points out the faithfulness of the Jews to
the Bible as an example to the Christians, and urges
them also to accept the Bible as is, without being discouraged by the contradictions that appear in the texts. Contradictions exist only for those who do not know how to
read the Bible. "To understand the Scriptures, one must
discover a meaning that reconciles all contradictory passages. It isn't enough to find one that fits a few consistent
passages. The need is for a meaning that harmonize even
contradictory passages."[4]

Pascal is convinced that all the words of the Bible have
a double meaning. The Scriptures must be treated like
a cipher. "The cipher has a double meaning, the first
meaning is clear and the second is hidden."[5] The cipher
is interpreted by a key. For Spinoza, who had already
considered the Scriptures as a cipher, a symbol, the key
had been reason and love. For Pascal, this key is Christ,
and all the Biblical words are prefigurations.

But why did God speak in ciphers? Why did he not
speak more clearly? He wanted to hide, "to blind some
and enlighten others." We recognize here the Jansenist
doctrine of grace, a doctrine aimed at affording peace to
souls that are tormented by the eternal question of divine
justice.

The Prophets had predicted the Messiah, but they
had not specified the time of his appearance. If the Jews
had been touched by grace, they would have recognized
that Jesus was the Messiah. The misfortune of the Jews
lies in the fact "that they were great lovers of predicted
things and great enemies of their fulfillment. As a consequence, the misfortune of the Jews, but not their defect,
lies in not being touched by grace, which should win them
the charity of those who possess it."

Pascal exhibits toward the Jews a great deal of benevo-

---

4. *Ibid.*, p. 631.
5. *Ibid.*, p. 684.

lence and interest, which were repaid to him by the interest that the Jews have shown for his work. The philosopher Léon Brunschwicg prepared the classic edition of the *Pensées*. He restored the original text and illuminated it by commentaries on many an obscure passage. It is an expression of thanks similar to the one given by the actress Rachel, who, after generations of conventional and academic interpreters, injected new life into Racine's plays.

Thus we see that, while Pascal starts and ends with the apology of the Church, he transcends more than once the traditional framework of Christian discipline, able neither to keep his private conscience from sympathizing where his religious conscience should have condemned, nor his reason from admiring and approving what the obedient believer should have despised. This freedom of judgment, what was it if not a triumphant ray of the century that we call the Enlightenment?

10
Shadows in the Century of Light

The sun of reason did not rise suddenly; for several centuries signs had been foreshadowing it. The humanitarian ideal brought to fruition during the eighteenth century is only the culmination of a liberating movement that began before the Renaissance and the Reformation. The Reformation was the freeing of conscience from the absolute authority of the Church that left its mark even in places where it had not been politically victorious. The Renaissance is defined in general as the discovery of man. The eighteenth century advanced the discovery of human personality and dignity by its struggle for better political and social conditions. The Enlightenment of that period was owing to the popularization of ideas that the preceding centuries had formulated. The humanists had discovered the individual value of man and advocated his moral and spiritual freedom; the eighteenth century rationalists conquered the rights of man and won his political freedom.

In the sixteenth century, the humanists, from Rabelais to Montaigne and the heroes of the Reformation, had demanded freedom of conscience. Descartes had claimed for everyone "the right to remain faithful to the religion of his nurse" and could brag "that he had written a philosophy in such a way that it could be accepted even

by the Turks."[1] In the seventeenth century the dignitaries
of the Church and the royal poets (in the two meanings
of the word), Pascal, Bossuet, Racine, and Corneille had
spoken courageous words. The last was certainly not
thinking only of the persecuted Christians of antiquity
when in *Polyeucte* he clearly formulated the ideal of
tolerance of an enlightened Catholicism:

> J'approuve, cependant, que chacun ait ses dieux
> Qu'il les serve à sa mode, et sans peur de la peine . . .

> I approve, however, that each man have his gods
> That he serve them in his way, without fear of reprisal . . .

The importance of the writers of the eighteenth century comes from the fire with which they developed and
spread the ideas they had inherited. Although they continued and perfected the sixteenth and seventeenth centuries, they diverged from them on an important point.

The spiritual movements launched by the humanists
were, in spite of their opposition to the official Church,
essentially religious. The abuses of clerical power were
opposed, but in the name of the spirit of the Bible.
The eighteenth century is characterized by a sudden
aversion for the religiosity of the preceding period. It
noted that by a skillful policy of concessions and retrac-
tions, the Church had succeeded in channeling the spiritual movement of the sixteenth century and depriving
it of its revolutionary edge. The philosophers themselves,
cautioned by the example of Giordano Bruno and Etienne,
were careful of the sensitivity of the clergy. Their broth-
ers-in-arms in the eighteenth century, seeing the deteriora-
tion of that noble effort, reacted violently against the
supple policy of the Church by extending their hostility
to religion in general. To fight the Church, they attacked

---

1. Charles Adam, *Vie et Oeuvres de Descartes* (1910).

the books that were its foundation, and in particular the Old Testament. That is the source of an anti-Semitic campaign that contrasted peculiarly with their purported enlightened and humanitarian tendencies. These summary remarks will help us understand the tortuous paths that the idea of tolerance was to follow before arriving at the Declaration of the Rights of Man of 1791.

Montesquieu

President de Montesquieu is the noblest figure, the most enlightened of the philosophers of the eighteenth century. He is the link between the somewhat pedestrian philosophers of his century and the bold innovators of preceding centuries. His thinking guided the moderate reformers of the Constituent Assembly. Eager not to destroy the past, purely and simply, but to adapt tradition to the needs of new times, he examined inherited institutions by freeing them of accretions that had deformed their original meaning. His work *Spirit of the Laws* contains a complete program.

His method, which consists in tracing the first origins of human institutions, leads him to very subtle psychological observations; it impels him to reject abuses, but also to give credit to the positive elements of institutions. This preserves him from the radicalism of his contemporaries. When he examines religions, he recognizes the usefulness of the apparatus employed by the churches to strengthen the people's faith. "The more a religion is wrapped in cult that impresses the senses, the more one becomes attached to that religion. We have a penchant for sensory things. We prize the things that continuously occupy us."

However, the external apparatus would in the long run lose its effectiveness if it were not based on a lofty doctrine. By external means, by the effects of skillful propaganda, it would be possible to direct a people for only a limited time. "For a religion to command allegiance, it must have a pure moral. Man, larcenous in little things, is fundamentally honest. This can be seen in the theater: the spectator will respond to emotion that morality endorses and will be shocked by those that it disapproves of."

Montesquieu finds in Judaism the two essential characteristics of a religion: a rich and impressive cult, and an elevated doctrine. The stubborn obstinacy of the Jews in maintaining their faith is due to the fact that ritual practices, wisely distributed, occupy them for a great part of their lives. Every Jew, even far removed from religious practices, is still bound to it by numerous ties of which he is not always aware. The ease with which primitive people change religion stems from the fact that they never change religious practices. Those of the Jewish religion, on the other hand, have too particular and distinctive a character to afford any chance of success to those who expect an easy conversion.

As for the spiritual value of the Jewish religion, Montesquieu evaluates it in these terms: "The Jewish religion is an old trunk that has produced two branches that have covered the earth; I refer to Mohammedanism and Christianity; or rather it is a mother that has given birth to two daughters who have wounded her deeply because, in the matter of religion, the closest are the greatest enemies. But in spite of the bad treatment she has suffered, she allows herself to take pride in having produced them; she uses one to encompass the whole world, while the venerable age of the other stretches through all time."[2]

This assessment of the Jewish religion clearly distinguishes the conception of a Montesquieu on religious tolerance from that of his contemporaries. Tolerance in the eighteenth century was basically the fruit of a general

2. *Lettres persanes*, LX.

skepticism. It was advocated for all creeds because they were considered various forms of the same fundamental error. Those who lack absolute convictions are indulgent toward the beliefs of others. It is only the awareness of possessing the truth that leads one to struggle against everything that is not this truth, unless opposing opinions are squelched for political purposes. The eighteenth century, through indifference to religion as a whole, considering it false *a priori,* lacking anything positive to oppose it, claimed indulgence for any particular confession. This form of tolerance does not result from a positive appreciation of the moral values of the tolerated religion, but from a contemptuous attitude for religion in general.

At the opposite end of this tolerance of skeptical origin, there exists a positive form of tolerance, coming from a profound respect for the particular form in which the search for unique and absolute truth has become crystallized. The superior and truly free minds (free from prejudices) of that period, such as Lessing in Germany and Montesquieu in France, respected the true, the good, and the beautiful in all its forms. For they recognized that pure truth is for God alone, and that the image that men conceive is of necessity conditioned by the particular forms in which the idea of divinity is revealed to them. This comprehensive indulgent spirit that informs the famous story of *Nathan the Wise* also inspires Montesquieu when he writes: "Zeal for the progress of religion is different from the allegiance that we owe it; to love it and observe it, it is not necessary to hate and persecute those who do not observe it."[3]

According to Bossuet, the Jewish religion strayed from the right road after Jesus Christ; Montesquieu maintains frankly that it all depends on one's point of view. In the *Very Humble Remonstrance to the Inquisitors of*

---

3. *Ibid.*

Spain and Portugal[4] he opposes to the aggressive defense of Christianity the reasoning of a Portuguese Jew: "We are the followers of a religion that, as you yourselves acknowledge, was once beloved by God; we believe that God still loves it, and you think that he doesn't love it any more; and because this is your opinion, you put to the sword those who commit the very pardonable error of believing that God still loves what he once loved. . . . We believe that the God we serve, you and I, will not punish us for having suffered death for the sake of a religion that he gave us in the past because we believe that he still wants us to have it."

The rest of this *Remonstrance* is a biting condemnation of the atrocities commited in the name of religion. The inquisitors, says he, persecute heretics more like personal enemies than enemies of the Church. The blows that Montesquieu strikes against the Church are especially telling, since they come from a philosopher who otherwise does not share the hostility of the philosophers of his time against Christianity. In the midst of a generation essentially destructive (destruction no doubt necessary, but which is not an end in itself), Montesquieu was a constructive genius. His thinking transcends in breadth, as well as in depth, that of his contemporaries who enjoyed a greater popularity, and every period could profitably take to heart the humanitarian ideal in which the author of *Spirit of the Laws* believed.

The resounding success of the *Lettres persanes* is confirmed by *Lettres chinoises,* and other exotic letters that appeared subsequently. Let us single out in the series of this exotic correspondence *Les Lettres juives*[5] by the marquis d'Argens. Through the pen of three educated and broad-minded Jews, he paints the picture of European

4. *Esprit des lois,* XIII.
5. Haag, 1736.

civilization in relation to the Jewish people. For an example:

"What do you think, my dear Isaac, of the confusion and the disorder that reigns in the customs of the Nazarenes? They daily extol the beauty and wisdom of their morality, and they consider adultery a form of gallantry. What a difference between the innocence of Israel and the debauchery of the infidels. Our women take their greatest pride in loving only their husbands; and if sometimes human weakness overcomes wisdom and reason, they mitigate their crime by the care they take to keep the knowledge of it from the public.

"Jewish women are the only ones in the world immune to the mores of their environment: they have everywhere the same freedom and the same reserve. They are equally virtuous in Asia, Europe and Africa; that is not the case with the women of other religions. The Moslems owe their virtues to locks, to doors, to the vigilance of the eunuchs; they have as great a penchant to unfaithfulness as the Nazarenes; and they are even easier to seduce. The restraints put on them impel them to take advantage of their first opportunity. Virtue alone is the rule of the daughters of Zion; they are as free in Asia as European women; and they have the propriety of the Moslems; they preserve it equally among the excesses of Nazarene countries without being won over or tempted by bad examples."[6]

The literary value of these letters cannot be compared to *Lettres persanes;* but they are proof of the friendly interest that the period, as a whole, showed to Judaism. In France, the people and the government showed in their behavior that humanitarian ideas had found a fertile ground. Tolerance toward the Jews, before its legal establishment by the French Revolution, was already practiced in fact, if not officially. Mercier in his *Tableau de Paris* notes that their business dealings are unrestricted, that their marriages are valid, and he mentions the anecdote of a German Jew who had come from Ger-

---

6. *Lettres juives,* part I.

many and was the proprietor of a *seigneurie*. Having defended in court his right to appoint priests to the parishes within his jurisdiction, he won his suit.

And yet, this friendliness towards the Jews was not unanimous. The difference of opinions among the members of the National Assembly, where in spite of the enthusiasm for the rights of man, the question of the emancipation of the Jews was to be the subject of a bitter struggle, was foreshadowed by the diversity of views of the writers who prepared the Revolution. A spiritual movement or a literary school is never so true to itself as it seems from a distance. And its representatives do not always act in accordance with the role which a naïve tradition has attributed to them. This observation becomes evident when one studies the anti-Judaic campaign conducted by the "king of the century."

Voltaire

Bossuet and the official representatives of the Church justified the wretched condition of contemporary Jews by their straying from the path of righteousness, but they were grateful to them for having given the Bible to the world. The philosophers of the eighteenth century, on the contrary, fought the Bible as the basis of the Church, but left contemporary Jews alone.

Voltaire adopts the criticisms of both camps, without making their allowances. An anticlerical philosopher, he fights relentlessly against Christianity; but at the same time he does not neglect the arguments of the Church when they strike against post-Biblical Judaism. He uses the same procedure when he analyzes the Judaism of his own time by explaining the ambulant trades that had characterized the life of the Jews from the Middle Ages on as an atavism from "their wanderings in the desert," and when he uses against Biblical Judaism criticisms born two thousand years later as a result of anti-Judaic legisla-

tion of the Middle Ages. His method is thus reduced
to a vicious circle.

Let us examine the arguments that he marshalls against
the Bible.[7] "It is a signal example of human stupidity
that we have so long considered the Jews as a nation
that has taught everything to the others.[8] The Jews
did with ancient history and ancient fable what their old
clothes dealers do with their used suits; they turn them
inside out and sell them as new as dearly as possible."
Here is a historical parallel more amusing than con-
vincing.

To establish the inferiority of the Jewish people and
of the Bible, Voltaire makes an extensive study of the
ceremonies and rites of the various religions of antiquity.
The Jews, he says, did not even have a word for God;
they must have borrowed it from the Phoenicians:
Adonai comes from the Phoenician word *adonis*. The
whole cosmology of Genesis is of Phoenician origin; the
creation of the world in six stages, the creation of man
by God's breath, the Garden of Eden, the serpent, even
the ten generations up to the Deluge. "Their stubbornness, their new superstitions, their confirmed usury are
the only things that distinctly belong to them. The story
of Loth and his daughters is only the imitation of an
Arab tale, whose theme is nevertheless more moral than
the Biblical version. Finally, it has been said that the
Garden of Eden resembles these gardens of Eden in
Saana, in happy Arabia, famous throughout all of antiquity; that the Hebrews, a very recent people, could
have been an Arab horde, and that they took credit for
whatever was most beautiful in the best canton of Arabia;
that they have always exploited the ancient traditions of

7. Cf. H. Emmrich. *Zur Behandlung des Judentuns bei Voltaire*, thesis
(Breslau, 1930).
8. Dictionnaire philosophique, *Abraham*. The articles on the Jews are
found in *Philosophie générale* and in *Dictionnaire philosophique*, "Oeuvres" (Paris: Aux Deux-Ponts, 1791–92), pp. 44–49 et pp. 52–63.

the great nations in the midst of which they were enclaved."[9]

The Egyptians have given the Jews the practice of circumcision, of the scapegoat on Yom Kippur (Day of Atonement), the immoral relations with the ram, and a great part of their mythology.

From the Chaldeans, they borrowed the name of Israel, the names of the angels and devils; during their Babylonian captivity, they adopted Babylonian writing and enriched their language with Chaldean words. "They borrowed everything from the Chaldeans, the Persians, even their language, their script, their numbers, and by adding a few new customs to their ancient Egyptian rites, they became a new people."[10] Voltaire forgets that Israel had been a clearly determined national entity long before its Babylonian captivity, and long before this first exile had the great regenerating effect announced by the Prophets.

Also very long is the list of borrowings from Greek mythology. According to Voltaire, apparently there is not a page of a Jewish book that is not plagiarized. The curiosity of a woman as the cause of the misfortunes of humanity corresponds to the Pandora motif. Pandora's box invented in Egypt, the egg created by Orosmade and pierced by Arimane who inserted in it mental and physical ills, are the pictures from which the wretched copy of Eve and the apple were made.[11] Isaac's sacrifice is just an imitation of the myth of Iphigenia; Samson is a pale copy of Hercules. The miracles of the Prophet Elijah are not in the least original, and his journey to Heaven on a fiery chariot is nothing but a crude imitation of the allegory of the god Helios. "This chariot of light, these four fiery horses, this whirlwind, this name Elijah have

---

9. Genèse.
10. Juif.
11. Sottisier.

led Lord Bolingbroke and M. Boulanger to think that
the adventure of Elijah was an imitation of Phaeton's,
who sat down on the Sun's chariot. Phaeton's fable was
originally Egyptian; it is at least a moral fable that shows
the dangers of ambition. But what does Elijah's chariot
signify? Jewish writers are always crude and clumsy
plagiarists."[12] The figure of Moses is drawn from Bac-
chus, who in Orphic poetry is called Mises, and the
pythoness of Endor was one of those wretches who tried
to earn a living by imitating as best they could the
pythoness of Delphi. However, Voltaire forgets that
the pythoness of Endor is in no way presented as an
admirable person (besides, the severest critics of Biblical
heroes are always found in the Bible itself).

Even though the Jews borrowed from Greek mythology, Voltaire questions whether there were direct contacts between the noble Hellenes and their wretched
copyists: "We think that Esdras himself never knew the
Greeks, and until the time of Alexander there was not
the slightest intercourse between Greece and Palestine.
Not that a few Jews could not conceivably have gone
to trade in Corinth and Athens, but that type of people
did not make up the history of Israel."[13]

It is unnecessary to prolong the list of the borrowings
of which Voltaire accuses the Bible. He seems to be unaware of the fact that a man or a doctrine has the right
to take useful material wherever it finds it without com-
promising its originality. He himself drew the elements
from his *Zadig* from various sources, without destroying
the original character of this charming tale due to the
genius of the narrator. "Let it not be said," wrote Pascal,
"that I have said nothing new; the arrangement of the
material is new." The selection of the different elements,
the order in which they are grouped, the new spirit that

---

12. The Bible.
13. *Ibid.*

inspires the whole, determine the originality and the value of a work or a civilization.

Similarly, it is undeniable that certain elements in the religious traditions of various people have a common source; the various stories of the deluge, for instance, undoubtedly go back to a great catastrophe which has remained in the memory of nations. But each people has endowed this common subject with a character coming from its own concept of the world, injecting it with its national spirit and placing in it a more or less imposing religious system. "A park in the style of Lenôtre and an English park, such as the one of Ermenonville, are made of trees, grass, flower, water, perspective; they create, however, decors and impressions that seem to have nothing in common."[14]

Voltaire, by "exposing" the Bible as "plagiarism," pursues two goals at the same time. First, the struggle against Christianity. The enlightened generation of the eighteenth century prided itself on having demonstrated the absurdity of ancient mythology. If it could demonstrate that the Bible was nothing but the crucible of all the mythologies, it would strip it with one stroke of its identity as a holy book. It would cease to be the preface to the New Testament. Christianity, which relies on the allusions to the arrival of the Messiah contained in the Old Testament, would lose the basis for its existence and the halo of its divine origin. Thus, one reason why Voltaire parodied every word of the Bible was to strike a mortal blow at Christianity.[15]

The other purpose emerges rather clearly from the tone of the preceding quotations. Voltaire has an implacable hatred for the Jews and does not miss a chance to stigmatize them. In this philosopher of the "enlight-

14. Daniel Mornet (R. C. C. 1938), p. 13.
15. "Voltaire is the Scarron of the Bible. He doesn't discuss it, he doesn't criticize it, he parodies it and smears it." F. Vigouroux, *Les Livres Saints et la critique rationaliste,* II (Paris, 1890), p. 273.

ened century" there persists a surprising vestige of the
Middle Ages, from which he is distinguished by generously conceding that "they should not be burned, however." Not only is his resentment manifested in his
polemical writing against the Jews, but it is hardly disguised even in so-called historical and scientific works.
What an ill-intentioned anachronism it is to attribute to
Biblical Jews the role of broker in Greek cities. Voltaire
exploits the most corrupt sources, as long they confirm
his opinion of that people. That is the state of mind
that explains his concept of Jewish history, of which
we give a brief picture:

"The Jews were only a troop of nomads, originating
in the desert between Egypt and Syria, who captured
gradually a few Phoenician villages. Their turn of mind,
their inclination for parables and unbelievable magic,
their extreme passion for robbery (*brigandage*), all
these things lead us to think that they are a recent
nation, originating from a small horde of Arabs." The
feast of the tabernacle is proof of their nomadic origin.
The destruction of Jericho testifies to their dislike of
cities. It is only in David's time that they have a capital.
"The Jews were originally nothing but Arab thieves
who, after they were chased away, grabbed, in time,
part of Palestine and then wrote their history the way
all ancient history was composed, that is to say very late,
with pieces of fiction, sometimes ridiculous, sometimes
atrocious."[16] Elsewhere, the Jews are a troop of lepers
chased from Egypt: "A tradition just as ancient and more
widespread claims that the Jews had been chased from
Egypt, either as a gang of undisciplined thieves, or as
a tribe infected by leprosy. This double accusation draws
its likelihood from the very land of Goshen where they
had lived and where leprosy, peculiar to the Arabs, must
have been known. It seems, according to the Scriptures

---

16. The Bible.

themselves, that this people had left Egypt unwillingly."[17] This claim does not prevent Voltaire from questioning Moses's existence on numerous occasions. "If everything in a man's life has the incredibility of fiction, from his birth up to his death, then we must require the most irreproachable reports of contemporaries; it is not enough that one thousand years later, a priest found in a chest, as he was counting money, a book concerning that man, and that he sent it by a clerk to a little king." Thus, Voltaire uses the existence or the nonexistence of Moses according to the thesis he is discussing.

Another example will serve to illustrate the method of Voltaire the historian. The freeing of the Jews from their Babylonian exile and the permission to return to their country are supposedly explained by presents they had given king Cyrus. They were able to afford presents thanks to the wealth they acquired by their usury. Let us note that the only existing sources for that period are the Bible and Josephus. Neither one nor the other makes the least allusion to anything of that sort. Besides, usury practiced by the Jews of antiquity is an indisputable anachronism.

Voltaire's method, therefore, is rather that of a pamphleteer than of a conscientious historian. Instead of studying historical data to deduce objective results, he uses them arbitrarily to support a preconceived judgment.

Hence it is less interesting to discuss Voltaire's conclusion than to try to understand the reasons for his bias, to delve into the origin of his anti-Judaism. We have to consider Voltaire's experiences with Jews, and we have to have some knowledge of his personality, to understand his reactions to his experience. In a word, to understand Voltaire the writer we must know Voltaire the man.

Voltaire reproaches the Jews in a thousand ways for their love of money, but everybody knows that he him-

17. Moïse.

self had a very pronounced taste for that commodity. He acquired a considerable fortune by participating in several questionable deals, then in speculating on food, military supplies, and grain.

During his stay in Berlin he had dealings with the Jewish banker Hirschell. He wanted to make money by manipulations on the stock exchange, and he therefore commissioned Hirschell to buy for him depreciated shares to cash in at par. The acquisition or the sale of these shares was forbidden. Voltaire defied the prohibition; then, to give the deal to another banker, he canceled the commission he had given Hirschell. A suit ensued between the two. They accused each other of fraud. The judges were never able to figure out this very confused affair. An agreement was finally reached, which, one fine day, was repudiated by Voltaire. He cheated, forged documents, then cried that he had been tricked. Hirschell was condemned to pay the expenses of the suit, but Voltaire did not come out of it too brilliantly. This affair provoked the indignation of Frederick II, who wrote a comedy in French verse, *Tantalus's Trial,* pastiche of Voltaire's trial. The king called him a crook who tried to trick a thief.

Voltaire, who was also characterized by inexhaustible spite, persecuted not only his personal enemy, but the whole Jewish nation. We know that Voltaire knew no bounds when it came to avenging his hurt pride. He stigmatized his opponents relentlessly, carrying on the struggle until they were completely annihilated. His opponents were in fact his victims. So, during his whole lifetime, Voltaire aimed his poisoned arrows at the Jews and at Judaism, modern and ancient, and every Jew had to expiate the fact that Voltaire compromised himself in a deal with just one Jew.

This portrait does not correspond to the prevalent concept of the man posing as the apostle of tolerance.

"Voltaire is intolerance personified, he preached tolerance to others, but never thought of practicing it himself."[18]

Toward the Jews at any rate, he demonstrates it only once, when he has Rabbi Akiba cry out, in a purported sermon delivered at Smyrna in 1761: "We have been a barbarian, superstitious, ignorant or absurd nation, but would it be fair to burn today the pope and all the monsignors of Rome because the first Romans carried off the Sabine women?"

Petit de Julleville adds these observations about Voltaire: "When one studies him for a long time, when one measures him by comparing him to the truly great men in the letters and the arts, one ends up by growing weary of a genius who excels only in malice, who lacked conscience, seriousness, elevation. It is possible to come back to him once in a while for entertainment, but not for instruction, and even less to exalt one's soul."[19]

This assessment does not date from today; it was already Voltaire's contemporaries'. After a period of enthusiastic Voltairianism, the public had returned to a more objective opinion of his works and to the judgment of those who were closely acquainted with him. Thus his outbursts against Judaism did not produce the expected effect. His era was more progressive than he in its approach to the Jewish question. As proof, we may mention the answer of Abbé Guéné, who, in the name of a few Portuguese Jews, undertook a public controversy with Voltaire. One quotation from this controversy deserves to be noted, because it shows the unconditional admiration that the Jews felt for genius, even if it was used against them: the Portuguese Jews "want to thank heaven

---

18. Petit de Julleville, *Histoire de la langue et de la littérature française,* VI.
    19. *Ibid.*

for your talent and bemoan your deplorable abuse of
it."[20]

Diderot

Voltaire's personal resentment aside, his attacks against
the Bible reflect the general attitude toward positive religions. The classic monument of this hostility is the
Grande encyclopédie published under Diderot's direction.
It would be useless, however, to look for frontal attacks
against the Bible. Those must be sought in secondary
writings, whose ban by censorship would have been less
consequential.

Just as Voltaire wants to shake the foundations of
Christianity by debasing the Old Testament, Diderot too
uses the Jews as an argument against the Church, but
he does it by assigning them a worthy role. Like Pascal,
he is impressed by the incredulity of the Jews, their
"stiff neck" in the presence of the miracles performed by
Jesus, but he goes considerably farther than the philosopher of Port-Royal by using the Jews as an argument
against Christianity. Their rejection of conversion is,
according to him, a greater miracle than all those performed by Jesus. "It must be admitted that the Jews are
men without parallel: everywhere people have been
swayed by one miracle alone, and Jesus could do nothing
with the Jewish people with the help of an infinite number of real miracles. . . . That is the miracle, the incredulity of the Jews; that must be emphasized, and not
that of the Resurrection."

If, in this passage, Diderot, by using the Jews as
witnesses against Christianity, attacks it openly, on other
occasions he does it less directly. It was not possible to
launch frontal attacks against the Church. She was still

---

20. *Lettres de quelques Juifs portugais et allemands à M. de Voltaire*
(Paris, 1769).

very powerful and her influence could have prevented the publication of the *Grande encyclopédie,* this gigantic monument of eighteenth-century thought. It was necessary to outwit censorship and this was done by means of the famous "encyclopedic method," by expressing heretical opinions in disguise. An example is the editorial remark made by Diderot. After quoting the heretical arguments of Abbé de Prades, he writes with charming hypocrisy: "Of course, however plausible the Abbé de Prades's system might be, it could not be adopted since the censure of several bishops of France and the faculty of theology have stated that it threatened the authenticity of the Holy Scriptures." Sophisticated readers knew how to interpret that remark.

Another form of disguise consisted also in using Judaism as a witness in reverse as well as—and that was the favorite device—to destroy Christianity by attacking its foundation. Without imitating Voltaire's spiteful diatribes dictated by personal resentment, Diderot adopts an attitude just as severe toward the Old Testament, going as far as biting satire in works such as *La Promenade du sceptique* and *La Moïsade.*

La Promenade du sceptique is an allegory where the life of religion is symbolized by a path of thorns, the life of pleasure by a path of flowers, and the life of knowledge by a path of chestnut trees. These interpretations give the work a tendentious nature from the beginning. God is called the ruler; the faithful are his soldiers, forced to wear a blindfold over their eyes. The ruler has given his state two codes, contradictory in all respects, which earns him the reproach of having badly chosen his secretaries. The first part is the work of an old shepherd who knew how to practice magic well. The exodus from Egypt becomes the mutiny of a few robbers, the Red Sea a little river, whose ford is unfortunately unknown to the persecutors. The Book of Genesis, whose naïveté has always enchanted the poets, is for Diderot, partisan of the rationalism of his time, an endless source of sarcasm. He speaks of Adam as the first soldier, who was disgraced because of the bad meal prepared by his wife. The life of the patriarchs is a series of immoral descriptions. Reducing to grotesque proportions the naïve character of the Bible is the only originality of this satire, of which Naigeon, although a severe critic of the Bible, has said: "the philosophical part, except for five or six pages where we can feel the lion's claw, seems in general superficial; and the two others, especially the first, are of no interest."

In spite of a few tasteless attacks, it appears that Diderot, unlike Voltaire, does not harbor any personal resentment against the Jews. He takes an interest in them only to the extent that they can be used to fight the Christian religion. But, on the other hand, he has no interest in applying to them his humanitarian ideas. He is completely indifferent to the fate of the Jews of his time. He wishes them neither good nor ill. However, he considers them more or less the representatives, consequently responsible for the Bible, so disastrous in the eyes of the philosophers. For, if Christianity is guilty, Judaism is even more so, according to this principle: the greatest objections to a doctrine must go to the doctors who created it.

Thus the variations of the Jewish themes culminate in a grotesque phenomenon. In the past, the arguments of the time were directed to its opposition to Christianity; henceforth, it was to be criticized for too great an affinity with it. How ironical is the history of the human mind! Opposition passes from a Christian anti-Semitism to an anti-Christian anti-Semitism. As the inquisitor says in *Nathan the Wise:* "In spite of everything, the Jew will be burned." The inquisitors pass on, their spirit remains. There will always persist an anti-Semitic trend that will fight the Jews for the most paradoxical reasons, either as capitalists, because there are capitalists among them, or as socialists, because there are Jewish socialists, but always for the same reason: because it is easy to vent one's resentment on those whose means of defense are limited. It seems that the human "animal" has a profound need to find a scapegoat.

Rousseau

In spite of the persistence of the anti-Jewish trend, the idea of tolerance spreads more and more. We have distinguished two forms of tolerance, one that is the product of a skeptical attitude toward all positive religion, whose representatives are Voltaire and Diderot, and one that respects absolute truth in its limited forms. The first believed that their only duty was to burn the gods of the past; and there were, no doubt, many things that needed to be burned. But the others salvaged from the ashes the values that deserved to remain. From this spirit true tolerance was to be born, the one that consisted of the respect for all beliefs.

It is from the second spirit of tolerance that Judaism benefited. Montesquieu was its first representative. A straight line leads from him to Rousseau, this solitary dreamer whose dreams have inspired the actions of the succeeding generations.

In Rousseau are summarized the positive tendencies of the eighteenth century that ultimately neutralized the disintegrating effects of an unbridled rationalism and a limitless skepticism. "Under the pretext of explaining nature," he says in *The Social Contract,* "they sow in the heart of man depressing doctrines, whose apparent skepticism is a hundred times more affirmative and dogmatic than the assertive tone of their opponents." What Rousseau demands is a return to faith. But what religion will be the right one, Catholicism or Protestantism? "It is important to the state that each individual have a religion conducive to making him love his obligations, but the dogmas of that religion concern the state, or its members, only insofar as these dogmas are related to morality. Everyone can have the opinions he wishes, without giving the ruler the right to intervene, and since he has no jurisdiction in the other world, whatever the subject becomes in the other life is not his concern, as long as he is a good citizen in this one."[21]

This idea of Rousseau has become one of the first principles of the Rights of Man of which we give an article: "No one can be persecuted for his opinions, even religious, as long as their manifestion does not disturb the order established by the law."

It is not through pity, or Christian love, that Rousseau wants the free profession of oppressed religions; it's through love of truth. True justice, true democracy cannot be based exclusively on the rights of the greatest number. "Do you know many Christians who have taken the trouble to examine what Judaism accuses them of? If a few have seen some of these criticism, it's in Christian books. Fine way of acquainting oneself with the arguments of one's opponents! But what's to be done? If one of us dared to publish a book openly favoring the Jews, we the author, the publisher, the bookseller, would be punished. This policy is convenient and guaranteed to be always right. It's a pleasure to refute people who dare not speak . . . I won't believe that I have heard the full explanations of the Jews until they have a free state, schools, universities where they can speak and argue without risks. Then only will we be able to know what they have to say."[22]

These words sound like the leitmotiv of emancipation (on the way to being realized). One more literary event hastened its march. In 1785, the Royal Society of Sciences and Arts of Metz adopted the Jewish question as the

21. *The Social Contract,* book IV, chap. 8.
22. *Emile,* book IV.

theme of a literary contest. Nine essays were entered. The prize was divided among three contestants: a lawyer, Thierry; a Jew, Salkind Horwitz, employed by the Royal Library; and finally, Abbe Grégoire, curate of Ember-menil. Of all the essays submitted, two only were opposed to the emancipation of the Jews. The author of one of them, imbued with the anti-Semitic outlook of Voltaire who had conceded that, "however, they should not be burned," drew the conclusion that at least they ought to be deported to the wilderness of Guyana. The other, a Benedictine monk, followed Innocent III's lead: the condition of the Jews had to be perpetuated, because their usefulness is priceless for the truth of the Christian Church. The essays of Abbé Grégoire, the man who was soon to fight for his ideas in the political arena, states the following: "Do you want the Jews to become better men, useful citizens? Grant them and protect all their rights of citizenship, and soon this fair constitution will place them among the most useful members of the state."

These words became the classic formula for those who represented emancipation in the National Assembly. Mirabeau intervened with his usual fire. . . . Robespierre, Rousseau's disciple, exclaimed: "The vices of the Jews are caused by the degradation to which you reduce them; they will be good when they are able to find some benefit in it." On September 27, 1791, just before it adjourned, the Assembly adopted this decree:

"The National Assembly—considering that the requirements for French citizenship and active citizenship have been set by the Constitution, and that any man, when fulfilling these requirements and taking the civic oath and promising to fulfill all the duties that the Constitution imposes, has a right to all the privileges it guarantees—revokes all postponement, reservations and exceptions introduced in preceding decrees dealing with

Jewish individuals who will take the civic oath, which will be considered the renunciation of all the privileges and exceptions previously introduced in their favor."

This decree meant the realization of an idea dreamed about by the noblest minds of the time and which had found its poetic expression in the play by Joseph Chénier (brother of André Chénier) *Nathan the Wise,* written a few years before the fall of the Bastille, and in which the poet, in Lessing's wake, exhorted his contemporaries:

> Du sang qui vous unit respectez mieux les droits!
> Une bague est échue à chacun de vous trois;
> Chacun de vous la tient d'un père respectable.
> Croyez tous trois avoir la bague véritable . . .
> Imitez envers vous son tendre attachement;
> Aimez-vous comme il dit, tous trois également,
> Eprouvez cet amour par votre bienfaisance,
> Consolez la douleur, secourez l'indigence,
> Dans son asile obscur cherchez l'adversité,
> Et de votre manteau couvrez la nudité,
> Quand des trois diamants la céleste puissance
> Aura de père en fils versé son influence,
> Un juge plus habile après mille et mille ans,
> Devant ce tribunal citera vos enfants.
>   Ainsi parla le juge équitable et modeste.

> Show greater respect for the rights of the blood that binds you!
> A ring was given to all three of you;
> Each has received it from a worthy father.
> Believe, all three of you, that you have the true ring . . .
> Imitate his tender care for you;
> Love each other the way he commanded, all three equally,
> Test this love by your kindness,
> Console unhappiness, assist poverty,
> Seek out adversity in its modest refuge,
> And cover its nakedness with your coat,
> When the heavenly power will have transmitted
> From father to son the influence of the diamonds,
> A cleverer judge after thousands of years,
> Will summon your children.
> Thus spoke the fair and humble judge.

Part III

EBB AND FLOW

Opposing destinies cannot be reconciled; excellence in one field is always paid for by a decline in another.
—*Ernest Renan*
Conférence d'Angleterre

To the powerful development of the social and spiritual life of the nineteenth century corresponds an endless ramification of the literary aspect of the Jewish theme. The question is reflected in socially oriented novels and plays.

The eighteenth century had witnessed the triumph of cosmopolitan ideas; the "Rights of Man" excluded all distinction of nation and religion. The nineteenth is the century of national movements; the unification of Germany and of Italy was achieved, with its repercussions on the neighboring states. A nation, it is said, must be one, homogeneous, of the same race. What will be the fate of Israel whose emancipation has been achieved under totally different conditions? A special genre of literary works deals with this problem.

New problems rise on the horizon of the modern era, new political, social, and spiritual tensions appear, and make the Jewish theme, the barometer of European society, increasingly complex. Its multiple and often contradictory aspects will come together in the Dreyfus Affair.

11

The New Social Doctrines

Saint-Simon and his School
The Count of Saint-Simon is both the philosopher of the
bourgeoisie and the initiator of the theories of Socialism.[1]
The two systems that subsequently became hereditary
enemies were easily reconciled in his utopian thinking. If
he advocated that the government be in the hands of
the industrialists, "the only productive class," it is because he considered it better qualified to accomplish the
salvation of the proletariat, "the more numerous class"
that remained the object of his humanitarian concern.

His social system presents a peculiar mixture of philosophical, economic, and religious ideas. Saint-Simon considered himself the only legitimate defender of the ideas
of the Great Revolution that he wanted to complete in
order to prepare for the coming of the Messianic period
on earth. After the "critical" period of the past, he said,
we are entering a creative, organic period thanks to the
principles of the Revolution which are perfectly compatible with a modern interpretation of the doctrine of
Christ. Science and faith are not mutually exclusive in
this "new Christianity": faith consists in believing in
science and art. They are to guide society toward the
great goal of the fastest possible rehabilitation of the

1. O. Warschauer, *Zur Entwicklungsgeschichte des Sozialismus* (Berlin, 1909).

poorest class."[2] The first commandment must be: "You shall work." The professions will be classified in a strictly hierarchical order according to their practical importance. The apex will be formed by the industrialists, the "priests" of Saint-Simon's state. The whole economic and spiritual life must be concentrated in the hands of the industrialists. This class must occupy the first place because it is the most important of all, because it can get along without the others and the others cannot get along without it; it alone exists on its own resources and personal initiative. Since everything is done through industry, everything must be done for it.

In this professional hierarchy, an important place will be reserved to the Jews, whose commercial training, cultivated since the Middle Ages, will be useful to the new economic system. But this favorable assessment is not the main reason that the doctrine of the philosopher, widely ignored, found an echo in Jewish circles.

Saint-Simon, exhausted by his long period of material difficulties, tried to commit suicide in 1823. From that time on, a few students gathered around him; this group included the poet Léon Halévy and the financier Olinde Rodrigues. The latter provided him with a livelihood and the time to finish his work. Right after the death of the philosopher, the group founded *Le Producteur,* a magazine dedicated to the spread of Saint-Simon's ideas. Olinde Rodrigues especially, Saint-Simon's "heir," undertook a tireless propaganda campaign to spread the ideas of his master. His brother, Eugène Rodrigues, an idealist with mystical tendencies, developed the religious framework of Saint-Simon's doctrine. The two brothers, in collaboration with Gustave d'Eichtal and the Péreire brothers, formed the first cell of the Saint-Simon movement that subsequently took on the dimensions of a vast religious movement.

---

2. *Le Nouveau Christianisme* (Paris, 1925), p. 12.

Saint-Simon's doctrine aimed to carry out the social teachings of a Christianity "betrayed by its false priests." Bought up by the power structure, they had preached to the underprivileged the ideal of renunciation on earth to win heavenly happiness. Saint-Simon, on the other hand, proclaimed happiness in this world, by the establishment of a better social order, a promise that earned him for a time the unlimited confidence of the masses. The major dogma of the new religion states: "Inherited property is theft," which is only the logical application of the master's maxim: "From each according to his ability, to each ability according to its work." The future social structure is to be a kind of state capitalism through the centralization of capital, through the creation of a production fund to supervise and subsidize industrial organization of national interest. Banks linking capital and industry will be subordinated to a general bank that will control them. The first practical result of this theory was the creation in 1852 of the "Crédit Mobilier" by the Péreire brothers.

The centralizing tendency of the new doctrine, that is, the tendency to organize all the public resources under the guidance of the state, led Saint-Simon's followers to study the structure of Mosaic law. They discovered in the Jewish religion an organic character that they wanted to reintroduce into modern civilization. An organic period is a period "where religion, politics, morals are only the various names of the same fact." In Judaism, all the forms of human life were organized around religion. "Therefore it is to Moses that the organic or religious chain of the European race must be traced back."[3] There was, therefore, an attempt to base Saint-Simon's humanitarian religion on the Jewish religion, but giving it a more universal character. A few priests of Saint-Simon's philosophy carried out a symbolic gesture: dressed in their

3. *Doctrine de Saint-Simon.* 5th session (Paris, 1829).

Saint-Simonian clothes, d'Eichthal, Barrault Lambert, and Félicien David organized a solemn procession to the synagogue during the Jewish New Year of 1831. The mysticism of the sect is fully revealed in the grotesque act represented by the expedition to Constantinople to look, according to predictions, for the bride of the Messiah.[4]

The success of Saint-Simonism as a religion was ephemeral, and its political influence was also weakened by the fact that it backed no specific party of the time. The theoreticians of Socialism saw in it only the capitalistic class that they had to oppose; on the other hand, landed capitalism, the great beneficiary of 1789, fought fiercely against this new form of capitalism that was going to take away its supremacy. It is obvious that the Jews, relegated since the Middle Ages to the field of commercial capitalism, were well prepared for the new economic constellation, and they managed to secure a solid foothold. As a result, the reactionary parties that represented the interests of landed capitalism, and the revolutionary parties serving the Socialist ideal met on the common platform of anti-Semitism.

Let us therefore not be surprised to find in Fourier, even though he was a member of the Socialist *avant-garde,* arguments borrowed faithfully from the vocabulary of the bourgeois and clerical reaction.

Charles Fourier

Fourier promises to change the structure of human society by a system based on a better knowledged of the human heart. He believes he has discovered its psychological secret, a discovery as significant as Newton's revolution of the physical world. "The first science that I

---

4. G. Weill, *Les Juifs et le Saint-Simonisme,* Revue des Etudes Juives, vol. 31, p. 267.

discovered was the theory of emotional attraction."[5]
Thanks to the intimate knowledge of human emotions,
society will be reconstructed on a new and more solid
foundation.

The whole social misfortune is caused by its moral
disorder. The interests of people are too contradictory
to allow the establishment of a harmonious life. The
doctor is interested in the perpetuation of disease; the
architect reacts complacently to the collapse of a house
or a bridge; the son secretly wishes for the death of
his father so that he may inherit his wealth; the lawyer
could not exist if his fellow citizens lived in peace. Only
a small number of people are happy with their fate.
Most men must painfully earn a living through a profession they did not choose and that does not represent
their personal taste. The only result of this joyless activity is being able to keep from starving (as was
Fourier's case).

We must strive to reconcile man with his fate. The
study of human emotions will reveal that the microcosm
of human emotions is governed by the same laws as the
macrocosm of the universe. The human soul is composed
of twelve major passions, mixed in such a way that one
or another predominates and thus determines what we
call the character of the individual. In the diplomat,
for instance, it is, above all, cabalism, the urge to scheme,
that is developed. Another basic emotion of human
nature is the need to form social families. The question
now is to organize closed associations, "phalanxes," in
which 400 to 1800 persons, chosen so that their characters will eliminate all rivalry, will live and work together, each according to his personal tastes. Three
phalanxes will be under the authority of a "duarche,"
twelve under a "triarche," etc. Finally all mankind will

---

5. "Théorie des quatre mouvements," in *Oeuvres Complètes* (Complete
Works).

be organized under the government of an "omniarche" of the world, a world transformed into a great garden of Eden. The lamentable results of a few "phalansteries" founded under Fourier's inspiration in France, in Africa, and in Brazil ruined the experiment even before the establishment of a "duarche."

Fourier was a Utopian. He belongs to the promoters of Socialism less by his constructive ideas than by his criticism of the established social order. And even there his lack of realism is apparent. He often scores accurately certain facts, but he is mistaken as to the causes. His writings reflect a man embittered by his resentment against his own very modest social position, supporting the malcontents of any political group. Accordingly, although he is far from agreeing with the principles of Catholicism, he adopts the complaints of the clerical reaction against the philosophers of the eighteenth century. "Under the name of philosopher I include only the authors of dubious sciences, political scientists, moralists, economists and others, whose theories are not compatible with experience and which have no other rules than the fantasy of their authors. All our evils are due to the reforms prepared by the philosophers of the eighteenth century. Their most disastrous work was the emancipation of the Jews; here is the origin of all our social difficulties."

On the other hand, Fourier does not hate the philosophers to the point of rejecting all their views. He adopts a few of them, those, for instance, that serve as sources for his anti-Semitic diatribes. Thus he is obviously inspired by Voltaire when he claims that "the Jews have kept their patriarchal spirit, which is the root of vile passions, and that degraded them, even in their days of power. Was there ever a nation more contemptible than the Hebrews who were indifferent to the arts and the sciences, who distinguished themselves only by the

continuous practice of crimes and brutality, whose tale
fills one with indignation at each page of their disgusting
annals?"[6]

Morally, below the philosophers stand only the businessmen, "the most lying class of the whole social structure." Even for that class there are extenuating circumstances, similar in nature to the philosophers'. "The
establishment of a thief or a Jew is enough to disorganize
entirely the whole merchant corporation of a big city and
leads the most honest people to crime."[7]

It is the Jews who push the businessmen on to the
path of sin. *Pars pro toto.* What a classic demonstration
of a method as old as it is effective: a social class defends
itself by sacrificing a part, a minority of its number, which
it saddles with all the wrongs of which it is accused.

Thus, of the two great social currents that we have
just examined, Saint-Simonism and Fouriérism, the first
seeks in Judaism the example of a harmonious synthesis
of all social forces, bringing to the individual and to
society, through a common ideal, the solution to the
various problems of existence; the other tries to impute
to Israel all the faults it has discovered in the organization of the society of its time.

These two doctrines, to which we ought to add the
vast literary production of the Socialist P. Leroux,[8] have
left important traces in the social history of the nineteenth century, and have strongly inspired the literary
movements which are its faithful mirror. We will find
these influences alternately preponderant in a great number of works, and we will see their decisive confrontation
at the end of the century, in a great historic crisis.

---

6. *Ibid.,* p. 61.
7. *Ibid.,* p. 235. For further details, cf. C. Lehrmann: "Das Humani-
tatsideal der sozialistisch-romantischen Epoche Frankreichs," in *Beitrage
zur Kultur de Romania* (Wurzburg, 19??), p. 9.
8. *Ibid.,* chapter on Leroux.

12
The Jewish Theme in Romantic Literature

Return to the Bible

Romanticism, whose aesthetic characteristic is an atmosphere of mysterious shadows, in its humanitarian doctrine also appears behind a shadow whose real background is difficult to define. Revolutionary and reactionary tendencies meet in a surprising manner, and contradictions exist not only among the various phases of this vast movement, but even in the same authors. These contradictions appear also in the different ways of treating the Jewish theme.

We note first a renewal of Biblical inspiration. The Bible, which under the attacks of the rationalists of the eighteenth century seemed to have lost all justification, and whose teachings, since the French Revolution, had been replaced by a so-called reasonable religion, was going to experience a resurrection. Saint-Simon had already read it in a different light from the philosophers who preceded the Great Revolution. The Romantic Movement is characterized by a return to the Bible, whose influence then reaches its apex. Anxiety, sensitivity, the need to escape, everything that characterizes the romantic soul, impelled it to seek out secret affinities in the feverish writings of Israel, with their violent lights and colors. When we think of the innumerable masterpieces inspired directly or indirectly by the Old Testament, we must agree with Brunetière who says:

If one were to imagine that the sources of Hebrew inspiration had dried up, the Germans would not have had Luther, nor the British *Paradise Lost,* nor the French Pascal, Bossuet, Hugo; the poets of the obscure and inaccessible, so to speak; those who have given us the thrill of the infinite; and those finally, who, among men, have maintained the notion of the divine. The Greeks had loved life too much. They had imagined it too radiant. They had not suspected that it had any other goal than itself. They had lacked the notion of the hereafter. This is what places Israel among the wonders of humanity.[1]

Numerous, indeed, are the Romantic works inspired by the Bible. *Moïse,* by Alfred de Vigny, grandiose poetry evoking the alienation of the man of genius, bears, even in its powerful and restrained style, the stamp of the Bible.

> Hélas! Vous m'avez fait sage parmi les sages!
> Mon doigt du peuple errant a guidé les passages.
> J'ai fait pleuvoir le feu sur la tête des rois;
> L'avenir à genoux adorera mes lois. . . .
> Hélas! je suis, Seigneur, puissant et solitaire,
> Laissez-moi m'endormir du sommeil de la terre!
> Or, le peuple attendait, et, craignant son courroux,
> Priait sans regarder le mont du Dieu jaloux;
> Car, s'il levait les yeux, les flancs noirs du nuage
> Roulaient et redoublaient les foudres de l'orage,
> Et le feu des éclairs, aveuglant les regards,
> Enchaînait tous les fronts courbés de toutes parts.
> Bientôt le haut du mont reparut sans Moïse.———
> Il fut pleuré.—Marchant vers la terre promise,
> Josué s'avançait pensif et pâlissant,
> Car il était déjà l'élu du Tout-Puissant.

> Alas! You have made me the wisest of the wise!
> My finger has guided the marches of the wandering
>   people.
> I have caused fire to rain on the heads of kings;
> The future on its knees will worship my laws. . . .

1. *Nouveaux essais sur la littérature contemporaine* (Paris, 1897), p. 232.

Alas! I am, O Lord, powerful and alone,
Allow me the sleep of the earth!
Meanwhile, the people were waiting, and fearing
   His wrath,
Were praying without looking up the mountain of
   the jealous God;
For, if they lifted their eyes, the black flanks
   of the cloud
Rolled and multiplied the thundering of the storm,
And the fire of the thunderbolt, blinding their vision,
Chained all heads, everywhere bent.
Soon the top of the mountain reappeared without
   Moses.—
His loss was mourned.—Walking toward
   the Promised Land,
Joshua came forward thoughtful and pale,
For he was already the elect of the Almighty.

This poem reveals in Vigny a profound knowledge of the Bible. "I knew the Bible by heart," says he in *Servitudes et grandeurs militaires,* "and this book and I were so inseparable that it always followed me, even during the longest marches."

It is also Victor Hugo's faithful companion. Even the subsequent loss of his religious faith did not make him relinquish his Biblical sources. *La Légende des Siècles* is the noble fruit of the inspiration he drew from the Holy Scriptures. As for Chateaubriand and Lamartine, they were not happy merely to resurrect spiritually the atmosphere of the Bible; they went to the scene itself to seek its vestiges. However, while Chateaubriand drew his enthusiasm for the Bible from the heart of a confirmed Catholic, for Lamartine, as for Hugo who saw in it the romantic work par excellence, it prevailed rather as a source of aesthetic inspiration.

Here is Zion! Here is the palace! Here is the tomb of David! Here is the scene of his inspirations and his pleasures, of his life and of his final rest! Place twice sacred for me, whose

heart this heavenly bard has so often touched, and whose mind
he has so often delighted. He is the first of the poets of feeling.
He is the king of lyric poets. . . . Never has the thought of the
poet aimed so high and cried out so true, never has the soul of
man unburdened itself before man and before God in expressions and in emotions so tender, so ingratiating, so heart-rending.
Read Horace and Pindar after a psalm! I no longer can.[2]

Just as Racine, starting with the intention of creating
Biblical works in *Athalie* and *Esther,* had discovered and
formulated the post-Biblical Jewish problem, Lamartine,
while delving in his subject in contact with the Holy Land,
meditates on the fate of a people separated from its
spiritual homeland:

Here is Judea, here is the site of this people whose destiny it
is to be proscribed at every period of its history, and from which
other people have tried to wrest even the capital of its persecutions, cast, like an eagle's nest on top of these mountains.
Yet this people bore the great idea of the unity of God, and the
element of truth in this elementary idea was enough to separate
it from the other nations, to make it proud of its persecutions
and give it trust in these doctrines of Providence.[3]

Lamartine feels mystical ties between Israel and Palestine and his meditations crystallize in an amazing vision
of the future of that country:

Such a country, repopulated by a new Jewish nation and irri-
gated by intelligent hands, made fertile by a tropical sun, producing on its own all the plants needed or enjoyed by man, from
the sugar cane to the banana, to the vine and the wheat of the
temperate zone, to the cedar and the pine of the Alps, such a
country, I say, would still be the Promised Land today if Providence gave it back a people and a policy of tranquility and
liberty.[4]

---

2. *Voyage en Orient,* in *Oeuvres complètes (Complete Works)* VI,
(Paris, 1861), p. 432.
3. *Ibid.,* p. 448. Cf. also p. 395.
4. *Ibid.,* p. 309.

One hundred years later, these words, which in Lamartine's time seemed Utopian, sound like a hymn in honor of the successful Zionist struggle.

If one sometimes finds in Lamartine's works expressions such as "the Judaic race of publishers," they can be explained by the fact that the word *Jewish* had become synonymous with usurer since the Middle Ages: it would not be warranted to infer from the occasional use of such a term an anti-Semitic attitude on Lamartine's part, who, as a poet and a politician, had championed the noblest humanitarian ideas. This poet-politician symbolizes the ideal of French Romanticism, tending to express itself in the world of action as well as in the world of dreams. The Romantic School is in France a revolutionary movement, not only on a literary plane, but also in its close connection with subversive political parties. However, in both fields its program contains many compromises and inconsistencies. It is therefore not surprising to find among the Romantics, side by side with a liberal attitude defending the principles of the Great Revolution, a persistent evocation of the Jewish usurer, as perpetuated by popular tradition since the Middle Ages, thus serving the interests of reaction. To elucidate this contradiction, we have to undertake a more detailed analysis of the Romantic drama.

THE DUALISM OF THE ROMANTIC POETS
THE "SUPER-SHYLOCK"

Victor Hugo: **Cromwell**

This drama was the first decisive attack of Romanticism against the stronghold of Classicism. In the preface Victor Hugo expounds his aesthetic program, which culminates in an apotheosis of Shakespeare. The enthusiasm that the young Hugo felt for this "god of the theater" did not allow him merely to imitate his ideal. He exaggerated enormously the characteristic traits of Shakespeare's drama. Thus, he created a play of grotesque proportions, which could never be staged. While Shakespeare, for instance, settles for one fool, Victor Hugo puts in four; while the fool's scenes interpolated in Shakespeare's tragedies aim at the psychological relief of the spectator and at imitation of life where the tragic and comic intermingle, these scenes become in *Cromwell* full-fledged comedies, whose proportions destroy the framework of the tragedy. Because of these exaggerations the tragic produces a comic effect and the comical becomes ridiculous. In a scene of the fifth act, Barebone implores the plotters not to execute Cromwell when he is on his throne so as not to ruin the valuable carpet by smearing it with blood! Consequently, *Cromwell,* far from fulfilling the promises held out in the preface, evokes in the reader's mind the figures of Quasimodo and other monstrous beings created by a fantastic and sometimes uncontrolled imagination.

What we have just seen in the play in general applies in particular to the Jewish characters it contains; Rabbi Manassé ben Israel is Cromwell's agent in his dubious intrigues, his astrologer, his "spy from heaven," and finally his spy in the prosaic sense of the word. This does not prevent the rabbi from indulging in counterespionage for the benefit of Cromwell's adversaries. Manassé has his private interests in the political plot. The simple way of life to which Cromwell subjects the nobility threatens to harm the Jew, who was getting rich on the prodigality of the nobility. Besides, Manassé is not at all satisfied with the profits he earns from the commercial transactions with which Cromwell entrusts him. This crowned bourgeois watches him too closely and leaves him only three-fourths of the profits! Finally, if Cromwell dies, that leaves one less Christian in the world.

Des deux partis rivaux qu'importe qui succombe? Il coulera toujours du sang chrétien à flots. Je l'espère du moins! c'est le bon des complots.

Of the two rival parties, does it matter which succumbs? Either way, Christian blood will flow in torrents! At least, I hope so! that's the advantage of conspiracies.

The thirst for Christian blood appears in another scene under an even more detestable aspect. Manassé is preparing Cromwell's horoscope, when the latter suddenly notices that Rochester is sleeping in his room. He does not know whether he ought to kill him to rid himself of an embarrassing witness. The Jew encourages him!

Frappe, tu ne peux faire une action meilleure. (à part) Par une main Chrétienne immolons un Chrétien.

Strike, you can't perform a better deed. (aside) By a Christian hand let us immolate a Christian.[5]

If we had not already pointed out Shakespeare's influence, these lines would suffice to remind us of the famous scene in which Shylock sharpens his knife to cut a pound of flesh from Antonio's body. This resemblance does not stem from a mere unconscious recollection. It is rather an almost learned reconstruction of the elements that make up Shylock's character: greed and an implacable hatred for all Christians. We find these two traits in one line put in Manassé's mouth:

Voler des chrétiens est chose méritoire.

To steal from Christians is a meritorious thing.[6]

But, while Shakespeare's Shylock is a living figure,

5. Act III, scene 17.
6. *Ibid.*

whose behavior remains comprehensible because it is determined by motives that the author is careful to bring out, Manassé's hateful character is cleverly and artificially constructed; the author painfully invents the most arbitrary situations (a rabbi who practices usury, espionage, and astrology) to provide the Jew with the opportunity to display the most abject vices. The English poet, as he analyzes Shylock's character and shows us the psychological causes for his atrocity, succeeds in humanizing him and making us understand his anger, without, however, letting us accept his excesses. Victor Hugo's creation, on the other hand, is a naïve collection of all imaginable diabolic elements in one character; Manassé is the infernal product of an exuberant imagination, a monster of Quasimodo's family.

And yet Victor Hugo, whose literary ideal was to allow nature and life to enter into art, had created the personality of the Jew on the model of a historical figure. Manassé ben Israel is the famous chief rabbi of Amsterdam, friend of Rembrandt and all the famous men of his time, among whom we find Cromwell, with whom he negotiated to obtain the abolition of the law preventing the Jews from settling in England. This highly respected personality becomes in Hugo's drama a criminal incarnating the principle of evil.

Such an arbitrary distortion of historical facts is explained partially by the romantic concept of historical truth.[7] "Often the myths of the people become the truth of the poet." It so happens that there exists a popular fable dating from the Middle Ages, that of the Jewish usurer, allegorical figure whose stubborn longevity equalled that of Ahasver, the wandering Jew.

Shakespeare's growing influence on the French theater is Victor Hugo's undisputed achievement, but the adapta-

---

7. Cf., Thoughts on truth in art, in the preface to *Cinq-Mars* by Alfred de Vigny.

tion did not take place without the frequent distortion of Shakespeare's drama. When he brought to life the *Merchant of Venice*, Shakespeare had also drawn from popular tradition, but he applied to an allegorical figure his analysis of human psychology, lending it moving touches that elicit our understanding in spite of the conventional façade of the dirty usurer. The Shylock type, adopted by Victor Hugo, assumed in his hands grotesque proportions for which Shakespeare is not responsible. If the one has created a Shylock, a figure with recognizable features, the other has created a super-Shylock, a theatrical monster, soon to become a cliché of Romantic Drama. Victor Hugo was to use it again in another of his plays, *Marie Tudor*.

Marie Tudor

In the cast appears "a Jew." He has no name; he is simply "a Jew." This fact indicates, no doubt, that the role, in the traditional sense of the word, is that of a usurer. Indeed, the character introduces himself with these words: "I am one of the main moneylenders of Kantersten Street, in Brussels. I lend ten and I get back fifteen. I lend to everybody. I would lend to the devil, I would lend to the pope." The cynicism with which the Jew admits his real faith, faith in money, is expressed again in the scene between him and Fabiano Fabiani, favorite of the queen and hated by the people. The latter's duplicity is surpassed, however, by the Jew's, if this be possible. Informed of Fabiani's criminal projects, he wants to get paid for keeping quiet. Fabiani gets rid of him by stabbing him, without succeeding in getting hold of the incriminating papers. Disappointed, the outwitted schemer exclaims: "lying and thievery, that's the mark of the Jew."

Far be it from us to consider, like Drumont, this sentence as Hugo's personal judgment. It is hard to conceive that the poet would put his opinion in the mouth of a criminal like Fabiani. Furthermore, with that kind of belief, he could not write a scene like the one found in *Torquemada.*

Torquemada
A Jewish delegation begs the king, while offering him a great ransom, to protect the Jews against the Inquisition.[8] What a contemptible role, full of bigotry and lust for money, the royal couple plays! The words of Rabbi Moses ben Habib are more a biting accusation than a supplication.

> Ayez pitié. Nos coeurs sont fidèles et doux;
> Nous vivons enfermés dans nos maisons étroites,
> Humbles, seuls; nos lois sont très simples et très droites,
> Tellement qu'un enfant les mettrait en écrit.
> Jamais le Juif ne chante et jamais il ne rit.
> Nous payons le tribut, n'importe quelles sommes. . . .
> . . . .
> Permettez-nous de vivre, nous, dans nos caves,
> Sous nos pauvres toits, presque au bagne et presque esclaves,
> Mais auprès des cercueils de nos pères . . .

> Have pity on us. Our hearts are faithful and meek;
> We live shut up in our narrow houses,
> Humble, alone; our laws are so simple and straightforward
> That a child could put them in writing.
> Never does the Jew sing, never does he laugh.
> We pay the tribute, whatever the sum. . . .
> . . . .
> Allow us to live in our cellars,
> Under our humble roofs, almost in the gallows and almost
>   as slaves,
> But near the coffins of our fathers . . .

Finally, the delegation presents a cash argument, the

---

8. Act II, scene 2.

only one the rulers deem worthy of consideration, a ransom of 30,000 gold marks.

The king calculates rapidly!

Trente mille marks d'or font six cent piastres.

Thirty thousand gold marks equal six hundred thousand piasters.

He is inclined to abrogate the decree against the infidels, but the queen finds a solution that conciliates her faith and her self-interest:

Monsieur, prenons l'argent et chassons tout de même les Juifs, que je ne puis accepter pour sujets. . . .

Sire, let's take the money, and let's still chase the Jews, whom I can't accept as subjects. . . .

Here Hugo plays his role of poet and apostle, the poet whose heart is touched by any type of suffering, and the apostle in the service of the humanitarian ideals of his time, rebelling against injustice, regardless of origin. Victor Hugo could never have found this plea moving, if he were really the die-hard anti-Semite expressing himself through Manassé ben Israel or in *Marie Tudor*. But the fact remains that several times Victor Hugo has presented Jewish figures in a repugnant light. We will deal with the problem created by this duality after we have taken a look at a few variations of the figure of the usurer revived by romantic literature.

George Sand: The Mississipians

In this play, the cliché of the Jewish usurer is modernized, placed in the society of early capitalism under Louis-Philippe. There is a new aristocracy that has climbed over the other classes, the moneyed aristocracy that has replaced the feudal aristocracy of the past.

George Sand, herself an aristocrat of the old school, is naturally on the side of the deteriorating class, and that is human and understandable. What is less understandable is the author's insistence that capitalism is exclusively a Jewish invention. But the tradition of the theater demands that the self-seeking man, the speculator, the Shylock be a Jew. Once again he is an abstraction of all the vices imaginable, the personification of usury and crime. Samuel Bourset is "a man capable of speculating with his own entrails." He explains his philosophy in these terms: "if we lose our fortune and honor, My Lord, we will only have our lives left, and the people enraged will take it from us, as vengeance for disappointments. As for me, I am ready, and as I have often said, such a martyrdom is worth those that have been faced and undergone because of religious quarrels."[9]

After such a confession, Georges Freeman's judgment calling Samuel Bourset a "modern Shylock" seems even too moderate. For Shylock had at least a religion to which he was attached, and he was overwhelmed when his daughter eloped with a Christian. Samuel Bourset's religion is money, and for money he sells his own daughter. Shylock is an innocent lamb compared to Samuel, this "super-Shylock" created by the Romantic School.

We feel in this play the fever of speculation and of fat profits that prevailed under Louis-Philippe. The Jew Samuel Bourset was not especially needed to excoriate this mentality. George Sand was led to this conception partly by the influence of her friend Pierre Leroux, who contributed to the anti-Semitic literature of his time by the pamphlet: *The Jews, Kings of Our Time,* and also by the tendency of the Romantic theater to revive the Shakespearian figure under a modern form.

Musset and Augier: The Green Suit; Comedy

---

9. Act II, scene 4.

This tendency became a veritable fashion that prevailed especially in comedies during the whole nineteenth century.

Stripped of its tragic pathos, placed in a lower-class environment, the scoundrel of drama becomes a petty thief whose swindles amuse the spectator, but even in this caricature remain the outlines of the Shylock original, as can be seen in *L'Habit vert,* a comedy that we present by way of example.

In the few scenes of this play, the authors manage to display all of Shylock's characteristic traits and to top them with a few vices. In design, the whole plot of *L'Habit vert* is an imitation in infinitely different proportions of *The Merchant of Venice.* Raoul and Henry correspond to Antonio and Bassanio. Marguerite takes the place of the wise Portia, which is indicated by the final remark: "Well, my poor Munius, today you have found your master." Thus Shakespeare's tragic figure had finally become a cliché, a ubiquitous character whose frequent use proves its unabating popularity.

EFFECT AT ANY PRICE

Let us now go back to the writer who introduced this character on the French stage, Victor Hugo, and examine the reasons that impelled him to give Shylock such a scope. A. Sleumer notes: "From the reading of the prefaces, one gains the distinct impression that the author aspired more to popularity than to the instruction of the people. . . . Even his revolutionary tendency was only a concession to the democratic current of his time."[10]

This verdict may be too severe. It would be unfair to explain the revolutionary tendencies of Romanticism, its concern for ordinary people, as a form of opportunism,

---

10. *Die Dramen V. Hugos* (Berlin, 1911), p. 315.

as a concession to the dominant political trend of the
time. But, while we must recognize the sincere idealism
that animated the Romantic Movement, we must also
admit that a popularity race was undeniable. It is possible that to be successful any young movement must
make concessions to the taste of the masses, concessions
that it considers of little importance in relation to its
goals.

The half-Jew Adolphe d'Ennery, a popular author at
the end of the nineteenth century, was asked if there
were any Jewish characters in his plays. "No, never, and
the reason is very simple. I believe that in the theater
the playwright should not fight against public sentiment.
. . . The first duty of the author is to please the spectator, that is, to respect his tastes and customs. If I had
portrayed a Jew, I would have been forced to make him
into a usurer, a crook, or a traitor, in short, a villain."[11]
Victor Hugo, eager to insure his personal success and
that of the literary movement that he led, did not hesitate, even as he played the role of innovator and revolutionary in art, to make concessions to the ingrained tastes
and habits of the public when they seemed useful to his
cause. The image of the Jewish usurer was deeply rooted
in the masses, who do not like to relinquish a preconceived idea. To invest that type with all the magic of the
theater was almost enough to guarantee its success on
the stage. The aesthetic conscience could reassure itself
by calling on the example of Shakespeare, the idol of the
Romantic Theater, who had created the prototype.
Hugo's temperament was responsible for transforming
Shakespeare's very profound concept into a garishly
colored theatrical figure drawn from popular legend.

But that is the very reason that the problem is transposed from the aesthetic to the ethical plane. Shakespeare

---

11. A. Dreyfus: *Le Juif au théâtre.* Actes et conférences de La So-
ciété des Etudes Juives (1898), p. 52.

did not know any real Jews; he examined what legend furnished him with his psychological genius, thanks to which he almost neutralized the effect of an ill-intentioned fable. Victor Hugo knew some Jews; they were even among his friends. He fought for the principles of the Great Revolution, this revolution which among other things broke with anti-Semitic prejudices. Yet with naïve inconsistency, he also strongly contributed to the perpetuation of a Middle Ages legend, even though he was aware of the responsibility of the author to his public: "The author of this play knows what a great and serious thing the theater is. He knows that drama, without violating the impartial limits of art, has a national mission, a social mission, a human mission. . . . The poet, too, has been entrusted with the salvation of souls. The masses must not leave the theater without carrying with them some deep and austere moral lesson."[12]

This responsibility of the writer toward "the masses" which Victor Hugo speaks about, he himself, and his followers, sold for theatrical effect. Without harboring any personal aversion against the Jews, they showed them in this hateful light that appealed to the public. It was for professional self-interest, nothing else. Nowhere does the eagerness to yield to the demands of the day, or the courage to resist them, appear more clearly than in the manner of treating a Jewish subject. Here Classicism and Romanticism, confronted with the same theme, gave it radically different interpretations. And if we can be allowed to pronounce a judgment that we deduce from the particular viewpoint from which we are studying French literature, it would be summarized this way: If Romanticism has conquered a whole generation by its charm, Classicism will maintain its appeal through every generation, for its subject is truth.

---

12. *Lucrèce Borgia,* preface.

13

The Jew in the Social Novel of the Nineteenth Century

THE BIG BUSINESSMAN

The Realistic novel originated by Balzac gives a faithful picture of the society of his day. Until then, literature in France consisted of works of imagination and contemplation. The problems of contemporary life appeared in literature only through a veil of conventions. Subjects were chosen from the past: by the Classical writers, in order to extract from ancient characters a human truth valid for all ages and societies; by the Romantics, with the purpose of reviving the traditions and legends where the most precious sources of poetry were to be found ("The myths of the people are the truth of the poet.") The Realistic novelists of Balzac's school, on the other hand, want to paint what is happening under their eyes. *The Human Comedy* is to serve as a vast documentation of contemporary society, of capitalism, then in full growth, and it is along these lines that the nineteenth-century novel evolves from Balzac to Zola.

In the collection of characteristic types of that period we naturally find a few Jewish characters. They are presented in a more or less favorable light, and often, especially in Balzac, with an admiring note for the grandeur of their vices as well as their virtues. Balzac and his disciples explain their characters by their milieus and their economic conditions. It is still surprising that the activities reserved to the Jews are always the same: they are cast either as businessmen or courtesans. There is, no doubt, an echo of the merchant of Venice and of his daughter, beautiful and too charming, an echo of which, perhaps, even the authors were unaware. On the other hand, they did discover in their characters new and interesting traits.

In *The Human Comedy* we find two characters who are among the most original created by Balzac, Gobsec and the Baron Nucingen. He casts them as two businessmen of demoniacal power, who drive toward their goal without regard for the traditional notions of good and evil. Balzac, who hates mediocrity above everything, harbors a secret admiration for the unscrupulous skill of a Gobsec who knows the innermost recesses of the human heart and manipulates it at will. When this usurer pursues his material interests with an inflexibility verging on cruelty, the author gives us to understand that his deeper motives are not limited to base avarice, but that he acts according to unusual concepts. His lawyer describes him thus: "Old man Gobsec is intimately convinced of one principle that rules his whole behavior. According to him, money is a merchandise that can be sold cheaply or dearly, depending on the situation. A capitalist is, in his eyes, a man who participates in advance in lucrative speculations and enterprises by the high interest he asks for his money. Aside from his financial principles and his philosophical observations that allow him to behave superficially like a usurer, I am intimately convinced that away from his business, he is the most delicate and most honest man in Paris. Two men coexist in him: he is a miser and a philosopher, small and big."

Money for the Gobsecs and the Nucingens is not loved

for itself; it is a form of will, it is a concentration of energy expressed at certain moments in superhuman and anonymous power. Let us note the dialogue of Gobsec and Derville: "There are a dozen of us in Paris, all silent and unknown kings, the arbiters of your destiny." Sometimes Balzac, transcending the assessment of money as a form of individual will, lends it the characteristic of a natural force. "If securities rise and fall, if stocks improve and deteriorate, this ebb and flow is produced by a natural, atmospheric movement related to the influence of the moon, and the great Arago is guilty of failing to give any scientific theory for this important phenomenon."

There have been attempts to classify the author of *The Human Comedy* among the anti-Semitic writers because of his ironical and unkind remarks about his Jewish characters. We hesitate to subscribe to this viewpoint and are inclined to detect in the author a certain admiration for the "Jewish race" (he readily uses that term). Balzac does not like the Jews, but he admires them; he notes without pity their vices or their idiosyncrasies, but he acknowledges a certain genius thanks to which they rise above the vulgarity of their profession and their social condition. After a Nucingen and a Gobsec, and without speaking of the courtesan Esther (one of the most compelling characters that Balzac has conceived), it is Elie Magus[1] who confirms our observations.

Elie Magus is a dirty old Jew afflicted with all the bad habits of his tribe. "During the Middle Ages, persecutions forced the Jews to wear rags to lull suspicions, always to complain, whine, cry poor mouth. These necessities of the past have become, as always, a popular instinct, an endemic vice."[2]

But a noble passion lives in this old miser: "This soul dedicated to profit, as cold as an icicle, melted when he

---

1. In *Le Cousin Pons.*
2. Les parents pauvres, *Le Cousin Pons* (Calmann-Levy, 1885), p. 138.

saw a masterpiece, just as a libertine, tired of women, is moved at the sight of a perfect girl and devotes his time to the search for flawless beauties. This Don Juan of painting, this worshiper of the ideal, found in this admiration enjoyment greater than the miser contemplating his gold. He lived in a harem of beautiful paintings."[3]

Elie Magus is a peerless art expert; he knows all the schools and can detect a masterpiece under a one hundred-year-old coat of dirt. Here is a scene where he identifies a few masterpieces:

> The salon where the major part of the Pons Museum was lodged was one of the old salons built in the style of the architects employed by the French nobility. Pons' paintings, 67 in number, were hung on the four walls of this salon, paneled in white and gold. . . .
>
> As soon as the Jew came into this sanctuary, he went straight to the four masterpieces he recognized as the most beautiful of the collection, and by masters that he needed for his. They were for him those "desiderata" that compel naturalists to travel from East to West, to the tropics, to the desert, the pampas, the bush, the virgin forest. . . .
>
> Elie Magus had tears in his eyes as he looked at each of these four masterpieces in turn.[4]

Jewish types from high financial circles appear frequently in the nineteenth-century novel,[5] but without psychological nuances as fine as Balzac's. In *Les Monach* by R. de Bonnières, the hero is the prototype of the self-made Jew. Coming from a very religious milieu in Frankfurt, he makes his fortune in Paris and breaks with everything that ties him to his origins, hoping in this fashion to become a member in good standing of Parisian high society. His only commendable character trait is a

---

3. *Ibid.*, p. 140.
4. *Ibid.*, pp. 160–62.
5. Cf. M. Debré, *Der Jude in der franzos. Literatur von 1800 bis Gegenwart* (Wurzbourg, 1909).

filial love that resists even his snobbish ambitions; to please his mother he practices certain religious rites to which he is completely indifferent.

The author thinks he has captured the type of the Jewish parvenu; he has only captured the type of the parvenu. The least Jewish traits are perhaps certain traits that the author presents as typically Jewish. An example is the scene in which Monach, during an elegant party he gives in his house, brags about his expensive furniture, quotes prices, and makes the guest feel the material of a blanket to make them aware of the silk and silver embroidery. A literary critic has pointed out very accurately: "How very Jewish, the author must have told himself, as he noted this trait. Well, it is not Jewish at all. A real Jew would rather walk on silk and silver to give the impression that this luxury does not impress him, and that he has identical blankets in his stables."[6]

In many other novels, Jewish financiers have the same traits as Monach. *Les Rois en Exile* (*Kings in Exile*) by Alphonse Daudet and *Cosmopolis* by Paul Bourget are two cases in point.

In order to give the complete social picture of his period, just as Balzac did of his own, Emile Zola chooses the Stock Exchange as the scene of his novel *L'Argent* (*Money*). He pits two businessmen against each other, the Jew Gundermann and the Christian Saccard. In his private life Gundermann, endowed with all the bourgeois virtues, is a hard worker, an affectionate husband, averse to frivolous pleasures. He is exempt from all passions save one: money. He wants to multiply his millions, not to enjoy them but to leave them to his children, who by increasing them will, in their turn, be able to acquire their share of worldly power. His nature is in the Gobsec tradition. This man has an enemy, the Christian Saccard,

6. A. Dreyfus, *Le Juif au théâtre* (Revue des Etudes Juives, 1886).

who accuses him of belonging to a nation of parasites, feeding on the blood of the host-nation. But this anti-Semite in the name of virtue is himself a financier that the author describes this way: "Peculiarly, Saccard the terrible wheeler dealer, this unscrupulous financial executioner, lost all self-awareness as soon as the subject of Jews came up, spoke of them with a harshness, with the avenging indignation of an honest man who lives from the labor of his hands, untainted by any usury. He would draw up an indictment of the race, that cursed race that had lost its homeland, its princes, that lived as a parasite among nations, pretending to obey their laws, but in reality obeying only its thieving, bloodthirsty and angry God: and he showed it carrying out the mission of ferocious conquest that this God had given it, settling among each people like the spider at the center of the web, sucking everybody's blood, fattening on the lives of others."[7] These two rivals engage in a pitiless duel during which Saccard almost destroys his opponent by a daring stock market operation, but from which Gundermann, thanks to his coolness and financial genius, recovers to triumph over Saccard, ruined by a woman. The Jew does not indulge in a base revenge. He refuses to destroy his weakened enemy, not through Christian charity, but because he is farsighted enough to realize that it is necessary to put out the fire that is destroying a neighbor's house before it spreads to one's own.

In short, the Christian financier plays a much more unpleasant role than the Jew. The latter is presented with his vices and his virtues, in accordance with the program of an author who strove for a literature patterned on life. Thus, Zola presents side by side with the Jewish banker a little tubercular Jew, a fervent idealist who, until the final agony, dreams of the reconstruction of society. The anti-Semitic vocabulary placed in Saccard's mouth is an

7. Les Rougon-Macquart, *L'Argent* (Paris, 1928), p. 95.

eloquent illustration of the fact, already noted in the chapter on Fourier, that the campaign against Jewish capitalism is often nothing more than a maneuver prepared by the non-Jewish opposition.

SHYLOCK'S DAUGHTER

"As for Jewish women," says Leroy-Beaulieu, "our gallantry has always been kind to their velvety eyes and long eyelashes. I don't know whether there has been any anti-Semitism toward them."

Indeed, Jewish women occupy a special place in literature. They appear as the ideal of physical and moral beauty.[8] Even authors who cast them as Aphrodite's worshipers endow them with a transfigured beauty, a rare nobility of soul, even in novels which offer the usual image of the Jewish usurer. This contrast, originating in the doublet Shylock-Jessica, recurs almost diagrammatically in *Les Mississipiens* by George Sand as well as in *Cosmopolis* by Bourget and *Les Monach* by Bonnières. In *Splendeurs et misères des courtisanes* (*Splendor and Misery of Courtesans*) Esther, the niece of the usurer Gobsec, is one of the most touching characters of Balzac's world. Divinely beautiful, she has for Lucien de Rubempré a pure and selfless love. "Even if I were to die by staying away from my beloved," she writes to the Abbé Carlos Herrera, "I will die purified like Maria Magdalena and my soul will become for him the rival of his guardian angel. I have given up all impure love and will follow no other path than the path of righteousness. If my body is weaker than my soul, let it die. . . ." In her last letter to Lucien she adds:

The soul aches like the body. Only the soul cannot allow itself

---

8. An exception is the half-Jewess Séphora in the novel by Alphonse Daudet, *Les Rois en exil.*

to suffer stupidly like the body. You gave me a whole new life the day before yesterday by telling me that if Clotilde still rejected you, you would marry me. It would have been a great misfortune for us. The world would never have accepted us. The world which bows before money and fame, refuses to bow before happiness and virtue, for I would have done good deeds. How many tears I would have dried: as many, I think, as I have shed. Yes, I would have wanted to live only for you and charity.

She kills herself in the belief that her death will contribute to her lover's happiness.

The title character in *Manette Salomon,* the novel by the Goncourt brothers, is a curious mixture of virtues and vices. She is both frivolous and naïve. She renders unto Caesar (read Venus) what belongs to Caesar, but raised in that milieu, does not see anything wrong in what she does. Personally, she detests wild pleasures and seeks a peaceful happiness in her home. She is indifferent to jewels and accessories, of which women are usually so fond. The authors explain this sobriety by her belonging to a "race without drunkards."

The coexistence of vulgarity and nobility in the soul of a young Jewess is also the subject of a short story by Guy de Maupassant, *Mademoiselle Fifi.* The Jewess Rachel, a woman of ill-repute, becomes an example of patriotism and moral courage. During the War of 1870-71 a Prussian officer, nicknamed Mademoiselle Fifi, is billeted in a chateau near Rouen with several comrades. To while away the time, they send for prostitutes, they eat and drink copiously. Since the patriotism of certain people increases with their consumption of wine, Fifi glorifies the victories of the Prussian army and makes fun of the defeats of the French. The French women keep quiet. They are offended but do not dare say anything. However, when Rachel, the Jewess, hears her country being slandered, she kills the offender and escapes through a window. A whole batallion is unsuccessfully mobilized to capture her, but Rachel has disappeared. The Prussian officer receives a solemn funeral to the sounds of the church bells. The French priest who since the invasion of the Prussian army has refused to ring the bells, this time has consented to do it! Otherwise, the Prussians would have occupied the church, in which he has hidden Rachel. She is saved, and at the end of the war she finds happiness in marriage.

Elsewhere a Jewess is the symbol of feminine virtue; it is Rebecca in the play of Alexander Dumas, Jr., *La Femme de Claude* (*Claude's Wife*). Dumas, who in the preface gives a cry of alarm against the moral decadence of his time, against its boundless selfishness, shows in Rebecca the symbol of renunciation of earthly happiness if it is to be bought by the violation of virtue. In her last farewell to Claude, Rebecca exclaims: "When death has freed us, you of earthly ties, and me of earthly obedience, you will find me a patient and immaterial fiancée, waiting for you on the threshold of what is called the unknown, and we will be joined in the infinite."

Certain writers have meditated on the origin of this amazing charm that all have found in Jewish women. Chateaubriand gives reasons of a mystical nature. He notes that Jewish women did not participate in the persecution and humiliation of Jesus; some even showed him pity. Therefore they have been spared the curse of the Jewish people, and they have retained a trace of Jesus' divine gaze on them. It is in virtue of this theory that in the play *Le Juif Errant* (*The Wandering Jew*) by Merville and Mailland, Ashaver's daughter is the personification of beauty and innocence. That might be an explanation of the contrast between Shylock and Jessica, so often repeated in literature. Victor Hugo, who has created a super-Shylock in the person of Manassé ben Israël, also praises the unearthly beauty of the Jewish woman:

> Que m'importe, juive adorée
> Un sein d'ébène, un front vermeil!
> Tu n'es point blanche, ni cuivrée,
> Mais il semble qu'on t'a dorée
> Avec un rayon de soleil.

> What matters to me, adored Jewess
> An ebony breast, a rosy forehead!
> You are neither white nor bronzed,
> But you seem to be gilded
> With a ray of the sun.[9]

Balzac looks for the source of Esther's beauty in her distant oriental origin: "After 1,800 years of exile, the Orient still shone in Esther's eyes and in Esther's face. . . ." And elsewhere: "Esther came from the cradle of mankind, the homeland of beauty: her mother was Jewish. The Jews, although so often degraded by their contact with other people, offer among their numerous tribes veins where the sublime type of Asiatic beauties still survives. . . . Esther would have won the prize in the harem; she possessed the thirty forms of beauty harmoniously blended. . . . Esther would suddenly attract attention by a trait reminiscent of Raphael's most artistic drawings, for Raphael is the painter who has the most carefully studied and best captured Jewish beauty. . . . Only the races born in the desert possess in their eyes the power to fascinate everybody, for a woman always fascinates someone. Their eyes no doubt retain something of the infinite that they have contemplated."[10] (Let us note that Nietzsche also seeks a racial explanation of the beauty of Jewish women: "In Europe the

---

9. "La Sultane favorite" in *Orientale.*
10. *Splendeurs et misères des courtisanes* in *Oeuvres complètes,* vol. 18, pp. 37–39.

Jews constitute the purest race; that is why the beauty of the Jewish woman is the most flawless.")

And here are two Jewish opinions, both of which look for the secret of the charm of the Jewish woman, that strikes Christians so profoundly, in the social conditions in which she lives.

Henri Heine claims that the awareness of the misery, the shame, the dangers in which lived her relatives who had to get out of the ghetto in the daytime to earn a living, has given the Jewess the dreamy and melancholy expression that transfigures her natural beauty.

M. Bloch, by way of explanation, addresses Jewish women in these terms: "Living at home, you have not furnished the public spectacle of our humiliation, the public spectacle of the grotesque vexations we have suffered and that were designed to destroy our dignity. This is what has weighed so heavily on the Jew when the novel and the theater seized upon him, to make of him the wretched character with which you are acquainted."[11]

All in all, the Jewish woman plays in literature a role that is as flattering as the male's is unflattering.

Even a writer of Roger Martin du Gard's stature[12] makes use of the cliché of the Jewish woman's mysterious eroticism. While in the most moving episode of the novel *Jean Barois,* the story of the Dreyfus Affair and the moral conflict it provoked in the French people, Roger Martin du Gard expresses his views on the Jewish question with his well-known integrity, in *Les Thibault* he lapses into the most common stereotypes when he wants to present the Jewish woman.

It looks as if these authors were acquainted only with the Jewish women who live on the fringe of bourgeois society, unless they were simply attracted by the facility

11. *La Femme juive dans le roman et au théâtre,* R.E.J., vol. XXIV.
12. We are anticipating somewhat, for the sake of the unity of this chapter, the analysis of certain authors whom we treat later within the framework of their period.

of the traditional clichés for the creation of minor figures.
Rachel Goepfert, Antoine Thibault's mistress, is no
exception to this tacit rule. She is "half-Jewish," loves
sausages with garlic, "has the pagan charm and even a
little of the simplicity of the girls who really love their
profession; but this charm unspoiled by anything equivocal or vulgar."[13] In her presence, Antoine, the calm and
realistic doctor, is suddenly inspired by the fervor of the
Song of Songs and he recites in Latin entire passages
from the book. More pedestrian, she answers the rhap-
sodic enumeration of her charms with: Maybe I'll become
a fat lady. Jewish women, you know. . . . But my
mother wasn't. I'm only half a loaf of Yiddish."

Nevertheless, this half-loaf has a brother called Aaron,
a purely Biblical name like hers, Rachel, which would be
rather funny in real life for an integrated family, but
this facilitates the treatment for the author. As for
Antoine, the son of a typically French family, his mistress's background gives him a slight shudder while at
the same time it increases the charm of his conquest:
"At the thought that she might be Jewish, the last trace
of Antoine's education was disturbed just enough to
spice his adventure with the flavor of independence and
exoticism." Ultimately his paramour jilts him to follow
the leanings of her heart and her blood toward her
former swain, Hirsch; but it is not because she listens to
lowly instincts, oh! no. Or only a little, because after all
she is a little bit Yiddish: "Hirsch is going to marry me;
he is rich, very rich; and at my age, in spite of what one
might tell oneself, marriage is something: it is hard to
live one's whole life on the fringe. But it isn't that either.
No, really, I am above these calculations, as much as a
Jewess, a half-Jewess can be."

Here is a portrait that for the Antoines, the readers
of *Les Thibault,* may be endowed with an exotic and

---

13. *Les Thibault,* I, p. 346.

mysterious charm, but which for the trained historian of literature offers nothing new and simply makes us regret that a writer of Roger Martin du Gard's stature succumbed so completely to the commonplace.

Sartre is the only one who avoids the beaten path when he portrays a Jewish woman. He is too thoroughly original to settle for the meaningless cliché of a literary tradition, even on minor questions. He criticizes the well-defined role assigned to the beautiful Jewess in the most serious novels, her degradation to a "sexual significance." Sartre meets the Jewish woman, not in the boudoir but on the crowded roads of defeated France, when the moral values learned during normal times crumble under the imperative of "every man for himself," and do not stand up to an anarchic situation. Only Sarah's kindness is unlearned, a generous and spontaneous kindness that "rises to her breasts like milk" (*La Mort dans l'âme* [*Sick at Heart*], p. 32) and is more than the animal instinct stopping at the protection of its offsprings. Sarah is severe only with her son, who asks to be carried, but she spontaneously offers her help to the old peasant woman: "I'll help her, I'll relieve her of her bundle, her fatigue, her troubles." She is humiliated when her generous offer meets with suspicion and she finds excuses: "Her idle kindness filled her like a gas. They don't want to be loved. They're not used to it."

She understands that no one in this crowd that has lost its soul believes in altruism; everybody seeks his salvation by any available means and supposes the same attitude to exist among those who share his fate, and who are not his friends, but his enemies. Even the hatred of the invader is forgotten. It has been diverted to the compatriot, now a merciless rival for a bed, for a piece of bread. That is the real victory of the aggressor, to have produced mutual hatred in the hearts of the vanquished, to have made them lose their human dignity, to have brought death into the soul of a nation that had already lost face.

Among those living corpses, Sarah, the Jewess, has kept her personality. Although dead tired and seeing no solution, she does not surrender to despair and its resulting irresponsibility. She is, so to speak, trained for this situation, to this "weariness of a mother and a Jewess, her weariness, her destiny." This hereditary fate has transfigured the best members of her tribe and freed in them their best impulses, where in others the lowest instincts have been unleashed. And thus, "she forgot herself, she forgot that she was Jewish, that she herself was persecuted; she was escaping in a great surge of impersonal charity."

For Sartre the true human values are manifested in the dramatic situations of life, and in the defeat suffered by bourgeois society in 1940 he looks for redeeming features in a rout that was more moral than military. He finds them, for the regeneration of the nation, in the historic reserves of the Jewish soul.

Guy des Cars, a third-rate writer, but with a large following, can claim credit for being "original" in this matter by combining the characters of Jessica and Shylock.

Le Château de la juive (*The Castle of the Jewess*) is the story of a misalliance between Colonel Eric de Maubert and Eva Goldski, born "almost" in "the most sordid ghetto of Europe." The author has obviously never heard of a heroic resurrection that makes the Warsaw Ghetto the most glorious ghetto in the world.

Eva was eight or nine years old at the time of the invasion of Poland by the German armies, and she was dragged into the concentration camps where her whole family perished. She herself owed her life to her erotic docility through which she managed to satisfy the base instincts of the German prison guards. That's when she swore that "the day would come when she would take a stunning revenge, when she would apply the law of the talion, an eye for an eye, a tooth for a tooth."

This is the only explanation for the amazing actions by which the Jewess of Warsaw tries to pollute French high society. The author goes back at least ten times to this law of the talion which seems to be the mainspring of Eva's soul, her very nature, her racial inheritance. If at least she had applied that law, presented as characteristic of her race, toward those who had made her suffer so much! But no, she takes revenge against the Germans at the expense of France, the country that welcomed her most warmly. It is a French officer, the Count of Maubert, who freed the beautiful prisoner in rags from a D.P. camp and made her his wife. Too sensitive, like a true Frenchman, to feminine beauty, he could not resist "Jewish splendor in all its aggressiveness."

What does this aggressiveness consist of? The author settles for adopting and exaggerating the cliché of the beautiful Jewess exuding a dazzling sensuality: "As for Jewish women," Leroy-Baulieu had said, "I don't know whether there is any anti-Semitism toward them." There is, since Guy des Cars's novel. It is even an unacknowledged new form of anti-Semitism that combines all the vices of a Shylock with those of the depraved woman, "the most admirable mistress," who uses her body to carry out her diabolic goals. "She had brought her intelligence, her beauty, her caresses. Three treasures to cash in on, and very profitably."

Armed with her deadly weapons, after the total conquest of her husband, she resolutely sets out to quench her thirst for revenge, for "how often she had dreamed of marking the proud Maubert line with the Jewish blood which was held against her." She wins absolute mastery of the Maubert estate, which becomes the Castle of the Jewess. She wages a merciless and victorious fight against her mother-in-law, who would like to defend the traditions of "La Tilleraye," whose moral value "is inaccessible to those who were incapable of understanding the nobility of a past." Notice that the author, as always when he wants to insinuate an anti-Semitic idea, switches imperceptibly to the plural, to implicate not just one person, Eva, but her whole race. But he forgets that "those who are incapable of understanding the nobility of a past" possess and cultivate the longest past in the whole human family, a past four thousand years old, encompassing the whole history of civilization. He forgets that the ancestors of Eva Goldski were writing psalms and canticles at a time when Rome, Paris, and "La Tilleraye" were still marshes.

Finally, fate, too long defied by Eva, strikes her down. She suffers a total defeat, just like Shylock in the scene where he is crushed by Portia's Aryan superiority. She becomes once again the hunted Jewess, despised by everybody, spewed out by the society in which she had intruded, and she loses her last protector as her generous husband is killed by the bullets meant for his wife.

In her bewilderment she discovers Judaism and overnight becomes converted to Zionism and, with militant enthusiasm, dedicates herself to the service of young immigrants. A real miracle, this sudden enlightenment followed by a full conversion and a complete confession in the style of the Salvation Army. The author becomes thoroughly ecstatic about the performance of the young state and the useful job reserved for Eva.

His sudden enthusiasm for Eva's new homeland, described in a more than superficial manner, contrasts so sharply with the general tone of the novel that his thesis is unequivocal. It seems to be saying: "Go with God, but go! Go back to your Promised Land; be happy there as long as you rid us of your presence."

The space reserved here to the analysis of a best-seller contrived with the most sordid means can be defended only as a warning against a pseudo Judeo-French literature.

14
Gobineau's Theory

The Count of Gobineau, historian and philosopher, in his *Essay on the Inequality of the Human Races,* developed the idea of race as a fundamental factor of history. He presents the Aryan, the blond dolychocephalus, as the superior type of mankind. The Aryans have been the real founders of all civilization, and among the Aryans it is the Germanic people who have had the most pronounced creative spirit.

The author of the *Essay* has emphasized the mission of the Germanic people in the world, but, while glorifying the Germans in the past, he refuses to grant them an important role in the future. The last Germanic alluvium disappeared during the early centuries of our era. If there is a nation that still possesses vestiges of the Aryan essence, claims Gobineau, it is not Germany but Great Britain.[1] Today's Germans, according to him, are not even of German origin. Two years before his death, he insisted "that the blood praised by Tacitus is not as abundant nor as widespread in Germany as has been believed."

Gobineau, while extolling the virtue of the German race, did not, by the same token, condemn the Jews. In fact, it seemed to him that during the era when the races were still pure, Jews were the most creative of the Semitic people: "Modern travelers know by what efforts

1. *Essai,* vol. II (Paris, 1884), p. 456.

agronomists of Israel maintained its artificial fecundity. Since this chosen race has stopped living in its mountains and plains, the wells where Jacob's flocks drank have been filled with sand. . . . And in that wretched corner of the world, what were the Jews? I repeat, a clever people in everything it undertook, a free people, a strong people, an intelligent people, and which, before losing bravely, arms in hand, the title of independent nation, had given the world almost as many doctors as merchants."[2]

In France, Gobineau's work was coolly received. Scholars, philosophers, historians, and writers were suspicious of its new ideas. The naturalist Quatrefages, criticized Gobineau for his ignorance in physiology and his contradictions. Toqueville was reluctant to accept the truth of a historical system that he found insufficiently substantiated: "I disapprove of the book and I like the author." Renan refused to believe that creative genius depended primarily on racial purity. "Zoological origins precede by far the origins of culture, civilization and language. The racial fact decisive at the beginning therefore keeps on losing its importance. Human history differs basically from zoology."[3] He also explains the difference between Jews and non-Jews, not by race, but by a difference of mores and habits. There is not one sole Jewish type but several. Jews of different races are alike, however, owing to the fact that they form a religious minority. "There is a psychology of religious minority and this psychology is independent of race. . . . Certain similarities are created that do not stem from race, but are the result of circumstantial analogies. . . ."[4] Thus Renan does not reject the racial theory entirely; he adopts it in a broader sense, rather spiritual than biological. For a Mediter-

2. *Ibid.*, vol. I, pp. 58–59.
3. E. Renan, "Qu'est-ce qu'une race?" in *Discours et Conférences* (1887), pp. 295–97.
4. "Le Judaïsme, comme race et comme religion," in *ibid.*, p. 371.

ranean country it is, of course, very delicate to base its concept of race on purity of blood.

Finally, let us note a recent theory. André Combris compares modern racism with Gobineau's theory and absolves him of responsibility for the conclusions drawn from it. "The practical repercussion of Gobineau's philosophy in Germany constitutes, all things considered, a rather unexpected phenomenon."[5]

The most important play dealing with the racial theme is the drama by Maurice Donnay, *Retour de Jerusalem* (*Back from Jerusalem*), whose crude partiality cannot convince any objective spectator, in spite of the remarkable theatrical qualities of the author. The latter wants to prove the inevitable disappointment that the Jewish girl Judith is to bring Michel Aubier. If Donnay had insisted in a general way on the drawbacks of a mixed marriage, everybody could have gone along with him. But to expound this idea, the author should have portrayed characters of the same moral value, even though of different races or religions. Instead, he is far from maintaining a balance between the two races. On the one side he sees nothing but the most rigid honesty; on the other, he represents people that he just falls short of calling swine.

The partiality is glaring in the choice of the main characters. Instead of choosing as a protagonist an uncommitted young girl, Donnay makes her an adulteress. Michel Aubier, who has abandoned his wife and children, is inevitably unhappy in his new marriage, to such a point that he abuses the Jewish religion, sees in its members nothing but enemies of the Aryan race and destroyers of the French soul. His reasoning in the face of such circumstances is unconvincing, even though Judith responds only with a fit of hysterics. For the cause of Michel Au-

---

5. *La Philosophie des races du comte de Gobineau et sa portée actuelle.* Thèse (Clermont, 1937), p. 237.

bier's mental disturbance is not necessarily the fact of committing himself to a Judith, but of having abandoned his wife and children for a futile passion. "If Judith had been called Claire, if instead of being Jewish she had been born in the Catholic religion, it is probable that Michel would have experienced the same remorse, the same disappointments."[6]

These noticeable flaws in the exposition of Maurice Donnay's racial thesis have brought him at least as many detractors as admirers. The race problem did not cause any excitement in France for the reasons we have already mentioned: this Mediterranean country is a crucible of several races. Drumont's terminology, which we are about to take up, must therefore come from other sources than French literature.

---

6. *A. Kahn, Le Théâtre social en France de 1870 à nos jours* (Berne, 1905).

15

From Drumont to Dreyfus

Hate is a passion that can lead to the most surprising accomplishments. There are geniuses of hate just as there are geniuses inspired by religious or artistic ideals. But, since everything serves a historic purpose whose total image transcends the horizons of a single generation, the works accomplished in the name of hatred contribute, although painfully, to a new and positive order.

Edouard Drumont has been one of these geniuses of hatred. Although a very mediocre writer, he drew from an inexhaustible source of inspiration, his hatred of Jews, and unleashed the avalanche of political passions that marked the Dreyfus Affair.

La France juive (*Jewish France*) by Edouard Drumont is an immense pamphlet and does not attempt to be a scientific work. The author uses any argument to prove, at a time when the Jews in France did not number more than 45,000, that they had overrun the nation and usurped all the important functions of the state. He proceeds by accusations that he does not bother to prove: "Even the religious question plays a secondary role next to the race question that takes precedence over all others. Even among those who have forsaken Judaism two or three generations ago the Jew recognizes his own, he detects by unmistakable clues whether a drop of Jewish blood flows in their veins. . . . It is to the Aryan that

we owe all discoveries, great and small. . . . The Semite
has only exploited what the genius and the works of
others have conquered. . . . The major signs by which
a Jew can be recognized remain the famous hooked nose,
the blinking eyes, the clenched teeth, the protruding
ears . . . the too long torso, the flat feet, the soft and
melting hands of the hypocrite and the traitor. Frequently one of their arms is shorter than the other."[1]

This flood of arguments can in no way be traced to
Gobineau's theory, except for the fact that since Drumont
anti-Judaism becomes anti-Semitism.

Drumont draws on all anti-Jewish sources without examining their origin. He exploits all the hostile legends,
from ritual murder and the "Jewish odor" to racism in
its most modern forms. He formulates against the Jews
the most contradictory accusations: they have waged war,
they have made peace. If there happens to be a Jew,
Gambetta, who saved the honor of the French army by
organizing "the national defense," Drumont is sure to
claim that his actions were motivated only by material
reasons. The Jew is responsible for both large-scale capitalism and for the Communist uprising in 1871, statement difficult to reconcile with the thesis of "Jewish
solidarity." This legendary solidarity, tirelessly de-
nounced by Drumont, should have intervened to protect
Jewish capitalism against the resurrection of the Commune, for which, according to Drumont, the Jews are
equally responsible. If Aryans have participated in the
revolt, Drumont forgives them in the same manner that
he accuses the Jews, without attempting to prove his
statements: "The Aryan, do I have to repeat it, is a
person of faith and discipline, and he keeps these feelings
even during a revolution. . . . The Commune, then, had
two faces: one unreasonable, unthinking, but courageous:
the French face; the other mercantile, grasping, pillag-

1. *La France juive*, I, chap. 1.

ing, basely speculative: the Jewish face. The French insurrectionists fought and died. The Jewish "communards" stole, murdered and burned to hide their thefts."[2]

One of Drumont's most frequent accusations against the Jews is their alleged espionage in favor of Prussia. "Most of the Prussian spies captured in Alsace are Jewish. No one could practice this vile profession better than the children of this degraded race that has had the contemptible fate of producing the most accomplished example of perfidy and treason."[3] The Jews are the ones who have persuaded the Germans to humiliate the French by the destruction of the column on the Place Vendôme, a memorial to French glory. "The Prussians, masters of Paris, would not have touched this column; they have respected everywhere the monuments of our victories and the pictures of our heroes. There are things that Aryans do not do themselves, but sometimes they have these things done by Semites as if to prove that they can be useful occasionally. . . . A man in front of the Prussians gave the signal to knock down on a bed of garbage the monument to our ancient glories; his name was Simon Meyer and he was a Jew."

"There are certain things that Aryans do not do themselves. . . ." And if it happens anyway, the author uses a very simple method: if the President of the Republic, Carnot, has been assassinated by an Italian anarchist, Caserio, Drumont merely spreads the rumor of the assassin's Jewish background.

By exploiting and modernizing all the anti-Jewish traditions going back to the Middle Ages, Drumont prepared in a defeated France the climate that lay at the base of the Dreyfus Affair. The affair itself arose from the allegation of Jewish espionage in favor of Germany, propagated by Drumont. La France juive was published

---

2. *Ibid.*, II, chap. 6.
3. *Ibid.*

in 1886. Three years later, the "National Anti-Semitic League" was founded. From 1892 the newspaper "La Libre Parole" (Free Speech) carried out a tireless anti-Semitic campaign, crowned in 1894 by the arrest of Captain Dreyfus.[4]

---

4. In the literature of the twentieth century we encounter a racist and anti-Semitic current in L. F. Céline, Drieu La Rochelle, etc.

Part IV

RECONSTRUCTION OF THE DEMOCRATIC IDEAL

The French genius was sleeping on a pillow of vipers. It looked as if it might suffocate in the disgusting knots of a civil war. But the bells ring the alarm and, behold, the sleeper wakes up in a surge of love.
—Maurice Barrès.
Les diverses familles spirituelles de la France.
(The various spiritual families of France.)

16
The Dreyfus Affair

"The Dreyfus Affair was a crucial event. It was an eminent crisis in three histories, themselves eminent . . . : in the history of Israel, in the history of France, in the history of Christianity."[1]

Its importance in the history of Israel will be the subject of the last chapter of this book. As for France, she rediscovered in this crisis her political ideal, the return toward the fulfillment of the principles of "the rights of man." The history of Christianity was settled for several generations, for France has the peculiar destiny that what happens within her borders has repercussions on the whole of Western civilization.

It is rather curious, and it recalls the formula of the "Jews as the salt of the earth," that a crisis with such far-reaching repercussions should have exploded around the humble figure of a minor Jewish officer. A minor officer, who did not even realize the importance of the cause in which his person was the pawn, became the focus of all the forces fighting for the future of France. It was like a phenomenon in a chemical experiment, where the minimum of a specific element added to a liquid produces a powerful reaction, regrouping the elements and ultimately creating a new crystallization.

---

1. C. Péguy, "Notre jeunesse," in *Cahiers de la Quinzaine.* Série XI, Cahier 12 (Paris, 1910), p. 54.

The Dreyfus Affair was not simply the symptom of an anti-Semitic current nor a judicial error and the review of a trial; it was tied to the whole spiritual life of the nation; to patriotic emotions because of treason, to political struggles because of the summary procedure of the military court, to nationalistic prejudices because of the race of the accused, to social conflicts because of the isolation of the aristocratic army from the nation and the role assumed by the Socialist party in the struggle for the judicial review, in short, to the whole material and moral crisis, to the French decadence of the second half of the nineteenth century, whose first symptoms had been the military defeat of 1870-71.

"France is dying, do not disturb its agony," exclaims Renan. Paul Bourget, in his *Essais de psychologie contemporaine* (*Essays in contemporary psychology*) notes a "deadly weariness of life, a dull disillusionment with the vanity of all effort."

The weakening of moral supports is frequently accompanied by an external stiffening; a morality, imposed like a suit of armor, replaces the moral sentiments that ought to guide the behavior of a nation. Reasons of state take over when plain reason becomes atrophied. The government becomes authoritarian when the principles which are the supports of a democracy lose their validity for a disillusioned and bewildered people. The army which has the noble duty to *serve,* to defend the civilization of the nation, proclaims itself the supreme institution to which all others must be subordinated. The spiritual movements whose free interplay determines the equilibrium and the wealth of a nation are suppressed in favor of a spirit of uniformity. This was the direction which France seemed to be taking at a moment of national weakness. The Dreyfus Affair was only the symptom of a moral and political crisis.

Charles Sénéchal, in a few concise sentences, summarizes the political consequences of the Dreyfus Affair. It was to result "in the army in the attempt to republicanize the officer corps; in education, it lay in control of the schools; in religious life, in the separation of church and state and the expulsion of religious congregations; in society, in a rapprochement between intellectuals and the proletariat; in political life, by abortive *coups d'état,* the growth of Republican and Socialist parties; in literature, by the awakening of conscience that brought writers close to life, that led them to take a part in events. . . ."[2]

Taken separately these reforms might not always have been successful. Nevertheless, taken *in toto,* once the storm abated they gave France greater strength than ever. The democratic idea was rejuvenated and filled with a new *élan.*

The trial of Captain Dreyfus had exposed the impasse in which democracy found itself. It was evident in the form that the solution to the Jewish question had taken.

In 1789, the inhabitants of the ghettos, who had got used to their way of living and had even found spiritual compensations in it, were told: "You are all French citizens; you belong to the body politic of this nation; the sweet land of France is your homeland, her cities, her fields, and her rivers are yours; in return you will be asked only to forget the banks of the Jordan and to see in Paris your new Jerusalem." Those who offered this alternative acted in good faith, according to the victorious principles of the Great Revolution. They asked the Jews only what they asked the inhabitants of the French provinces: to give up their clannishness in order to become citizens of France. Guided by the spirit

---

2. Cf. Sénéchal, *Les Grands Courants de la littérature française contemporaine* (Paris, 1934), pp. 16–17.

of the Enlightenment, they wanted to reorganize society on new foundations. They would have, had they had the power (the Napoleonic wars fostered that idea), reorganized Europe by asking its citizens to give up their national loyalties to become European citizens. The Jews, in the last analysis, were asked to break completely with their past, to be assimilated by French society. "To the Jews as individuals everything, to the Jews as a nation, nothing," Clermont-Tonnerre had declared to the National Assembly and the program of assimilation began, in various degrees, in all the countries where Napoleon had brought the principles of the French Revolution.

But equality carried to extremes ended up in that "uniformization" that is quite the opposite of the democratic idea.[3] In exchange for the political equality granted all citizens, the Jews were asked for a complete conformity of mores and beliefs. In Dreyfus's time, the chauvinist elements were calling for a restriction of the ideal of total fusion of all the inhabitants of France, because, meanwhile, the new racist theories had made their appearance. Either they had to be applied, or the creed of the Republic had to be revised.

The French writers who stepped into the arena to fight against a miscarriage of justice did not at the beginning grasp the full scope of the conflict. Such was the case of Zola and Anatole France. They dedicated themselves body and soul, especially Zola, to the struggle against injustice. They hurled all the slings of their indignation and irony against the theories of racism and anti-Semitism. But they were not farsighted enough. It seemed to them that once the immediate danger had been averted, they could return to the former state of things—the best, in their eyes. They saw the Dreyfus Affair with the eyes of the nineteenth century, of which

---

3. Cf. J. P. Sartre, *Réflexions sur la question juive.*

they were the offspring. In this respect, even Marcel Proust and Rogert Martin du Gard still reflect the century in which they were born.

Others discovered gradually the scope of the struggle in which they were engaged. Among them were even anti-Dreyfusards who had evolved toward new principles. Maurice Barrès is not only an example but the symbol of the transfiguration of the national idea in France that was to add a vigorous new branch to the venerable tree of French literature: a Jewish literature, written in French. It was created not only by Jewish writers, but also by Christians who were attracted by the color of Jewish life and were curious to discover the "Jewish soul."

In this profound transformation, Judaism only slowly took an active part. For the Jews, too, were far from understanding the full implications of the Dreyfus trial. The important Jews even took sides against the accused: when the Affair turned into a moral crisis, through the opposition of practical justice and absolute justice, a number of Jews (such as Bernard Lazare) threw themselves into the battle to defend not the Jew Dreyfus but the principle of justice. As the anti-Semitic edge progressively sharpened, Israel's instinctive solidarity did not take long in emerging in its scattered camp. First it was the wounded ego, then pride, that became more exasperated by anti-Semitic attacks. Finally, it was a new self-consciousness, a return to forgotten tradition, a renaissance of Zionist ideas, a resurrection of the spiritual heritage forsaken for untroubled happiness, and an effort to reconcile the Jewish idea with the French humanitarian ideal.

After sketching this evolution in its broad outlines, we intend in the following chapters to develop it step by step.

17
The Peerless Knights

Both Emile Zola and Anatole France proclaim themselves champions of the disintegrating humanitarian ideal. They are frightened by the sudden intrusion of political methods that threaten to destroy all the conquests of which the nineteenth century was so proud. They do not understand how necessary a revision of these conquests is, but they understand that this revision cannot be undertaken along the lines proposed by the anti-Dreyfusards, and they deserve our admiration for the courage with which they fight for their convictions, falling thus within the best traditions of French literature.

Emile Zola

This writer formulated his opinions on the progress of mankind in an unfinished cycle: *Les Evangiles* (The Gospels) in which Matthew, Luke, and Marc Froment are the apostles of Fecundity, Work, and Truth. It is in *La Vérité* (*Truth*) that we find the substance of the Dreyfus Affair.

The novel deals with a crime analogous to the "ritual murder" trials that had often taken place in several European countries. A child has been murdered. The crime, committed by Brother Gorgias, is imputed by his congregation to Simon, Jewish lay teacher, with the double purpose of discrediting the lay school and of increasing anti-Semitism. "Does a dirty Jew deserve the truth?"[1] Marc Froment, another lay teacher (vaguely reminiscent of Picquart and Bernard Lazare) takes up the cause of truth. The trial excites the press and the country, just like the Dreyfus Affair. France is divided into Simonists and anti-Simonists. "The few Simonists were crushed by the uncontrolled and ever-growing floods of anti-Simonists. Hired thugs threatened Jewish shops. . . . Terror reigned: cowardice became immense."

For the sake of pacifying the nation, some reasoned, Simon had to be condemned. He had to be guilty, otherwise "it would be too great a misfortune for the country." Thus Zola satirizes the nationalistic thesis for which Maurice Barrès found the formula: "Let us judge everything, even metaphysical truths, in relation to the interest of France."

Let us skip the incidents of the Simon Affair, which correspond in all details with those of the Dreyfus Affair as Zola saw it at its conclusion. Although he had the tragic fate of not seeing the triumph of the cause to which he had devoted his life, he lived that triumph in his mind, and the Simon Affair has an epilogue that fulfills all the political wishes of the author. Simon is pardoned, the Simonists rehabilitated. Clericalism (which had committed itself strongly to the anti-Dreyfus campaign) is severely punished. "There is justice only in truth, there is happiness only in justice";[2] the program of the teacher Marc is on the march. Truth will triumph, as ignorance, which is maintained, according to Zola, by Catholicism, disappears. "The new generation did not understand why the Jews were accused of all crimes. There were no more Jews, since there were only citizens freed of all dogmas. Only the Catholic Church had used and exacerbated idiotic and fierce anti-Semitism to re-

---

1. *Vérité* (Paris, Fasquelle, 1903), p. 33.
2. *Ibid.,* p. 749.

capture the questioning people, and anti-Semitism had disappeared as the Church itself had been discarded among the dying religions."

We subscribe to these conclusions only to the extent to which they express the idea that anti-Semitism is a "socialism within the reach of the ignorant," which is only one of the multiple aspects of the Jewish question, of which Zola, product of the nineteenth century, had too simplified a view.

Anatole France

While he does not have so robust an idealism as Zola, Anatole France shares with him his hatred of ignorance. This highly cultured Epicurean hates nothing worse than human stupidity, the original sin that threatens all mankind with relapse into barbarism. The Dreyfus Trial is a symptom of this stupidity, whose spiritual children are lies and injustice. In numerous articles and novels, he struggles against human stupidity that is revealed as an invincible monster. Each head cut off is replaced by two new ones which grow in its place. Lies are stronger than truth because they multiply while there is but one truth. One of the forms of the "thousand-headed" lie is anti-Semitism in its infinite variety.

Here is the Duke of Brécé, who dreams of the creation of an ante-1789 society that he calls "Christian France," where the Protestants and the Jews will have no place.[3] It is the sharp and kindly Abbé Guitrel who plays down the aggressive Christianity of the Duke of Brécé. The anti-Semitism of M. de Terremondre is more opportunistic. He is "anti-Semitic in the country, especially during the hunting season. During the winter he dined with Jewish financiers whom he liked sufficiently to sell them paintings at a good price. He was nation-

---

3. *L'Anneau d'améthyste* (Paris, 1899), chap. II.

alistic and anti-Semitic at the Conseil Général in view
of the opinions prevalent in his county seat."[4]

To this intermittent anti-Semitism, ready to sound the
most ringing patriotic notes, Anatole France opposes
Bergeret, who expresses the author's ideas: "I think it
is pernicious to make racial distinctions in a country. It
is not race that makes the fatherland. There is no people
in Europe that is not formed by a multitude of races
mixed and integrated. Gaul, when Caesar came in, was
populated by Celts, Gauls, Iberians, each different from
the other in origin and religion. To this human mixture,
invasions added Germans, Romans, Saracens, and all
that created a nation, heroic and charming, *France,*
which even in the past, taught justice, freedom, and philos-
ophy to Europe and to the world."[5]

In the short story *Crainquebille,* a little masterpiece in
which the thesis is completely absorbed by the artistic
form, Anatole France draws a pathetic picture of the
essential problems of the Dreyfus Affair. Although he
returns to the same subject a few years later, he now
treats it with the resigned smile of the skeptic. Thus we
find in *L'Ile des pingouins (Penguins' Island)* a delightful summary of certain aspects of anti-Semitism. The
ironical tone can only mislead those who do not recognize
the master's art in *ridentum dicere verum.* Any commen-
tary would weaken the effect of this charming story:

"Shortly after the flight of the admiral, a Jew of
humble circumstances called Pyrot, eager to associate
with the aristocracy and wishing to serve his country,
joined the Penguin army. The Minister of War, who
was then Greatauk,[6] Duke of Skull, could not stand him:
he criticized him for his zeal, his nose, his vanity, his
love of learning, his thick lips and his exemplary be-

---

4. *Ibid.,* chap XIX.
5. *Ibid.*
6. General Mercier.

havior. Everytime the perpetrator of a misdeed was sought, Greatauk would say: "It must be Pyrot!"

One morning, General Panther,[7] his chief of staff, informed him of a serious matter. Eighty thousand bundles of hay earmarked for the cavalry had disappeared. Greatauk exclaimed spontaneously: "Pyrot must have stolen them!" He looked thoughtful a while and said: "The more I think about it, the more I am convinced that Pyrot has stolen the eighty thousand bundles of hay. I see his handiwork in the fact that he stole them to sell them at a minimal price to the Marsouins (Porpoises), our implacable enemies. Unspeakable treason!"

"There is no doubt about it," answered Panther, "All we have left to do is prove it."[8]

All Penguiny was shocked to learn about Pyrot's crime; at the same time everyone felt a sort of satisfaction in learning that this theft, compounded by treason and verging on sacrilege, was committed by a little Jew. To understand that reaction, we have to know public opinion toward the big and little Jews. As we have had occasion to say in the past, the financial caste, universally hated and overwhelmingly powerful, was composed of Christians and Jews. The Jews which formed part of it and against whom the people concentrated its hatred were the big Jews. They possessed immense wealth and owned, it was said, more than a fifth of the Penguin fortune. Outside of this fearsome caste, there was a multitude of little Jews of modest means, who were not liked any more than the big ones, and were much less feared. In all civilized countries wealth is a sacred thing. In democracies it is the only sacred thing.

Consequently, they acquired a religious respect for

7. Commander DuPaty de Clam.
8. Did Maurice Barrès not write: "Nobody has to tell me why he committed treason. In psychology all I have to prove is that he was capable of treason"?

Jewish as well as Christian millions, and, since greed was stronger in them than aversion, they would have preferred to die rather than to harm a hair of these hated big Jews. Toward the little Jews they felt much less respectful and, whenever they saw one fall, they crushed him. That is why the nation learned with such fierce satisfaction that the traitor was a Jew, but a little Jew. They could take revenge on him and on all Israel without fear of endangering the public welfare."

The conclusions that the great skeptic Anatole France draws from the outcome of the Dreyfus Affair are rather discouraging: "Victorious, the defenders of the innocent tore each other apart and hurled insults and slander at each other. The great Jews and 700 pro-Pyrots turned away contemptuously from their Socialist comrades whose help they had humbly begged in the past."

Roger Martin du Gard

The most intense literary expression of the Dreyfus Affair is found in the novel *Jean Barois*, a faithful reflection as well as a philosophical vision of a dramatic episode in French history. The major portion of this biography of a man who seeks his truth amidst ready-made creeds and opinions, is devoted to the description of the moral, political, and social convulsions provoked by the Dreyfus Trial. The humble little Jew Woldsmuth is the first to shake the self-assurance of Barois, editor of the newspaper *Le Semeur*, on the subject of Dreyfus: "I beg of you, in the name of all that is noble and just, reject all preconceived opinions, forget everything you have learned through the newspapers two years ago and all the stories that are being told . . . yes, it is easy to be interested in humanity in general, in the anonymous masses . . . but that is nothing, no, really nothing. Loving your real neighbor, loving those whom you find suffering one fine day, right here, next to you . . . that is love, that is goodness!" This heartfelt cry awakens Barois, who begins to study the question, and becomes, along with Zola, Bernard Lazare, Clemenceau, an ardent advocate of the review of the trial.

Many obstacles had to be overcome, psychological ones, first of all, that public opinion raised around the central figure, Captain Dreyfus. He has been criticized, up to the present, as not being worthy of the stakes. "Reality does not coincide with our imagination. Many of us have not forgiven him for it." The author defends the accused with moving simplicity: "He is a simple man, whose natural energy is internal. He is weakened by incarceration, by the unprecedented emotions he has experienced. He is sick, he shivers with fever. How can he rise to the pitch of this frenzied audience, three quarters of which hate him like a public enemy while the other quarter adores him like a symbol? Isn't this overwhelming role above human strength? He does not have the energy to shriek passionately his innocence, as he did in the courtyard of the Military School. The little strength he has left, he uses it, not against the others, but against himself: in not getting depressed, in looking like a man. He does not want to be seen crying.

"The heroic, unrewarding grandeur of that conception escapes popular aesthetics. He might have won over the crowd by a more theatrical attitude. But the self-control that he maintains by dint of great effort is criticized as indifference, and those who have been killing themselves in his behalf for four years resent it."

The central problem of the Dreyfus Affair is that of national security, the established order that French officialdom intends to defend at the price of an individual, even innocent. The rebellion against this reason of state is the glory of the Dreyfusards: "there is a French scholar, says a member of the *Semeur* staff, who has already answered this argument of national security. He has said . . . that there is no reason of state that can prevent a court of justice from being just."

To the argument that the national order and public order are well worth the sacrifice of an individual, the Dreyfusards oppose that of national honor. "An illegal act, openly committed, even in the name of national security, if it is officially accepted by all, creates difficulties a thousand times more serious than the temporary troubles of a people. It compromises the only acquisition in which men can take some pride, those sacred liberties with which, in the past, French blood enriched the nations of the world. More precisely it compromises the right to justice of the whole civilized world."

Credit for this rebellion goes to the handful of Dreyfusards, not to the mass of those who subsequently rushed to the rescue of victory. After the victory, a deep uneasiness subsisted in a divided France. Still, the price was not too high for the result obtained. The temporary disequilibrium was more than made up by the preservation of the principles which are the true justification of a civilized nation. The mobilization of all the moral forces of a nation for the defense of just one Jew saved France from the catastrophes suffered by her neighbor across the Rhine. The author summarizes the meaning of the trial as follows: "Let us remember that in fifty years the Dreyfus Affair will be only a minor episode in the struggle of human reason against the passions that blind it; a moment and no more, in this slow and marvelous evolution of mankind toward a greater good. . . . The strict duty of each generation is to go in the direction of truth to the extreme limit of what it is permitted to glimpse, and to maintain its position as desperately as if it hoped to reach Absolute Truth. That is the way to man's progress."

Jean Barois, as well as the protagonists of the novel

Les Thibault, dies a broken, disillusioned man because he was not able to carry out in their complete purity the noble goals he had set for his life as a humanist. But is it so little a matter to have fought on the right side, to have contributed to the victory of a good cause, even if this victory loses its fruits if it is not won over and over again by succeeding generations?

Jacques de Lacretelle

Once again it is the atmosphere of the Dreyfus Affair that is reflected in the novel *Silbermann* by Lacretelle. More than that, this schoolboy story is a microcosm of the whole Jewish question in France, from the social and the moral viewpoint, although the author might perhaps have meant to study the broader problem of the individual in his social context and the drama which often arises from it. Classical tragedy introduced fate as a crushing force. Lacretelle, as a disciple of classicism, has a similar concept of society, as environment which crushes the individual who refuses to conform to its laws.

The hapless young hero of the story *Silbermann* is a boy who in spite of his superior intelligence is reduced to the role of Don Quixote by the hostility of his classmates. They do not accept him; they reject him, in fact, in spite of his superiority, or because of it.

Yet, it was he, the Jew, who could interpret the great French writers with a sensitivity unsuspected by the others, who revealed to his only friend, the narrator, such sophisticated subtleties that he captures the eternal truth of great literary works and their everyday meaning. Contrary to Charles Maurras's chauvinistic thesis, according to which a Jew will always be unable to understand Racine, it is Silbermann who reveals to his classmates the beauty of the French spirit. But the young

readers of the newspaper *Le Français de France,* blinded
by the mirage of a false patriotism, were of the opinion
"that knowing how to land a punch was more useful in
life than everything we were taught in class."[9]

And Silbermann, whose greatest ambition is to be
accepted, is systematically excluded, psychologically first,
and soon in actuality, thanks to a transparent pretext
built into an affair. Like the writer Henri Franck, who
delighted in the challenge of his position as teacher, Jew,
and Frenchman, Silbermann saw in his double role of
French Jew the best condition for doing great things:
"I use my qualities to know and to understand this intellectual inheritance that is not mine, but that one day
may be enriched through me. I want to appropriate it!"
But this alliance was rejected and Silbermann was condemned to universal hatred.

When he is suspended from class, it is not for the
crime attributed to his father, but "for the disturbance
of which he was the cause." Thus, it is the reason of
state seen through a microscope, this same "public interest" invoked by the groups seeking the condemnation
of Captain Dreyfus.

The narrator is deeply disturbed by the episode of
his early youth. "Why this explosion of anti-Semitism?"
He has no illusion about the fragile morality of his
bourgeois milieu and the indictment he puts in the
mouth of his classmate is strikingly reminiscent of Shylock's plea: The Jews are grasping? "Don't all men who
work try to earn money? They're thieves? Ah, my friends
if you knew the shady deals that the most illustrious
names in France propose to my father, you would agree
that our way of getting rich in business is quite honest."

Jews are foreigners? "Isn't everyone in the same
nation, and in spite of a common background, subject to

9. Cf. J. P. Sartre, *Jeunesse d'un chef.*

the various currents of his heredity, class heredity, religious heredity? Among the various families of the French nation, there are as many differences as among the types of distinct races."

Silbermann's departure, symbolizing the expulsion of the Jews, leaves a void in the life of the narrator that no other classmate is capable of filling. "Did I see at least one, even among those who appreciated intellectual matters most, who was fired with an intellectual passion similar to that of the young Jew?"

The profound analysis of the Jewish problem made by Lacretelle, his objectivity toward the Jewish spirit understood as a creative element, is an important contribution to the discussion of this problem. This little book, which in virtue of its numerous aesthetic qualities is a great novel, also has its place in classical literature through its high moral stature.

The same cannot be said for the sequel to this youthful novel. In *Le Retour de Silbermann* (*Silbermann's Return*), Lacretelle modifies his outlook in a manner reminiscent of André Gide in *Retour d'U.R.S.S.* (*Return from the U.S.S.R.*).

His classmate, who had expatriated himself to the U.S.A., did not make good. His lack of realism, that is to say money sense, his taste for advanced ideas, that is to say, subversive ones, made his life in the new world difficult and he goes back to Paris. Still materially disinterested, independent to the point of pride, he descends even lower on the social ladder. "No doubt, I would have imagined a brilliant career for Silbermann, facilitated by outward qualities that struck all those who met him, by his ambition, by tenacity, by a sure instinct. But I, more than anybody, knew the existence of a totally different inclination hidden in the inner recesses of his nature, like a grain of poison, capable of destroying everything, a secret admiration for the misfortunes of his race."

He dies at twenty-three, frustrated, abandoned. Before dying, he is dealt the surprise of seeing a classmate, the one who was called the "shlemiel" because he was last in his class, gain fame as a novelist. Could it be that the various and brilliant gifts of David Silbermann were worth less than the hidden talent of the "shlemiel"? He admits it bitterly and explains the misleading aspect of his Jewish superiority: "I have only been one of these precocious little rabbis who, at 10, knows the Torah by heart and can copy it, *in toto,* or discuss a word for hours. That's why I ranked first in my class four times. But when it came to creating something, to writing a book, nothing. . . . It's the Christian who did it."

This self-discovery of the Jewish failure seems to the author the definitive explanation of the allegedly superior intelligence of the Jews. It's a flash in the pan, without creative power. The gods that Lacretelle had admired as a schoolboy he burns as a grown man, though he never abandons a certain warmth toward the Jews. He tries to erase the effect that too great an admiration for the Jewish spirit might produce. He condemns Silbermann to failure because "that faculty to understand which, in a classroom, seemed a prodigy to us, stemmed perhaps from gifts that produce their results immediately but never develop."

The dying Jew has let his beard grow just like Heine, who returned to his origins on his deathbed. According to the author, he would have been better advised to remain among his own people and not to mix in French civilization. "The little rabbi was wrong to listen to the stories of the Christians. . . . He was wrong to look up at the churches. He should have remained among his own kind. . . . For the 'goim' poisoned him."

Le Retour de Silbermann is obviously Lacretelle's recantation of the generous opinion that he had expressed as a young author on the Jewish question and that perhaps was no longer suitable to an author consecrated by the Academy.[10]

---

10. If Charles Péguy, another peerless knight, does not occupy in this chapter the place he deserves for the nobility of his thinking, exalted and deeply creative, it is because we refer to it frequently in relation to the ideas born from the Dreyfus Affair.

18
Discovery of the Jewish Soul

Maurice Barrès
In spite of Anatole France's bitterness and skepticism, a
sharp about-face, a decisive evolution took place, although of a nature different from the one advocated by
Zola. Anatole France and Zola belong, in spite of their
militant attitude, to the nineteenth century. They could
conceive progress only in the spirit of the rationalist ideas
that had filled the century of liberalism. During the crisis
a new ideal had emerged, capable of reconciling the
cause of nationalism, which had provoked the crisis, with
the humanitarian ideal of the Great Revolution. Henceforth the idea of the nation will be based on a new support: the right of the individual to self-realization, and
the right of ethnic or spiritual groups to go back to their
roots, to draw from them their substance, to nourish
with it the common tree. The ideal, no doubt, is not
realized in its purity, but is stated as a new orientation
for future generations.

The undisputed leader of French youth at the beginning of our century offers a living example of the
transfiguration of the democratic ideal. At first, Maurice
Barrès professed a nationalism based on the notion of
blood and race: "Our difference in blood strengthens my
repugnance towards Protestantism (secular education different from mine) and towards Judaism (race opposed

to mine)."[1] Later, his nationalism is transformed, enlarged, elevated. Instead of suppressing all individuality, he urges that it be put to the best use: "Be aware that you are made to feel as Lorrains, Alsatians, Bretons, Belgians, Jews."[2]

This is the direction that French democracy was to take; it was the new directive for democracy.

Here, finally, is the formula that saw the Jewish problem in a new light. The Jews were no longer asked to renounce their origins as the price of emancipation. It was realized that assimilation did not have to consist in suppressing the past. It was understood that a nation is that much stronger if it leaves its members, either as individuals or as groups, the freedom to develop their spiritual being. The World War was the fire in which the ideal proved its strength, where it was to be tempered. Maurice Barrès, in looking for the source of that strength that saved France, finds it in the voluntary union of the various spiritual families of France. In a chapter devoted to French Judaism, he mentions among others, the case of a Zionist, second lieutenant Rothstein, a volunteer, who died for France in 1916 and whose last wish was to sleep under the sign of the Mogen David.[3] This patriotism is not an irrational instinctive element, like the attachment of a child to his mother. It is a spiritual patriotism, an act of will, a choice of the spirit. It is, as the Countess of Noailles says, "the great contribution of those who, born in France and participating in her

---

1. Maurice Barrès, *Scènes et doctrines du nationalisme,* I (Plon), p. 67.
2. *Ibid.,* p. 16. Romain Rolland enlarged this idea and gave it a more universal scope at a private interview: "In my opinion, the most natural thing is for each one to base himself on the distinctive characteristics of his people. I am cosmopolitan, but as a Frenchman. I see the world through a French way of thinking and feeling which I hold dear. . . . Just as I am European as a Frenchman, it seems equally logical to me to be European as an Englishman, Italian, or Jew, each in his own way by developing the values of his own nature nurtured by his tribe."
3. The Star of David, the Zionist emblem.

life, rediscover by study and meditation, the meaning of their origin and offer their very own qualities to their country."[4]

Even writers like the Tharaud brothers, who have not always been kindly inclined towards the Jews, accept this definition when they say: "The Jew can be a good citizen of the country in which he lives, even an excellent patriot, as the war has shown, and nevertheless identify himself with his heart and mind with the race to which he belongs. Zionism is only the extreme expression of the rediscovered Jewish feeling by those intellectuals who had neglected it for such a long time."[5]

The general about-face of public opinion in favor of the Jews is reflected in a literary vogue, where Christian writers, attracted by the color of Jewish traditions, discover "the soul of Judaism." Numerous novels on Jewish themes see the light of day, such as *Silbermann, Le Puit de Jacob (Jacob's Well), Le Juif Errant est arrivé (The Wandering Jew Has Arrived)*.

J. and J. Tharaud

In this literary trend the Tharaud Brothers occupy a leading place. They take up Jewish subjects that, at times, they are able to treat with remarkable insight. According to their own testimony, they have discovered poetic material in the Jewish quarters of Eastern Europe or simply in "Jewishness." In several novels[6] they have evoked the Messianic mysticism of the Jewish Eastern Europe with a friendly smile and an understanding not previously shown by any Frenchman. Is not this village in the Ukraine a kingdom of God, where murder and debauchery are unknown, where it is taught that everything in the world except man is sin, and everything in

4. Henri Franck, *La Danse devant l'Arche,* preface by Anna de Noailles, p. 14.
5. *Petite histoire des juifs,* p. 277.
6. *A l'Ombre de la Croix; Un Royaume de Dieu.*

man that is not God is sin? The authors succeed in
capturing in the historic traditions of these Oriental Jews
all the spirituality it contains. They bow with emotion
before the clownish dance of two old Jews who hold
each other by the beard to celebrate "joyfully," according to their religious precepts, the tradition of the Law,
and who force themselves to rejoice while the pogrom
is rumbling. In several other works, the Tharauds explain Judaism to their French readers. Thus in *L'An
prochain à Jerusalem* (*Next year in Jerusalem*) they
present in several *tableaux* the Messianic and political
aspects of Zionism. They pay tribute to Theodore Herzl,
"the prophet about town" ("le prophète du boulevard"),
to Ben Yehuda, the son of Judea, thanks to whom
Hebrew became once again an official language, to Sarah
Aronson, who died for the liberation of Palestine. There,
in the struggle for a national home, the Tharauds see
the natural solution to Israel's anxiety. If they were
Jews, they say, they could only be Zionists. "I mean a
real Zionist, and not one of those, so numerous among
us, who are not in a great hurry to inhabit the ancestral
land personally, but dream of sending to it their bother-
some compatriots."

It is unfortunate that, subsequently, their intimate
interest in Jewish subjects turns into intimate hostility.
Quand Israël n'est plus roi (*When Israel Ceases to be
King*), published in 1933, marks a surprising volte-face
on the part of the two brothers and constitutes a tribute
to a movement that according to some observers was
directed only against the Jews.

Perhaps such divergent ways of treating Jewish themes
can be explained as a symptom of the survival of an
attitude that made a sharp separation between historical
and contemporary Judaism. Just as the Romantics were
able to look for inspiration in the Bible, to exalt its
poetry, and to bring back its events to life while drawing

a picture of the contemporary Jew that could actually
be odious, in many modern writers there prevails a
tendency to value in the contemporary Jew only what
goes back very far, to the beginning of time, to the
burning climate of Judea. Among modern Jewish aspirations, only Zionism seems to them the logical and organic
extension of a prodigious past.

But Israel's destiny is not limited to the pure and
simple return to Zion. The latter is only one of the
multiple aspects of Judaism analyzed by the best French
writers of the twentieth century.

Romain Rolland[7]

Among these writers, Romain Rolland is the one who
best formulates the various tendencies of emancipated
Judaism.

He sees "three different trends in the thinking of the
freest and sincerest Jews." Most of the time these three
trends mingle and oppose one another. They cannot
all be followed at the same time. Each Jew ought to
follow the one that can give him the most satisfaction
for himself, and be of greatest benefit for others.

The first solution is the generous union of the Jew
with his adopted land. Romain Rolland believes that
for a certain class of Jews, for whom their religious
ties are too tenuous, there is no other solution than the
one urged by Zola and Anatole France: the slow absorption by the host country.

Another solution is the Jewish state. The thousands
of scattered and persecuted Jews must find a home. The
Zionist ideal must be the best solution for these Jews,
too attached to their origins to be assimilated by the
people in whose midst they were raised and for whom

---

7. B. Krakowski. *La Psychologie des peuples allemand et juif dans les
romans de Romain Rolland* (Toulouse, 1931).

the struggles provoked by this alienated existence contain too much suffering and humiliation.

Finally, the Jews scattered through the world must be "the children of the law," the highest role in Israel's destiny. Although conscious of their origin, these Jews must nevertheless not leave the country where they were born to found a new nation. Romain Rolland expects more from this Jewish elite. He entrusts it with the sacred mission of "God-bearer, the champion of the new law in the old world of Europe and America." Their mission goes beyond the frontiers of nations and becomes a question of the highest importance for all mankind. Their mission is "to be the people of Justice for all, of Universal Right." Romain Rolland elaborated on this idea in a letter from which we quote, without fear of repetition, a typical passage that summarizes the substance of his thinking about Judaism: "We have, all of us, elected them to form the nucleus of a new universal humanity. But for you Jews, this duty is the very essence of your deepest traditions."

Let us add that Romain Rolland portrayed in *Jean-Christophe* numerous Jewish characters who are depicted with integrity and with friendly perspicacity. And in *Dialogue de l'auteur avec son ombre* (*Dialogue of the Author with his Shadow*) that constitutes the prologue to *La Foire sur la Place* (*Fair on the Square*), Christophe declares on the subject of the Jews: "I know all the greatness still to be found in their race. I know all the capacity for dedication, all the proud selflessness, all the love, all the desire for progress, the tireless energy, the obscure and stubborn labor of thousands of them. I know that there is a God in them. And that is why I resent those Jews who have rejected him, those who betray the destiny of their people for a degrading success and vulgar happiness."

Georges Duhamel

A new idealistic humanism characterizes the great novelists of the first third of the twentieth century who follow in the wake of Romain Rolland. Moral values based, not on faith in an absolute God, but on man's inner powers, must guide him through the labyrinth of existence. Instead of traditional religions, Romain Rolland advocates a fighting, uncompromising pacifism: his friend, the half-Jew André Suarez, aesthetic emotion; Roger Martin du Gard, integrity, honesty, justice; André Maurois (Emile Herzog), moderation, practical optimism; Jules Romains, fraternal solidarity, unanimous effort. In this brilliant humanistic phalanx, Georges Duhamel occupies a leading place.

He, too, seeks a reason for existence for a world that has lost its moral and social equilibrium. His work is a meditation on the human condition, but without the religious inspiration of Claudel, Bernanos, or Mauriac. He is not interested in metaphysical salvation, but in the reconstruction, the reorganization of human society on the basis of common goals and interests. If his doctrine ignores superior ideals, it has the considerable merit of trying to resolve practical problems facing each generation because "between the miracle and the practical achievement, I choose the achievement."

Duhamel was, at first, committed to Jules Romains's ideal of Unanimism. He soon divorced himself from it, because, in his eyes, the individual took precedence over the group: "Civilization is in the heart, or it isn't anywhere." He describes his Unanimistic experience in *Le Désert de Bièvres,* a work that is a part of his great cyclical novel *La Chronique des Pasquier.* The central figure in this episode is the Jew Justin Weill.

The adventure of the "Unanimist" group is strikingly reminiscent in its lesson on anti-Semitism of the school

experience told by Lacretelle. The big difference is that
Justin Weill is not just a youthful friendship, quickly
forgotten, but an intimate, lifelong friend, the one who,
after the musician Cécile Pasquier, represents the spiritual
nobility that other human beings see intermittently and
only through a veil. As early as high school (*Le Jardin
des bêtes sauvages—The Garden of Wild Beasts*), Laurent Pasquier has for Justin "an enthusiastic, admiration,
uncontrolled, no doubt, and most often rewarded." In
a society eaten up, like the Pasquier family itself, by
materialism, Justin represents poetry, intellect, the reflection of a better world.

"We have been criticized," says Justin to Cécile Pasquier (for whom he feels a selfless love, capable of
sacrifice and renunciation), "for not being able to produce
great artists. Well, even admitting that this absurd idea
is true, what would happen to the great artists if we,
Jews, were not here to understand them and to celebrate
them? *We are the enthusiasm of the world.* When you
perform in Paris, London, New York, in one of the
great intelligent cities, you know that a third of the souls
who came to listen to you are fervent Jewish souls."

Another prejudice of Christian society against Judaism
is its belief that it represents an inferior form of morality,
lagging behind the one preached by the Gospels. Even a
mind as progressive as Laurent Pasquier's finds nothing
better to say in order to praise his friend's virtue than
"these beautiful words are Christian words." Embar-
rassed, he accepts Justin's correction: "You imagine,
perhaps, that we are still at the stage of the law of
the talion? You imagine that, ethically, we are still sav-
ages in the desert. But ideas evolve for everybody, old
man, for me as well as the others. You are a *Dreyfusard*.
And you seem to think that we are twenty years behind
the times. Then in what way do you like me? Like a
wild beast?"

Justin, naturally, assumes the leadership of this group of writers, painters, and musicians, hungry for freedom, purity, fraternity. It is he who organizes life into a phalanstery in the "abbey." It is he who formulates its moral rule, as for the volunteers of a monastery. "We must have regulations from above. We must have a Law." He fights the violations of the rules, he is the vigilant conscience of the group. They were accustomed in the desert (of Bièvres) to see Justin rowing against the currents and the breezes." (What a delicate symbol of Judaism!)

As a result, he becomes unpopular. The situation takes a tragic turn when his comrades, disappointed by their solitary existence and their youthful experience, need a scapegoat to blame for their failure. . . . It begins with snide remarks such as: "I'm sick and tired of dedicated people!" Or Sénac's: "I am *Dreyfusard* rationally and anti-Semitic by inclination. Everything for Dreyfus, granted, but provided that the Jews don't poison our lives."

The situation deteriorates and Justin, suffering in silence, foresees the impending catastrophe. Finally, he is humiliated, beaten by Sénac with the others' consent. The group is dissolved; each one takes his belongings and goes home. It is Justin who remains to take care of their obligations to their creditors. When Laurent, absent during the feud, invites him to return to Paris, Justin, highly discouraged, thinks only of returning to his "crowd," his coreligionists, to await with them the final pogrom, the massacre or expulsion. Barbarism, smoldering under the thin layer of nineteenth-century humanism, had for a moment unveiled its hideous, threatening face, awaiting a more propitious moment to explode without restraints and to free itself from "the malaise in civilization."

Even in the depth of his despair, an almost prophetic

surge of emotions grips him once more and orders him to pursue from one failure to another the ideal of brotherhood: "You think you understand Jesus! No, you don't. He was one of us, a little Jew like me. Only I haven't done anything. I'm a failure in a very small matter."

In spite of the insults and the humiliations, he starts dreaming again and hoping again: "Our failure doesn't prove anything for the mass of other people." Who will pick up the flag of mankind, if not the vanquished, the humble, the disgraced? Justin's attitude is the only glimmer of light in the lamentable adventure that cured each of the protagonists of his "idealism," an easy idealism expecting salvation from the gift of others, and which, afterwards, is replaced by a more solid and traditional materialism.

Duhamel's optimism is not of this nature, and his support does not go to proud and useless animals. The gentle perseverance of his Jewish friend, his positive humanism, counting not on a miracle but on works, revives his own hope and saves his faith in the future of mankind: "And I began to understand that Justin was not cured of dreams and not even discouraged."

If Duhamel is willing to see the Jew as the gadfly of mankind, "the child of the law" in Romain Rolland's definition, "the people of justice for all" (and the name "Justin" has no doubt a symbolic meaning), he has, on the other hand, no understanding of the Zionist solution. Yet it could have been the logical reaction of a Justin ill-used by those he wanted to serve. Instead of waiting for the "last pogrom," he should have gone to look for his martyred brothers and attempted with them a new experiment, not in the desert of Bièvres, but of Judea. "Take your staff, gird your loins and walk!" Justin won't consider it, for on another occasion he has made an anti-Zionistic profession of faith (*La Nuit de Saint Jean —The Night of Saint John*): "Jerusalem may be the homeland of my eternal life, it is not the homeland of my earthly life." And he traces the road of his assimilation: My grandfather was called Abraham. Listen carefully, Laurent, all this means something. My father is called Simon. I am called Justin. I may call my first son François."

In the light of this reasoning by one of the best-intentioned Frenchmen, Georges Duhamel, who wishes for the integration of his Jewish friends in the French nation, not as Jews, but as a stimulating element, as a spring graft, it is easy to understand the decision of the Goncourt Academy, thirty years later, to award its prize to *Eaux Mêlées* (*Mingled Waters*) by Roger Ikor, a book that glorifies the attempt at fusion and disappearance of "the sons of Avrom," who are called successively Yankel, Simon, and Jean-Claude.

Paul Claudel

In *Le Pain dur* (*The Hard Bread*)[8] Paul Claudel introduces two Jewish figures, Ali and her daughter Sichel, who take an active part in the crimes committed in this play. The author, afraid of being suspected of anti-Semitism, feels obliged to explain in an introductory note that Jews had to appear in a drama showing the collapse of traditions and the dislocation of a world. If Ali and her daughter do not elicit our admiration, no more than the other characters in the play, this is in no way a reflection on Claudel's attitude on Judaism, since these Jewish figures are shaped by the plot. Judaism is too serious, too important a subject, according to Claudel, to be judged by a few protagonists in a play. Besides, he proves his sincerity by an impeccable attitude under the German occupation.

Ali and Sichel symbolize the alienated man of the

---

8. Julius Bab, *Juden bei Paul Claudel*, "Der Morgen," 1929.

period of Louis-Philippe. The Jew's homeland is God; if he loses this homeland, he is more alienated than the others. He becomes the symbol of alienation.

Claudel is concerned with those Jews who take their political emancipation for a definitive liberation that they eagerly pay for by the repudiation of their origins and their spiritual sources. Sichel hates her blood, her tribe, the Jewish past in which her biological roots are sunk. But the break with the past, so pathetic for the Jews, is the general characteristic of the times: the Catholics take the same road to sin by abandoning the values of their religious traditions: piety, faith, love.

In the following play, *Le Père humilié* (*The Humiliated Father*), we encounter Sichel once more. She has made a "calculated marriage" with the Comte de Coufontaine, ambassador of France to Rome. Their daughter Pensée, a dazzling, almost immaterial beauty, is blind. The Pope's two godsons, Orian and Orso de Homodarmes, are in love with her, but each one is ready to give her up for the other. The young girl, so gentle, so delicate that she seems the incarnation of pure thought, inspires the young men with the noblest affection. Her name is symbolic, just like her whole enigmatic appearance. "I am like the Synagogue of the past, as it was represented on the portals of the Cathedrals. My eyes have been blindfolded and everything I want to take is broken."

The author seems to express the idea that the emancipation of the Jews, their admittance to society, their desire to be accepted by their entourage, have not brought them the hoped-for happiness. This applies even to those who strive for total liberation by making a "calculated marriage," through baptism and mixed marriages. "It takes a lot of water to baptize a Jew. The habits of so many centuries are not so easily forgotten. It seems to me that I carry with me all the centuries since the creation of the world."

As for Claudel, he does not see misfortune in this
inheritance, but rather a sign of aristocracy, of incomparable nobility. It is the substance with which Gods
are created. Orian, alluding to the execution of the "son
of man" receives this proud answer: "This God, it is
we who have given him to you. If there is a God for
mankind, he could only come from our hearts."

The dialogue that follows is a severe indictment of
the moral and social defects of Christianity, an exposition of the thesis of Judaism, and an almost metaphysical
explanation of its militant attitude toward the problems
of the time. Judaism gave a God to Christianity, but:
"What have you done with him? Is that why we have
given him to you, so that the poor be poorer, the rich
richer . . . for half-demented kings to reign over besotted
people? . . . And it is forbidden to change things in the
slightest? Because all power comes from God?"

In opposition to Christian resignation, to the pact
with Caesar and the powerful men of the earth, Judaism
maintains and Claudel concurs that "there is no resignation to evil, that there is no resignation to lies. There is
only one thing to do about what is bad, and that is to
destroy it!"

The Jewish and Christian theses confront each other
once more in their full metaphysical dimensions on the
importance that they attach to earthly things:

Pensée Where is happiness if not in life?
Orian Above life. . . . Making each other happy here on
earth, Pensée, is this the greatest good?

Fundamental opposition, not of character—both are
noble—but of the conception of the world, of responsibilities toward earthly affairs. "You who can see," exclaims the blind Pensée, symbol of the Synagogue, "what
did you do with the light? . . . Show me Justice and it
will be worthwhile opening them (i.e., my eyes)."

Although this remark betrays the Christian hope of an eventual conversion of the Jews, it is a rather metaphysical hope. The dialogue expresses above all the religious anguish of the fervent Christian that Paul Claudel was, his understanding and his friendliness toward Judaism that he does not want to judge merely by traditional dogmas. The play, like every work of the poet, is suffused with a Biblical lyricism that casts a transcendental light on all the characters. The dialogues between Orian and Pensée have a beauty that draws its substance from the Song of Songs, just as the other episodes contain images and comparisons inspired by the Bible, whose essence has entered into Paul Claudel's whole poetic creation.

François Mauriac

Mauriac is the chronicler of the bourgeoisie of Bordeaux, its clannish spirit, its provincial pettiness, its bigotry, its prejudice, a penetrating and pitiless chronicler, possessing a psycholoanalytic orientation, although of Catholic inspiration. The contemptuous prejudices of this provincial society towards outsiders, "the others," naturally applies also to the Jews, a prejudice made up of religious, racist, and social considerations. In the novel *Thérèse Desqueyroux,* it is Jean Alzévédo, a young student apparently from a family of Portuguese Marranos who came to France in the sixteenth century, who typifies the Jewish intellectual that Mauriac describes with all his qualities and faults. We see him first through the eyes of the two protagonists of the novel, Thérèse and her husband Bernard. The latter embodies the whole virtuous, right-thinking respectability of his region. His young wife asks why his parents were hostile to the marriage of his sister Anne to Jean Alzévédo. "He thought that she was making fun of him, begged her not to indulge in paradoxes:

"First, you know that they are Jewish. Mother knew

the grandfather, the one who refused to be baptized."

But Thérèse (the unfortunate criminal because of her nonconformity, who receives the author's grieving sympathy) insisted that there were no older names than those of these Portuguese Jews. "The Alzévédos were already prominent when our ancestors were wretched shepherds shivering with fever on the banks of their bogs."[9]

"Come on, Thérèse, don't argue for the sake of argument. All Jews are the same."

On the other hand, Mauriac does not hide certain unfavorable traits that are sometimes found among Jewish intellectuals, a passion for formulas that say everything and nothing, for brilliant and empty definitions. And also, "such a lack of reticence, this readiness to confide, it was such a contrast with the silence which every one of us keeps about his inner life! . . .

"But he was the first man . . . for whom the life of the mind mattered above everything else . . . he belonged to a small elite, those who exist."

Mauriac—who shocked his milieu because he criticized a hidebound morality and religiosity, and whose support goes to passionate people even if they are guilty, to receptive spirits even if they are suspect to a bourgeoisie resting comfortably on its prejudices—shows the same lack of conformity toward the Jews. His admirable attitude during the years of the Nazi night is the best testimonial to the value of that nonconformity.

Paul Nizan

In the novel *La Conspiration* (*The Conspiracy*), Paul Nizan introduces nonconformists, even rebels, during the years 1928-29. They are a group of young intellectuals led by Bernard Rosenthal and his magazine *La Guerre*

---

9. Thérèse's remark resembles almost word for word Chaim Weizmann's who told his host Lord Balfour: "We already possessed Jerusalem when London was nothing but a marshy plain."

Civile (*The Civil War*), which is committed to a new
way of life. But their rebellion against traditional education and social inheritances leads to no new horizon
and is an irrational denial of the moral principles on
which bourgeois society is founded.

As for the leader, Bernard Rosenthal, this rebellious
attitude turns inevitably against his Jewish background,
which fills him with a shame mitigated by a bit of pride:
"At times, among his friends, he began a sentence with
those words: 'I, who am Jewish . . .' But he only had
to be among his own people to tell himself that the Jewish
bourgeoisie was more horrible than any other."

A young French bourgeois like Laforgue, when he
feels like rebelling against the dictates of his class, finds
the break a less complex affair. He has only to solve,
according to Jean-Richard Bloch's apt expression, an
equation to the second degree. But a Rosenthal, confronted with an equation to the third degree, "did not
really know where to jump, whom to be faithful to.
Rabbinical ancestors are no joke. What can one do in
Paris with their advice, full of Zohar, of Talmud?" The
French rabbis of his generation seem even more simple-
minded than the old-fashioned rabbis, who at least drew
their inspiration from the authentic sources of their religion. He resents them, not without justification, for
settling too comfortably in the chairs and living rooms
of the rich bourgeoisie that he detests for its materialism
gilded over with a few religious rites. "Bernard thought
of his sister-in-law only as a property that his family
had acquired during a solemn sale, with flowers, an
elaborate luncheon, a religious orchestra that played nup-
tial marches and selections from *Moses* by Verdi . . . ,
cars to the end of Villejust Street, and an amazing speech
by the rabbi . . . of the Copernicus Street Temple on
the virtues of the Rosenthals and the dignity of sur-
gery" (p. 125).

There remain the vast number of those who have not yet been able to tear down the social barriers either through money or baptism. "But the most downtrodden of his own people did not disgust him less than the most successful, the richest, those who had finally a Catholic's self-confidence, as if Heaven and Hell also belonged to them." In short, he does not consider the Jewish proletariat a special entity deserving more consideration than the proletariat in general. Like Heine, who had found it more useful not to separate the Jewish cause from the general emancipation of the people "because Carthage must be defended before the gates of Rome," Paul Nizan is of the opinion that the Jews do not have the right to "their private liberation, a new act of alliance with God: he expected this liberation to be amalgamated with a general emancipation, where their name, their misfortunes, their vocation would disappear together." (p. 16)

Paul Nizan did not have the time to mature, to recognize the special place, in spite of it all, of the Jews in Western society, as was the case of the aging Heine, author of *Hebraic Melodies*. Killed at the front in 1940 during the Dunquerke retreat, he has not known the unbelievable extermination of European Judaism, by the German war machine, no doubt, but under the eyes of certain Western powers who refused to exchange a million concentration camp inmates for 10,000 trucks because they did not know "what to do with a million Jews." That is why Sartre, Nizan's classmate, richer in experience, has been more qualified than he in modern problems of Judaism and anti-Semitism.

Jean-Richard Bloch

The present chapter is in principle reserved to non-Jewish authors examining the Jewish soul and modern Jewish problems, but there is a book, written at the end of the *Belle Epoque,* that is such a vivid illustration of the thesis just outlined that we find it suitable to speak of it immediately. It is the novel . . . *Et Compagnie* (. . . *And Company*) by Jean-Richard Bloch, which even now retains its value as a chronicle of three generations of Jews in France, between 1871 and 1914. The Simler and Company firm, siding with the defeated fatherland, liquidates its business in Alsace and establishes itself in the interior of France to start once more the painful climb toward commercial success and social status, which it wins slowly through the united efforts of a big family in which every member subordinates his private tastes and desires to the overriding interests of the business. In reality, it is neither trade nor money that counts, but the desire to remain in the land that has become the fatherland, to win acceptance, to serve it by courageous initiative. There were numerous Jewish families in France that sank roots into the native soil, and gave it their energy and strength. "We strongly became citizens, bourgeois, property owners, mayors, then, pow, the Almighty gets angry and sends us to the devil." For, in case of economic crisis, "it is, of course, the Simlers who are accused, even though they are guilty of no other crime than forethought."

Old man Simler, who watches like a patriarch over the purity of the hereditary moral values, upholds them as superior to material goods. As he lies dying, he awakens from his long agony to snatch from his fleeting mind and his unresponsive body a last exhortation that he addresses to his grandchildren, stuttering in his Alsatian accent that acquires a kind of moving grandeur: "Kinder . . . factory . . . honest . . . work . . . rich . . . not necessary. Be fery careful . . . money . . . not necessary."

If his children still respect these principles that the father has taught them by his example, it is different with the third generation raised in unearned prosperity. The grandson, Justin, although brilliantly gifted, loses interest in unprofitable studies, betraying one of the most beautiful traditions of Judaism. Because "a Jew," says the author, "would sell his shirt to learn to read and go without bread to educate his children. . . . The only prestige these people have ever been impressed by is that of the scholar. They don't have priests, but doctors. . . . Accustomed by necessity to buy everything, they know that knowledge is the only thing that cannot be obtained by money." Justin becomes "an ass, the intelligent ass who doesn't know where to direct his ambition and slowly becomes a wretch." As compensation, he becomes adept at playing the arrogant lord when confronted with the demands of his workers, and at defending the prerogatives of the boss he has become without lifting a finger. "These people who in the past wore out their soles just like the workers, now have horses, carriages and stables! If the oldest don't use them, the young ones, on the other hand, have completely lost the habit of mingling with the ordinary mortals. Monsieur Justin, who started in the factory only five years ago, has brought with him insolent manners unknown here up to now."

And we can foresee the decline of a business founded by Hyppolite Simler, expanded by his son into Simler and Co., and winding up as an enterprise without soul or vital energy. "Simler suffered the fate of all those who start a business; the business devours the man, the 'Company' devours Simler."

The founder manufactured textiles like a doctor of the Kabbala and not like a weaver. "Hyppolite is dead and you have sold the sword to gild the sheath." And that is the whole story of modern Jewish society.

But the degeneration is followed by a rebirth, thanks to an offspring who becomes a new "founder," who rebels against apathetic complacency and launches new projects, who throws away the sheath and takes back the sword.

Louis Simler is the new pioneer who, in his own way, honorably resolves the problem of being a Frenchman, a bourgeois, and a Jew. "Other men have an equation to the second degree to solve; ours is to the third degree." He learns that it is not by being like other people that one is of service to them, and he seeks within himself the deeper reason that makes his tribe different and makes it last. For every conscious Jew carries in him a spark of the Jewish mission that forces him to take a stand and assume his responsibilities, as a supporter or a rebel, according to the situation. And in the labyrinth of new problems that face each generation, the alternative for the conscious Jew is not the worker's side or the boss's side, but the side of justice. And that is the most difficult: an equation to the third degree.[10]

10. In the novel by Irene Nemrowski it is the reverse from *Simler and Co*: the house "Golder and Marcus" is transformed, thanks to the brutality of the strongest partner into "David Golder, purchase and sale of all oil products." This petty Russian Jew who has gathered a fortune by belated speculations, does not seem to have any God but money and is killing himself in order to acquire it. But his splendor hides a deep wretchedness. This pitiful rich man works only to satisfy the insatiable demands of a frivolous wife and a spoiled and vulgar daughter. He is a self-sacrificing Père Goriot.

19

In Search of a Lost Judaism

Among the three attitudes analyzed by Romain Rolland,[1] it is the last two that gave rise to a Jewish literature in the French language. The first current could not have produced a truly Jewish literature. As long as the idea of Jewish emancipation meant only, according to Clermont-Tonnerre's formula, a complete break with the past in order to be integrated in French society, the role of Jewish thinkers such as Salvador or J. Darmsteter, consisted in proving that the teachings of Moses and the prophets had been invalidated by the works of the National Assembly. The social aspect of Moses' doctrine was admired, but nobody realized that it was the basis of a particular culture consecrated by 3,000 years.

An original literature was not possible as long as there did not exist a Judaism conscious of its own value, as long as the aspirations of the Jews tended only to deny their origins in order to prove their patriotism, an attitude scored by Edmond Fleg in a delightful scene from his drama *The Pope's Jew*. Mosé Latino, to demonstrate his patriotic loyalty, reports his fellow Jews to the Inquisition and justifies his attitude with the following reasoning:

---

1. Cf. p. 109.

. . . Is Molco my brother?
Where does he come from, by what roads?
He has travelled so much! I am Roman
Dear Lords, a Roman whose ancestors
Romans before Caesar, had Remus as master . . .
. . . Jews from France, Poland, the Empire
My brothers?
My name is Mosé, but Mosé Latino! I am Roman:
When they conspire against you, they conspire against me!

(The Cardinal Inquisitor makes a weary gesture. Latino is led
away and retires with numerous bows.)

Yes, Yes, Christian Lords, I am Roman
Roman only the way a Jew can be
For a Roman who is Roman
Because he is Roman, is much less Roman
Than a Roman who is Roman because he wants to be Roman.

A moving symbol of the tragic error that consists in
denying one's origin and originality is represented by the
person and the work of the Jewish-German poet Heinrich Heine.[2]

Heine is a dazzling poetic genius. In German lyricism
only Goethe has produced more moving harmony than
he, and if he is compared to French men of letters to
whom he is more closely allied than to Germans, both by
his birth and his life, his sparkling mind and his struggle
for freedom have earned him a place near Voltaire. And
yet, Heine has found no disciples, either in Germany or
in France. The Germans doubt the sincerity of his lyricism, and the French of his humanitarian impulses. For
the Germans he has remained a Jew; the French saw in
him a German; and in the eyes of the Jews he was an
apostate.

There is an inexpressible tragedy in the unfulfilled

---

2. Cf. C. Lehrmann, *H. Heine, Kämpfer und Dichter* (Editions A.
Francke, Berne, 1957).

life of this man, and this tragedy is that of his whole
generation. If his message does not ring true, it is because
of his equivocal situation, the situation of all those who
have just escaped from the ghetto, but still carry it inside.
At the end of his life only, during the seven years that
he lay bedridden by disease, he finally realized the great
mistake of his life. By examining himself, he discovered
the substance of his soul, a substance he should have expressed to give his life full meaning. He had wanted to
dedicate his life to poetry, to beauty, to contemplation,
like a Goethe, a Novalis, a Holderlin. Like them, he had
considered himself a son of Hellas, he had cultivated
beauty for its own sake, and he had bought without hesitation, the "ticket that gave access to European civilization." Now, he recognized that if Judaism and Hellenism
are the two sources of Western civilization, his place
should have been on the side of Judaism. It is less easy,
less serene, but equally necessary for the equilibrium of
civilization. And ultimately he even saw that Judaism is
not the denial of the world of beauty; its beauty is just
on a different level. Moses is not a lesser creative genius
than the man who made his famous statue. His marble
was that stiff-necked people, a poor tribe of shepherds,
out of whom he sculpted a people that defies the centuries. And the beauty of his work is manifested every
time Jews die at the stake with the *Shema Israel* on their
lips, proclaiming that their God is, in spite of everything,
a God of justice. . . . Thus the poor exile rediscovers
in Paris, on his bed of pain, the Judaism that he had
ignored during his life and he writes this proud confession: "If pride of birth were not a mad contradiction
for a man who has fought for the ideal of Democracy,
the author of these lines could take pride in the fact that
his ancestors belonged to the noble House of Israel and
that he is a descendant of those martyrs who have given
the world a God and a morality, and have fought and

suffered on all the battlefields of the mind."[3] When he finally recovered his inner peace, his poems reacquired that purity that speaks to the heart and which has won for him a place among the greatest names in world literature. And it is then that his *Hebrew Melodies* were also born, thanks to which Heine gained immortality in Jewish literature.

Marcel Proust

Proust offers another example of the tendency to break with Judaism, a break which Heine, during the alienation of his youth, judged necessary to the full development of his genius. It seemed that Proust would be more successful than the German poet since, Jewish only on his mother's side and raised in his father's Catholic environment, he did not, like Heine, have to pay a ransom to be forgiven for his birth. In the work that insured his fame,[4] a work that might be considered autobiographical, Proust keeps a discreet silence over his Jewish background. He preserves his integrity by identifying with the Jew Charles Swann, the leading character of the novel next to the narrator. Thus he has divided his "I," formed by a complex heredity into a Jewish and a non-Jewish character. He seemed to have felt some embarrassment in this camouflage of his origin, as his analysis of his half-Jewess Gilberte indicates: Married ultimately to the Marquis of Saint-Loup, she is the type of woman who tries through snobbishness to compensate for an inferiority complex. When she manages to have herself accepted by the Guermantes circles, she snubs a Jewish woman of her acquaintance, Lady Israel. "Gilberte belonged during these years to the most widespread variety of human ostriches, the kind that hides her head not in the hope

---

3. Hugo Bieber, *Heinrich Heines Confessio Judaica* (Berlin, 1925), p. 257.

4. *A la Recherche du temps perdu.*

of not being seen, which she considers unlikely, but of not seeing that she is seen, which seems quite a lot already, and allows her to leave the rest to chance."[5]

Elsewhere, the novelist draws an even darker picture of the mental disorder that afflicts the Jew who wants to be assimilated, by comparing the Jews of his time and country to a group of homosexuals leading a double life, always ready to hide, to camouflage that unhealthy inclination that torments their senses.

Nevertheless, while recognizing the humiliating aspects of assimilation, Proust considers the absorption of the Jews by their environment an inescapable eventuality.

And yet, the Dreyfus Affair produced in him, who had gone further than Heine toward assimilation, a reaction at least of pride, that led him to proclaim loudly what he wanted to hide. "These are his roots!" notes Cécile Delhorbe:[6] "With a Catholic father and a Catholic religion, he felt at this moment, the moment of persecution, a part of the race of his mother, of that mother whom he adored, of whom he was proud to be the reflection. His republican roots do not interest him, they are too short. But he is proud of his Jewish roots."

Even though the people he happily associated with were naturally anti-Dreyfusard, he became immediately a staunch partisan of Dreyfus. In a conversation between Swann and the narrator (that is to say, the two aspects of Proust's soul) the former says "I would like to live long enough to see Dreyfus rehabilitated." One cannot reasonably expect Proust to discover strong links with a Judaism he has not known, but the feelings of solidarity and spontaneous affinity are strong enough to make him feel proud of his affiliation with "the strong Jewish race, the vital energy, the resistance to death in which even the individuals seem to participate."

5. *Albertine disparue*, II.
6. *L'Affaire Dreyfus et les écrivains français*, thèse (Lausanne, 1934).

It is true that these flattering considerations on the race to which his beloved mother belonged and an occasional attack against anti-Jewish prejudices are all the conscious elements that survive in Proust of his Judaism. Yet, the Jewish spirit in his work is much more considerable than he thinks. Let us forget the fact that his novel contains so many Jewish characters, and that he paints very objectively both the people and the disappointment they encounter in the society to which they want to belong. (We have only to glance at *A L'Ombre des jeunes filles en fleurs* to be struck by the accuracy of his description of the various Jewish circles). Let us speak of what is apparent at first sight, his amazing style that makes him so inaccessible to the average reader.

Much has been written about the complicated and diffuse nature of Proust's style, considered unique in all French literature. As he pursues an idea, a sensation that appears vaguely in the inner recesses of his soul, the author wanders off in byways, discusses all the psychological possibilities imaginable. Like a Biblical verse in the Talmud, the basic idea is accompanied by commentaries and super-commentaries. The reader thinks he is lost in the inextricable labyrinth, when suddenly a luminous idea appears as a reward for the strenuous effort. This style, although Proust is placed in the classical tradition of great French novelists,[7] is not the product of his literary education. He created it himself as the only language suitable to his psychological approach, he found it in his soul, a soul where his mother's influence prevailed. Never has Buffon's dictum been more accurate: "Style is the man." In his style Proust reveals his soul, shaped by his mother's tribe.

One part of Proust's work is called *Sodom and Gomorrah*. The evocation of a Biblical epic is achieved not only by the title, but also by the tone, by the secret melan-

7. Jacques Rivière in N.R.F. (1920).

choly melody that recalls Biblical lyricism. When the
author describes the decadence of a brilliant society, he
sometimes does it, to be sure, with the irony, distance,
and restraint of a Parisian; but very often, he seems to
echo a pathetic page from the Bible. "In spite of his
thorough Parisian sophistication, he retained much of the
apocalyptic moral capacity of the Jewish prophet. This
tone of lamentation that is heard throughout his book is
really not very French. It seems more related to Jewish
literature."[8]

Proust, however, does not want to assume the role of
a moralist. His morality is strictly conventional : respect
for customs, the proprieties, good taste, this ideal of the
French gentleman that he inherited from his father and
that he adopted as a lifelong guide. It is when he describes the perversity of a decadent society that the objective observer, perfectly assimilated by the depraved
upper class, yields to the severe and implacable moralist.
Overwhelmed by the despair produced by the vision of a
declining world, he intones, like a modern Jeremiah, a
pathetic lament full of anguished images. When in *Le
Temps retrouvé* (*Time Recaptured*) Proust describes the
party at the Guermantes attended by all the luminaries
of society that he has known in his youth, and who now
reappear chastened, senile, crippled, it sounds like the
dark rumbling of the prophecies announcing the vanity
and punishment of prideful grandeur.

Proust, in search of bygone time, penetrates the human
soul to depths that make us shudder. He aims to describe
"man as having the length not of his body but of his
years."[9] Siegfried van Praag[10] describes his work as the
living illustration of Bergson's thesis. Along with Bergson
and Freud, he has conceived a world where time expe-

8. E. Wilson, *Axel's Castle,* quoted in G. Cattaui, *L'Amitié de Proust,*
Cahiers M. Proust, p. 8.
9. *Temps retrouvé,* II.
10. *Revue Juive de Genève* (May-July 1937).

rienced becomes the only aspect of reality and in which the soul acquires a new dimension: depth. The spiritual kinship between Proust and Freud is very strong. Proust and Freud have in common the tendency never to remain on the surface of things, but to find for the simplest idea, the slightest sensation, the roots that sink into the personal and racial past of the individual.

It is Gide who treated Proust as a "camouflager" because, unlike himself, he did not frankly admit his homosexual tendencies, while analyzing them precisely, almost scientifically, through other characters in his work. This observation is also valid for the Jewish consciousness of the great novelist-sociologist, the more so since he himself on several occasions has compared the homosexual and the Jew in society, and noted an analogy in their social behavior dictated by the necessity to hide their differences. Proust even seems to see a virtue in this pretense, a sign of discretion and propriety. And he is right as long as he is dealing with abnormal sex practices. But he compares the lack of inhibitions of those who would like to live as Jews, as Zionists, to certain homosexuals who cynically admit their deviations instead of wearing, in both cases, a mask to remain unobtrusive in their milieu.

Thus, a Jewish background becomes a social defect, more unforgivable than any other sin. When Gilberte, the daughter of the sensitive and exquisite Jew Swann and the courtesan Odette, manages to gain an *entrée* in society, she is more ashamed of her father than of her mother. And the same aristocrats who after his death have forgotten even the name of their former friend, so admired in the past because he dared take the defense of Captain Dreyfus, welcome Odette, his mistress, his wife, who has become Princess of Guermantes through marriage. In the eyes of society the *demi-monde* is a less heavy burden than Judaism.

Proust's social circumstances imposed upon him his

philosophy of dissimulation, which permitted him to remain in a circle to which he felt an attraction so pathological that he himself must have been ashamed of it. For he did not spare his criticism, again through another character, Albert Bloch, of this social ambition ready to pay by countless humiliations its entry into high society. Ultimately, Proust freed himself of the ambition of his youth and by a pitiless description took revenge on the aristocracy. There is a suggestion of his Judaism in his anguished images, as well as in his extraordinary style that imitates the rabbinical method that comments and overcomments a text, in the exclusive interest of truth, and without seeking the least aesthetic effect. Be that as it may, it is not a coincidence that the orientation of his mind links him with Freud and Bergson by revealing to him a new dimension, depth and duration, and make of this "Franco-Semitic doublet" so thoroughly assimilated, a typical example of the stubborn survival of hereditary traits of the "strong Jewish race" grafted on the tree of French thought.

Proust did not directly create disciples, but the French novel has been strongly influenced by his psychoanalytic art. He has not been imitated, either in his investigation of abnormal passions or even in the extravagance of his style; but the horizons opened by him have not been forgotten and the words of François Mauriac spoken at Proust's death have not yet lost their value: "Our generation of novelists is the first that was not born under the sign of Balzac. It was born under the sign of Freud and Proust" (*Nouvelles Littéraires,* May 26, 1923).

About Converts: Max Jacob

Would it be advisable to open a parenthesis to speak more generally about Jewish writers converted to Christianity? Their number is considerable and the title of this work devoted to "the Jewish element" without religious differentiation would justify a chapter about the anonymous contribution of Judaism to the French genius. It would be extremely difficult to define such a subject, in view of the fact that the whole of Christianity is tied to Judaism not only as to doctrine, but also by its founder and its early supporters. Besides, in modern times conversion did not have a purely religious character: when it does happen, as with Gertrude Stein, the problem is of a theological rather than of a literary nature. There are no doubt exceptions too, as in the case of Max Jacob, converted under the influence of an apparition, but without consequences to his general and literary behavior. He remained, according to André Billy's felicitous expression, a "bohemian of art and poetry, bohemian of religion." When one day worshipers in a basilica saw a man, Max Jacob, bowing down in prayer, striking himself violently on the chest, and uttering exclamations, the priest reassured them by explaining: "He is a converted Jew."

Max Jacob did not have dramatic apparitions; his friends used to tell about a vision he had at the Sacré-Coeur of Montmartre. The Virgin appeared to him: "How ugly you are, my poor Max"—"Not as ugly as all that, dear Virgin!" he answered with dignity. And he left the church, disturbing the whole congregation. Even during the time of mystical trance experienced in his new faith, his Jewish irony did not abandon him, nor did his expiatory contrition, the result of three thousand years of practice.

He knew he was destined to martyrdom and, like so many other converts, was haunted by the thought of violent death—a fate he met at Drancy in 1944, after undergoing all the agonies of the Jew hunted and sacrificed, in the midst of his former coreligionists on the altar of his French fatherland.

Marcel Proust, in spite of his conformity, announced

the awakening of Jewish consciousness after a 100-year
eclipse of French Judaism. His contributions to French
thought do not have a consciously Jewish character.
Neither have those of Henri Bergson, of Julien Benda,
of Max Jacob. It is only by their temperament, their
distinct spiritual make-up, that these authors bring a distinct note to French intellectual life. Lacretelle, in a novel
that we analyzed elsewhere, tells how the young Jew
Silbermann reveals to his Christian friend certain subtleties in Racine that are not usually seen on stage, and how
he calls his attention to the beauties of the cathedrals
from a viewpoint that the other had not noticed until
then. It is also true that among the greatest interpreters
of Wagner, Mozart, and Beethoven are found many
Jewish musicians. The reason is that in any given civilization a different temperament, adding its particular accent, produces a new harmony unnoticed by those who
really belong to it.

But alongside the unconscious contribution of the Jewish temperament to Western civilization, there is a conscious contribution, the work of a group of French writers
who tried to express their soul discovered during the
moral crisis caused by the Dreyfus Affair. The characteristic note of this Judeo-French literature is the painful
search for a new spiritual position in the modern world,
the attempt to integrate the Jewish heritage into Western thought.

20

Jewish Literature in the French Language (Up to the Second World War)

In a beautiful poem by André Spire,[1] we witness the painful birth in the soul of the French Jew of his Jewish vocation, repressed during a century of happiness. One day, around Easter 1905, that is to say, after the great pogroms of Russia, the poet sees on the southern portal of the Strasbourg Cathedral two pink sandstone statues that symbolize the Church and the Synagogue. The young Law victorious, triumphantly facing the old Law, vanquished, defeated. Suddenly he realizes that he, who could live in the kingdom of joy, of aesthetic happiness, who thought that he was the lucky heir to Franco-Hellenic art and gaiety, who had celebrated the charms of love, the beauty of the French earth, also possesses a faculty that shows him the hidden face of things where others see only its bright side. Beauty seems to him a luxury, luxury an abomination, its enjoyment a theft.

Tu voudras chanter la force, l'audace;
Tu n'aimeras que les rêveurs désarmés contre la vie

1. André Spire, *Poèmes juifs*. Definitive edition, Collection *Présences du judaïsme* (Albin Michel).
    Cf. C. Lehrmann, *Du Symbolisme au Sionisme* in *L'élément juif dans la pensée européenne;* P. M. Schuhl, *L'oeuvre poétique d'André Spire,* Cahiers de l'A.I.U. (Sept–Oct, 1959).

Tu tenteras d'écouter les chants joyeux des paysans
Les marches brutales des soldats, les rondes gracieuses des
    fillettes
Tu n'auras l'oreille habile que pour les pleurs
Qui tombent des quatre coins de l'univers.

You will want to celebrate strength, daring;
You'll only love the dreamers defenseless against life
You'll try to listen to the peasants' cheerful songs,
The brutal marches of soldiers, little girls' graceful dances;
Your ears will only be responsive to the tears
Shed at the four corners of the universe.

His roots are here. His social inclinations do not come
from a transitory generous mood. It is the historic heritage of a Judaism thirsty for justice that speaks consciously in him and that opposes the naïve joy of life and
enjoyment that fills his previous poems. He could, like
the others, turn a deaf ear to the lamentations of the
persecuted Jews and enjoy the pleasures of life. Isn't he
a free French citizen? But the voice that speaks within
him is stronger than anything else. It is a voice that cries
for justice, justice before beauty.

It is the old struggle between Hellas and Judea that
is reborn in the modern Jew.

The struggle that in the past was waged between the
Syrian armies and those of Judah Maccabee continues
nowadays in the heart of the modern Jew, who carries
in his age-old soul conflicting tendencies. In another poem,
A La France, Spire reflects on this duality. He begins by
a tribute to this "lovely country" that has absorbed so
many races by imposing its form, to this "French spirit"
made up of reason, joy, balance, light-heartedness, serenity. And the author feels "more than half captivated" by
the atmosphere he breathes, like another Jewish poet,
Henri Franck, who is entirely captivated and exalts it
with enthusiasm and emotion:

O raison ancienne en chaque siècle accrue
O courage du monde et coeur de l'Occident
Nation inventive et sensée, ô vivante

O ancient reason and growing with every century
O courage of the world and heart of the West,
Inventive and rational nation, o living. . . .[2]

Unlike Franck, whose beautiful equilibrium has never been disturbed—perhaps because he died very young— Spire feels in himself a spirit of rebellion. He is made suspicious by the ease of assimilation, and he rises against the alluring charm of his homeland:

Politesse, moi aussi, tu voudrais m'affadir
Blague, tu voudrais jouer à retrécir mon âme
O Chaleur, ô tristesse, ô violence, ô folie
Invincibles génies à qui je suis voué
Que serais-je sans vous? Venez donc me défendre
Contre la raison sèche de cette terre heureuse.

Courtesy, you would like to deaden my spirits too!
Joke, you would like to play at shrinking my soul!
O warmth, O sadness, O violence, O madness,
Invincible genii to whom I am pledged,
What would I be without you? Come and defend me
Against the sterile reason of this happy land.

This distinct element that he sees in his soul does not paralyze him any more. He begins to feel his horizons broaden, his heart grow fuller as he becomes aware of the other component of his personality. The Hellenic equilibrium and serenity surviving in the French soul clash with the Jewish melancholy and anxiety.

Similar themes can be found in a whole generation of Jewish writers who have participated actively in the spiritual preoccupations of their times and country and one day notice that in their soul vibrates a different string,

2. *La Danse devant l'Arche.*

whose strident sound jars the harmony of the concert.
And even when they are not aware of it themselves, their
readers notice in their works a strange tone that comes
from their long-repressed heredity. Thus, as we have
seen, critics have pointed out even in Proust—"more than
half captivated", by the atmosphere of his native land,
French by his father, education, and aesthetic tastes—
undeniable traces of the moralizing attitude of the
prophets.

Certainly these French Jews would like to celebrate
with their whole heart, and they often do, the sky, the
earth, the cities, and the rivers of sweet France, just as
they feel "more than half captivated" by the serene and
welcoming atmosphere of this lovely land. It would be
so wonderful to listen to the happy songs of the peasants,
the graceful farandolas of little girls, to admire strength
and daring, to dedicate oneself to the joys of creation in
the blessed realm where the Greek spirit reigns! Ah! if
one could be a poet, nothing but a poet. By the compelling
rhythm of his free verse, by the splendid color of his
"Jewish Legend of the Centuries" (*Ecoute Israël—
Listen, O Israel*),[3] a Spire or a Fleg would belong among
the great lyric poets of French literature. But the ear
straining to listen to songs, suddenly hears the lament
that rises from the four corners of the earth, the cries of
the underprivileged and the downtrodden. What does it
matter? That's life; let us sympathize with misfortune,
let us write elegies about their tragic fate, and "let us
live our vigorous lives," for we live but once! . . . But
how can we live, when in this country there is a pogrom,
in another human fanaticism demands victims, and in a
distant continent innocents are threatened? Does not
mankind everywhere live on top of volcanoes? How can
we enjoy beauty when there is no justice in the world?

---

3. Translator's note: this refers to Victor Hugo's poem *La Légende
des siècles,* an epic of the history of mankind.

Art, si je t'acceptais ma vie serait charmante
Mes jours fuiraient légers, bienveillants, dilettantes;
J'aurais à moi, j'aurais pour moi le fugace présent

Mais, mon coeur satisfait pourrait-il encore vivre
Si tu l'avais châtré de son rêve splendide
Le demain éternel qui marche devant moi.[4]

Art, if I accepted you, my life would be delightful.
My days would go by, light, kindly, dilletantish;
The transitory Present would be for me, would be my own.

But could my contented heart still live
If you had castrated it of its magnificent dream:
That eternal Tomorrow that walks in front of me.

This eternal Tomorrow is the historical dream of Israel, the dream of universal peace, a theme formulated at the beginning of time by the Prophets and recaptured by their children in their minds whenever they meditate at the foot of the Wailing Wall.[5]

Actively to prepare for tomorrow is the quintessence of Messianism. In this respect the Jewish ideal differs from the Hellenic and the Christian ideals. Judaism differs from Hellenism in the fact that the latter aspires to the complete possession of the present, while Jewish Messianism is characterized by a tireless march toward a better future, even if it is a march toward the infinite. Circumscribed and *limited perfection,* serenity—for the Greeks these are the aims: Phynicos, a tragic poet, was fined for having disturbed the consciousness and the equilibrium of the Athenians by the description in *La Prise de Milet* (*The Capture of Milet*) of misfortunes that could have been avoided. The Jews, on the other hand, are warned against "false prophets," those who weaken

4. André Spire, *Le Messie.*
5. Poem by Edmond Fleg.

our vigilance, the readiness of our hearts to react against the moral and social defects of life. Jewish Messianism rejects relative harmony in the present to aspire to *unlimited perfectibility*, to the preparation of a better future.

Christianity is closer to the Greek world than Judaism, and occupies, so to speak, an intermediary position between the two. It teaches an ideal fulfilled in the past; that of Judaism is to be fulfilled in the future. For the Christian, God has already sent his heavenly messenger to earth; for the Jew, man must make a continual effort to uplift himself and win heaven by the divine potential that mankind possesses. Thus the Jew takes a militant attitude toward evil, while Christianity tries to overcome it by nonresistance, meekness, and resignation. In this acceptance of the material world (summarized in the maxim "render unto Caesar what belongs to Caesar") the Christian attitude corresponds in practice to the Greek. Spiritual enemies, they come together in practice, forming the basis of Western civilization. It is well, perhaps, that Judaism maintains its uncompromising attitude of active struggle against the flaws of established order, counteracting the more accommodating, not to say indulgent, morality of the Western world.

Albert Cohen in his *Paroles juives* (*Jewish Words*) opposes the Biblical ideal to that of Jesus, through the words of the Prophet Jeremiah:

Ils voudraient guérir à la légère les plaies de mon peuple
Paix, paix! disent-ils;
Mais il n'y a pas de paix.

They would like lightly to cure the wounds of my people
Peace! peace! they say:
But there is no peace.

The Jew does not settle for a peaceful life as long as

there are misfortunes and iniquities in the world. He tends to reject the serenity of contemporary life to prepare a better future where, he hopes, real peace will reign. This rejection of serenity has produced the anguish that characterizes the Jew, and for which he is often criticized as a destructive element. The restless fever that consumes him, and his instability, can be disturbing if they produce trouble for the sake of material benefits only. But when these attributes of the soul are spiritualized, they become what Spire calls "his ancient protectors,"[6] keeping the Jewish people, and through them humanity, from succumbing to self-satisfaction, complacency, *das erbärmliche Behagen* before a world yet to be created, to be perfected. The Jewish elite was able to transform this element of anxiety, of instability, into a tireless search for an ideal of peace and universal justice. It is this elite that Romain Rolland has entrusted with the mission of being "the bearer of God, the champion of the new law in the old world of Europe and America."

Such a transfiguration of the anguish that characterizes Israel transforms the notion of being accursed that the world has attributed to the Wandering Jew. The Wandering Jew is not the symbol of a curse, but of a vocation. "They know the joys of exile, and their sadness contains light," asserts Henri Hertz.[7]

The conscious Jews take sad pride in the tragic mission that has been assigned to them: to go on until the end of time, until the day true peace is achieved. "Blessed are those who will die for peace, for they will see God!"[8] exclaims Fleg's Wandering Jew. It is a theme that the author deals with repeatedly. Thus in the play *Le Juif du Pape* (*The Pope's Jew*), when David Molco is disappointed in his hope of a new era based on the agree-

6. "Tu as raison" in *Poèmes juifs* by André Spire.
7. Ceux de Job in *Vers un monde volage*.
8. *Jésus raconté par le Juif errant* (Albin Michel).

ment of the spiritual and the political powers of the earth, he does not give up the struggle after his tragic failure. Just as in the legend the Wandering Jew comes back to life after each death to resume his march, Molco rises again with a painful effort to resume his mission:

> Qu'il est long le pèlerinage
> De lieux en lieux, d'âge en âge
> De travaux en travaux!
> On pense arriver: la fin du voyage
> Est un nouveau départ vers un départ nouveau.

> Il faut aller pourtant, fut-ce en la solitude,
> Et quand on est tombé, se remettre debout
> Il faut ne se lasser d'aucune lassitude
> Quel que soit le chemin, la lumière est au bout.

> How long is the pilgrimage
> From place to place, from epoch to epoch,
> From work to work!
> We think we have arrived: the end of the journey
> Is a new departure towards a new departure.

> But we must go on nonetheless, even alone,
> And if we have fallen, get up again.
> We must not get weary of any weariness.
> Whatever the road, the light is at the end.

This instability, so pronounced in the Jew, is only a fundamental quality of mankind. "The human condition: restlessness, boredom, anguish," said Pascal. And let us remember Romain Rolland's words: "Any free and enlightened spirit of other races has the same duty. But this duty is for you, Jews, the very essence of your deepest traditions."

These deep traditions are not the result of philosophical meditations. The passionate pursuit of justice for all is characteristic of men who have suffered injustice too often. The teachings of the Prophets of Israel could not have been perpetuated and have remained alive if its substance had not been revealed to each generation through the lessons of suffering.

It is in that sense that André Spire calls anxiety and sadness "his ancient protectors." Thanks to the suffering, to the sadness of its destiny, to the instability to which it was condemned for centuries, Israel has remained faithful to the role that Providence assigned to it in the concert of nations.

External blows are not sufficient to explain how Israel succeeded in remaining aware of its thankless historical role. Too many misfortunes deaden, stifle enthusiasm, degrade. A spiritual counterweight was needed, stronger than the material destiny, capable of transfiguring it into a metaphysical duty. This counterweight came to Israel in every period of its history, and today with renewed reality it comes from the Promised Land.

Although the pioneers of the new resurrection are recruited in the main among the Jewish youth from Poland and Germany, French Judaism plays an honorable role in the rebirth of Zionism. It is in France that the most important spiritual battles have been waged. It is French Judaism that first obtained political emancipation and gave impetus to the Jewish communities of other countries. It is in France that Heine wrote the immortal *Hebraic Melodies*. It is in Paris that the Jewish thinker Moses Hess lived and meditated. He was a hermit who, around 1860, under the influence of the unification of the German Empire and of Italy, first formulated the concept of national Jewish emancipation in Palestine. It is also in Paris that 30 years later, under the influence of the Dreyfus Affair, Theodore Herzl wrote *The Jewish State*, which has become the political program of the Zionist movement.

For French Judaism, the new Israel is a spiritual center in the sense given it by Achad Haam, as well as a political and geographic reality. According to the latter, the political, economic, territorial existence of a Jewish state is of value only if it is the support of the prophetic ideal. The Jews of the Diaspora must be the messenger of a reunited Israel as well as the medium through which the values of Western civilization will converge towards Israel.

"If a new message is being prepared over there, don't we need messengers everywhere to transmit it?"[9] It is this aspect of Zionism that appears in the Jewish literature of France. The Jewish writers are waiting for the Promised Land to become once again a center of Jewish culture, a source from which they can draw to renew their Jewish consciousness, while on the other hand, they want to enrich this Jewish home with all the wealth of Western civilization. Israel must become again

Un Peuple saint, un Peuple pur,
Aux flancs féconds,
Aux pensées chastes, au droit austère,
Mais qui a tant appris sur les routes du monde
Qu'il n'aura plus peur de son vieux péché,
Et qu'il laissera ses yeux, indulgents
Jouir du mouvement, des lignes, des formes
Que jadis il nommait une abomination;
Un Peuple où il y aura des pères et des mères
Mais aussi les garçons amoureux
Et des jeunes filles dansantes
Des fronts tenaces, des mains vaillantes,
Mais des mains caressantes aussi,
Qui sauront disposer les soies et les laines
Qui broieront les couleurs, pétriront la glaise
Et glorifieront, dans le marbre,
Ta beauté, Israel.[10]

9. E. Fleg, "Ma terre d'Israël," in *Vers le monde qui vient,* Collection *Présences du judaïsme* (Albin Michel).

A holy people, a pure people
With a fruitful womb,
With chaste thoughts, with an austere law,
But one that has learned so much on the roads of the world,
That it won't be afraid anymore of its old sin
And it will allow indulgent eyes
To enjoy movement, lines, forms
That in the past they considered an abomination.
A people where there will be fathers and mothers,
But also boys in love
And dancing young girls,
Stubborn brows, courageous hands,
But also caressing hands
Able to arrange silk and wool,
Grind colors, knead clay
And glorify in marble
Your beauty, Israel.

This is the general tendency of Jewish literature in France in the twentieth century. It does not matter if a few do not participate in this renewal of Jewish culture, this new self-awareness. It does not matter even if these indifferent Jews are in the majority. Jewish history has always been "the struggle of a minority against a majority, even in the midst of the Jewish people."[11] The Prophets of Israel have always been a weak minority rising against the overwhelming majority of the complacent, nevertheless imposing their law and building the future. The majority of Jews, as Péguy writes, "are led to their great, painful appointments with fate only under the urging of a handful of malcontents, an active minority, a wild and fanatic gang, a gang of madmen . . . which is precisely what the Prophets of Israel are. Israel has furnished innumerable prophets, heroes, martyrs, countless warriors . . . moreover, it is itself a prophetic race. . . . But it asks only this: not to give the Prophets a reason to intervene. It knows what it costs. . . .

10. André Spire, "A La Nation juive," in *Poèmes juifs.*
11. Hans Kohn, *L'Humanisme juif* (Rieder), p. 175.

Twenty, forty, fifty centuries of tribulations have told it. . . . Fifty centuries of misery, sometimes gilded. They know what it costs to carry God and his agents, the Prophets. The whole policy of Israel is not to make any noise in the world, to buy peace by a circumspect silence. But the whole mystique of Israel is for Israel to fulfill in the world its resounding and painful mission. . . . The disavowal of the Prophets by Israel and still the leadership of Israel by the Prophets, that is the whole story of Israel."[12]

It is this active minority, driven by the mystique of Israel, that has given birth to a literature that seems to be a rejuvenated branch of the old historical tree, a branch that has kept its original character under different skies. This literary branch, although of Jewish inspiration, although linked to the most sacred traditions of "the prophetic race," nevertheless participates in the spiritual excitement of France. It is a plant made fruitful by the dew of the Promised Land, but nourished by the fertility of the French earth. Its distinctive characteristics, the spiritual anguish, the compelling need to denounce injustices, to drive humanity toward progress in spite of itself, have most happily enriched the French genius, one of whose typical tendencies is the progressive assertion of human rights. The emphasis on this tendency by Franco-Jewish writers had noticeable repercussions on French literature for "in the intellectual field, France grows through the devotion of those who choose her and serve her."[13]

---

12. Charles Péguy, *Notre Jeunesse,* in *Oeuvres complètes* (N.R.F. 1916), pp. 101, 102, 104, 109.
13. Anna de Noailles in her introduction to *La Danse devant l'Arche* by H. Franck.

Part V

CONTEMPORARY LITERATURE
(1945 - 1960)

Dough does not like yeast. But often this yeast was needed to produce admirable manifestations. . . . Works produced this way are not any the less French. . . . Perhaps no other literature was as greatly impregnated without losing its own identity and characteristics.

—André Gide
Journal

21

The Patriarchs and Their Successors

At the head of contemporary Franco-Jewish literature we still find the two venerable patriarchs who were its founders at the beginning of the century, Edmond Fleg and André Spire. The republication and the translations of the latter's poems prove the vitality and the relevance of his message, while Fleg does not cease to amaze the modern generation by a creativity renewed after every blow of fate. The new generation pays tribute to a Fleg so "unphlegmatic," and a Spire so "inspired" even in the tenth decade of his life, two masters who teach hope and regeneration through the spirit.

Alongside, Armand Lunel has acquired the status of a classic author of Franco-Jewish literature, thanks to two very colorful novels that established his reputation between the two wars: *Niccolo Peccavi* and *Esther at Carpentras*. If he occupies so little space in our work it is not an argument against Armand Lunel, but a criticism against present-day literary history. This lacuna can only be excused by the fact that his novels have already been amply analyzed by qualified critics such as André Spire in *Quelques Juifs et demi-juifs* (*Some Jews and Half-Jews*).

Another Provençal writer would have deserved a substantial study, Emmanuel Eydoux, a Resistance name that subsequently became a well-known literary pseudonym.

His spiritual itinerary is typical of the Jewish generation immediately preceding and following the Second World War. He belonged at first to an assimilated milieu. The shock of events prompted him to read the Bible, first in French, then in Hebrew. Afterwards he tackled the study of the Talmud, and "discovered" Philo, Hassidism, Zionism—all this simultaneously with his daily pedestrian work, for he is an office worker who does not earn his living with his pen.

He began his writings with poetry (*Le Chant de l'exil —The Song of Exile*), continued it with three Biblical epics in dialogue form and with an attempt to formulate Biblical poetry in today's scientific terms (*La Science de l'être—The Science of Being*). Then he uttered a cry of indignation before the lethargic lack of comprehension of his time, before stupidity, intolerance, fanaticism, ignorance, indifference. It is a series of *Litanies,* one of which, *La Litanie des deux orphelins* (*The Litany of the Two Orphans*) devoted to the Finaly Affair, illustrates the tragedy of martyred children, by-product of the great Jewish tragedy of the Second World War.

André Néher undertook to revive the words of the Bible in modern terms on an even larger scale. This philosopher, writer, theologian, straddling Biblical and modern thought, has marked the postwar generation with his impressive spiritual presence. His presentations of the Prophets of Israel are not merely learned commentaries, but successful resurrections of the prophetic genius, for they bring out the incorruptible actuality of its doctrine. It is not surprising to rediscover a Biblical idea in Existentialist terms or others, for it is readily apparent that the most modern terminology, far from betraying bygone eras, helps us to understand the intentions of the Biblical seers, those men possessed by their mission of injecting the Eternal into the Temporal. Writing in the most classical tradition of French clarity, but introducing in his lines an ardent passion drawn from an even loftier tradition, André Néher by his themes and by his style has added an indisputably original accent to the literary world of his native land.[1]

It is too bad that Albert Cohen did not pursue the path that his two pre-War novels *Solal* and *Mangeclous,* two picturesque and vigorous works, led us to expect. But the book that he has recently brought out, *Le Livre de ma mère* (*My Mother's Book*) confirms the worth of this writer. The book is the moving tribute of all ungrateful sons (and what son is not ungrateful, to some extent?) to the mothers of the world, sources of life, torrents of love and devotion. It is more than a book, it is a hymn. Three authors have, in the twentieth century, built monuments to the memory of their Jewish mothers. Marcel Proust, Romain Gary (*La Promesse de l'aube—The Promise of Dawn*), and Albert Cohen. Such a work does not lend itself to critical analysis. We can only quote some significant excerpts:

". . . Listen, my son, even though you don't believe in our God, because of all those scholars . . . , still go to the synagogue once in a while," she begged sweetly, "do it for me."

"Son, explain to me why you enjoy going to the mountains. Don't you know that all these demon skiers break a leg? They like that, they're pagans, inconsiderate. Let them break a leg if they enjoy it. But you are a Cohen, from the race of Aaron, the brother of Moses, our master."

I reminded her then that Moses had gone up to Mount Sinai. She was stunned. Obviously the precedent was impressive. She thought it over for a minute, then she explained that Mount

---

1. The major works of André Néher:
Amos, contribution à l'étude du prophétisme (*Amos, Contribution to the Study of Prophetism*)
Moïse et la vocation juive (*Moses and the Jewish Vocation*)
L'Essence du prophétisme (*The Prophetic Existence*)
Jérémie (*Jeremiah*)

Sinai was only a little mountain, and besides, Moses had only gone there once, and furthermore, he didn't go up for fun, but to see God.

Son, you see, men are only animals. . . . But one day during ancient times, our master Moses came and decided to change these animals into men, into children of God, through the Holy Commandments, you understand. He told them: you won't do this, you won't do that, it's bad, animals kill, but you won't kill. . . . You know how Jews are. They must always have the most expensive. When they're sick, they immediately call the biggest professor of medicine. So Moses, who knew them so well, told himself: if I tell them that the Commandments came from the Almighty, they'll pay more attention, they'll show more respect.

My mother is dead, but I am hungry and so, in spite of my grief, I'm going to eat. Sin of life. Eating is thinking of oneself, it's wanting to live. My tearful eyes are mourning for my mother, but I want to live. Thank God, living sinners soon become the offended dead.

Sons of mothers still alive, do not forget that your mothers are mortal. I won't have written in vain, if one of you, after having read my funeral song, is gentler with his mother one evening because of me and my mother. Be gentle with your mother every day. Love her more than I did my mother.

The writer would like to take the liberty of evoking the image of his mother, deported and killed somewhere in Poland, far from the nine children she had brought into the world, but together with the man, the pious and venerable scholar, who had shared her heroic existence until the supreme martyrdom.

This woman was a torrent of love, a torrent whose source was God. For her faith was of the kind that moves mountains, to the point of what we intellectuals disdainfully call fanaticism. Was it not fanaticism in the middle of the First World War to insist on lighting a candle for each of her children on the eve of every Sabbath? And she always found these extremely scarce candles. After the ceremony her heart was calmed by her renewed alliance with God on the fate of her family. Irresistible torrent of love when the life of a child was at stake, irresistible even to the commander of a concentration camp. When a son was incarcerated in one of those camps, she managed to obtain his freedom, without money, without connections, by her tears alone. And when the two old people were deported to Poland, accompanied by their youngest child, they managed again to get her out of the great cemetery that land represents. God was faithful to the covenant concluded over the candles on the Sabbath.

Ah, yes, their fate is only that of six million others. There were millions of mothers who tried to cover with their fragile bodies the lives of those God had entrusted to their safekeeping. But since our imagination is incapable of grasping the tragedies that hide behind these figures, by honoring the memory of our mother we pay a heartfelt tribute to the suffering mothers of all nations. Judaism has neither saints nor angels to comfort and support the weak; in their place, living and dead mothers, down-to-earth and sublime, assume the roles of angels sent directly by God. Albert Cohen's elegy is a Song of Songs in their honor.

In the strictly literary field, one of the outstanding members of the new generation of Franco-Jewish writers is Arnold Mandel, incisive novelist (*Les Temps incertains—The Uncertain Times; Les Vaisseaux brûlés—The Burned Ships*) and essayist, a lucid and pitiless observer, but receptive to all the currents of modern Judaism, with a very personal wit that makes him a disciple of Heine. Another is Rabi, author of tragedies (*Varsovie—War-*

saw; Judas) a sensitive and fiery temperament, marked by the great catastrophe of European Judaism and by "the mystery of Israel." A third is Albert Memmi who with talent and sincerity introduced the theme of North African Judaism (*La Statue de sel—The Salt Statue; Agar*) and its problems so eternal in their individuality.

22
Sartre

In his *Réflexions sur la question juive* (*Thoughts on the Jewish Question*), published shortly after the end of World War II, Sartre analyzes the phenomenon of anti-Semitism, which had seemed an anachronism, but subsequently revealed its destructive force in the very heart of a civilization as advanced as the West. While he discusses the problem, Sartre asserts "that he refuses to recognize as an opinion a doctrine that is aimed specifically at individuals and that attempts to destroy their rights or exterminate them. Anti-Semitism does not belong in the category of ideas protected by the right to free opinion." Anti-Semitism, under the appearance of a doctrine, is nothing but an emotional reaction, an expression of mediocrity, of inferiority before a superior individual that the anti-Semite tries to humiliate and sometimes put to death. Albert Camus concurs when he notes: "I do not believe, in spite of the claims of Maurras' school, that anti-Semitism has a real logic. It is more a question of an emotional complex in which we must distinguish an attempt at self-justification as well as the gratification of hatred."[1] In modern society, anti-Semitism, afraid to admit its inherent sadism, hides it under the cover of a doctrine and indulges in its perversity only behind the anonymity of the crowd.

1. *Evidences,* Paris (January 1952).

Before this analytical examination of the anti-Semitic mentality, Sartre had already made a luminous description of it in his short story *L'Enfance d'un chef* (*The Childhood of a Leader*). He shows a group of "camelots du roi" (royalists), high school students belonging to the upper bourgeoisie and knowing that they are destined to be the future leaders of their country, for long before their birth they already had their place in the sun. In spite of their intellectual mediocrity, they are full of self-esteem, for they have "rights" by virtue of their origin, their relationship to "the land and the dead." A few phrases from Barrès and Maurras, opaque, inexhaustible, mysterious, such as "renewing tradition" or "France for the French" are the basis of their nationalistic philosophy in whose name they hurl invectives against the "kikes" and even assault them when the odds are overwhelmingly in their favor. Lucien Fleurier, an adolescent paralyzed up to now by his inferiority complex, feels his strength and self-confidence swell when by a bold blow he manages to blind in one eye a Jewish passerby, already beaten unconscious by the gang of royalists.

Lucien Fleurier is the prototype of this Uncle Justin (*Reflexions sur la question juive*), whose social respectability is based on the fact that "he hates the British." He, Lucien, discovers that "he hates Jews," whom until now he had hardly ever met and against whom he had no reason to complain. But the discovery of anti-Semitism as a philosophy fills him with the pride of carrying out a sacred mission. He finally finds a way of standing out from his entourage by the fierce hatred for Jews for which he is known. First, the Jewish stories he has borrowed from his father are found entertaining. All he has to do is start in a certain tone: "Van day, Lefy meets Plum," to delight his friends. Soon people refer to him respectfully as "the man who can't stand Jews," or "Léon Blum's closest friend." It is already quite an achievement to hear his name mentioned with that of the Socialist leader. Thus he is revealed to himself by the image that he reads in the eyes of the others, for he is the man who can't stand Jews! "The metamorphosis was completed." He was going to be "a leader among the French."

After this sharp description of the anti-Semitic mentality, Sartre seeks a definition for the innumerable and contradictory aspects of the Jewish phenomenon in the world. "It is society, not God's decree that made him a Jew." But there are two basic expressions of this phenomenon, both caused by the gentile environment; a Jew is whomever his entourage considers a Jew, which creates for him a hopeless situation, a sort of inescapable closed world.

This Jewish society is based not on the nation, the land, or religion, but on an "identical situation." A minority, however, recognizes its fate and affirms it: these are the authentic Jews, tied by no common bonds except the contempt they show the society that surrounds them. As they become aware of their situation, they accept it unconditionally and keep at least their moral equilibrium.

The nonauthentic Jew,[2] on the other hand, deep down confirms the judgment that his environment has passed against him and develops a guilt complex, even though he does not know the reason for the indictment. As in Kafka's *Trial,* he knows neither his judges nor his lawyers, nor what he is accused of. But he plays the game by pleading guilty. If one were to try to summarize the positive criticisms, the concrete defects attributed to the Jews, the real reasons invoked against their integration in the nation, the qualities demanded of them "to be accepted as a true Frenchman, how many Frenchmen would be worthy of being Jewish in their own country?"

2. Cf. also the distinction made by Pierre Aubery in his work *Milieux juifs de la France contemporaine* (*Jewish Milieus in Contemporary France*) (Plon, 1957).

One of Sartre's disciples, André Gorz, in a novel entitled *Le Traître* (*The Traitor*) has undertaken to illustrate this congenital nonauthenticity by portraying a poor Austrian wretch fleeing his Jewish environment and background (and only half-Jewish at that), trying to manufacture a new homeland, in Germany, in Switzerland, in France, and succeeding in creating at last in French literature an ideal, abstract homeland and taking root in it in an illusory and purely formal manner. André Gorz attempts to give a living interpretation of his master's thesis (who, incidentally prefaced his book) by conceiving Judaism solely as a form of human frustration imposed on the Jews by the others. It never occurs to him that Judaism presents a "choice" with a positive content, a civilization of essentially ethical inspiration and strict guidelines through the jungle of life.

Sartre's arguments, in spite of the nobility of his outlook, are weakened by an insufficient appreciation of the deliberate civilizing action of Jewish thought. The solution that he proposes to the dilemma inherent in the existence of Jews in an inadequate world, redemption through reason, is in the best French tradition. True, "there is no French truth, or a German, Negro, or Jewish truth. There is only one truth, and the best man discovers it." But it is in the name of this principle that Clermont-Tonnerre declared: "To the Jews as individuals everything, as a nation, nothing," inaugurating a century of tragi-comical camouflages and errors whose consequences have been analyzed in the other chapters of this work.[3]

On the other hand, Sartre's analysis of the Jewish problem during the Nazi era, his pitiless investigation

---

3. Cf. the anecdote told by Simone de Beauvoir in *La Force de l'âge* (*The Prime of Life*), p. 172, and her conclusion: "On a number of points, I was, and Sartre too—dreadfully abstract."

of moral responsibility to the ultimate limits of European society and bourgeois morality, elicits the admiration of all those who for years have been trying to clarify the problem of collective guilt.

For, fifteen years after the end of the National-Socialist nightmare, this event has not yet taken its place in what is called objective history. It continues to torment the survivors and keeps creating a malaise. As always, Sartre is able to formulate in dramatic dialogue the deepest emotions of his contemporaries, the various aspects of a moral problem that plagues the minds in spite of the disappearance of the conditions that gave it birth. It is the problem of the real responsibility for the horrors perpetrated by a gang of crime specialists that is presented in the play *Les Séquestrés d'Altona* (*The Prisoners of Altona*).

Franz von Gerlach, son of a big industrialist, has served on the Russian front. After Germany's total defeat, he shuts himself up for thirteen years in a room that he transforms into an altar dedicated to the cult of the Führer. Completely committed to the gospel of National-Socialism, he cannot accept the survival of a defeated Germany. "I know that everything is getting worse every minute . . . razed cities, broken machines, industry ruined, the sharp rise in unemployment and tuberculosis . . . we are defeated, we're being slaughtered."

He cannot accept the recovery of Germany without Hitler for yet another reason: was it not to protect her against annihilation that he blindly executed his orders, that he killed and tortured without pity? What other justification did the fatherland have, except self-defense? A prosperous Germany would be a horrible refutation of that belief. It would be the true condemnation of a generation of assassins, a condemnation beyond appeal.

"And since the German people accepts the abject ignominy forced on it, I have decided to keep one voice to yell: no! no! not guilty!"

His conscience atrophied by the poison of a sinister propaganda rationalizes with the reasoning: "Every time you spared the life of an enemy, even in the cradle, you took one of ours, or more simply: 'Germany is well worth a crime!' This perverted generation needs an agonizing Germany to prove the necessity of its inhuman behavior. Not all have invoked these reasons to carry out the acts demanded of them. Some practiced mental restrictions like Lieutenant Klages, the son of a pastor, who 'condemned the Nazis in his soul to keep from himself the fact that he served them with his body. . . .' He said to God: 'I disavow what I am doing!' But he did it."

Sartre, however, looks for the truly guilty ones in a completely different class of men, "the fathers" who had coldly speculated on the advantages that Nazi militarism would bring them: "These people are the masses on the throne. But they're waging wars to find us markets."

Thus, while detesting Hitler and Co., while disapproving of their methods and their massacres (after all, they had a humanistic education, didn't they? and, besides, they were good Christians), they made their peace with the government and reaped the maximum profits. Whereupon the son remarked accurately: "You provided Hitler with his warships and I provided him with corpses. What more could we have done if we had worshiped him?"

Seen from this angle, collective responsibility is not an empty word and extends even to the massacres and the systematic extermination of Jews. Certainly, they did not want that. But what could they do since they were powerless? This bourgeoisie, not at all anti-Semitic, "had chosen powerlessness," had comfortably ensconced itself in that position and consoled itself of having to submit to, although not necessarily to endure, events which it was "useless" to resist. Thanks to this tacit consent of a population resigned in advance (and who found this resignation to its advantage), Himmler was able to build his concentration camps and to proceed to "the final solution" of the Jewish question, without the knowledge of a world that never saw and never heard what went on behind the barbed wires.

It is, therefore, the compliance of the elders that was at the root of the depravation of millions of young Hitlerites who enthusiastically carried out the orders of the Führer. The son of an industrialist, Franz had at first obeyed his humanitarian impulse by saving the life of a Polish rabbi who had escaped from the camp and taken refuge on the von Gerlach estate. Franz discovers the poor man who, paralyzed by fear like a hunted animal, does not even hide, and he conceals him in his room. When the hiding place is about to be discovered, the father uses all his important connections to save his son, but he makes no move to defend the Jew who is shot before Franz's eyes. Once more the father compromises, since he has to survive. He, the Jew, does not survive, "but it is not my fault."

Franz's life, bought with that of the rabbi, has been deeply affected by his father's deal. The latter has handed over the prisoner to prevent the danger of discovery. "Doesn't that ever keep you from sleeping?" asks his daughter-in-law. "Never," the father answers calmly. For the father-generation has a clean conscience and the sons are not long in noticing that everything is allowed in a world where the results are the ultimate judges of one's actions. And they begin to practice the lessons they have learned on millions of other prisoners left to be shot.

The accused, in Sartre's play, are not only the Nazis, not even the German people alone, but a cowardly generation who had chosen helplessness and nonresistance to evil, who had chosen to compromise with it, and with apparent innocence, to enjoy its benefits. Fifteen years ago, Sartre had already written: "The Jewish blood that the Nazis shed falls on all our heads." And thus, before posterity, it is the whole period that is accused. The persecution of the Jews has developed into a formidable persecution of man. The rabbi, a real and symbolic figure, like all of Sartre's characters, is the key figure around which the drama of mankind is unfolding, going from catastrophe to catastrophe to its conclusion—perhaps its final conclusion by the atomic bomb—like the lamb in the song *Had Gadya,* whose cowardly murder provokes the series of disasters at the end of which appears the inexorable power of universal justice, presiding over the void.

23
Manès Sperber

The novel *La Baie perdue* (*The Lost Bay*) is an epic of the European underground under the German occupation. The most moving part, published separately with a preface by Malraux, is the section entitled *Qu'une larme dans l'océan* (*Only a Tear in the Ocean*) describing the war of extermination waged against the Jews. A series of hallucinating scenes evokes the atmosphere of indescribable terror that reigned in Poland during the time of the Einsatz-kommandos. Even though the author insists that there is only a loose connection with contemporary events, the situations he presents are marked by such realism, the characters of the protagonists in the various camps are so lifelike and drawn with such subtle insight that this dramatic tale has all the earmarks of truth.

The author makes us privy to the fate of the little town of Wolyna, one of hundreds characterized by a sizable Jewish population known for its piety and poverty. From the information provided by the author, Wolyna could be Strzyzow on the Wisloka, and the author himself probably comes from that province of the Austrian Empire that is now part of Poland. He is as familiar with the mentality of the Polish underground fighter as that of the Ruthene collaborators and the Nazi officers who ran the infernal death machinery. But above all, he understands and explains with infinite compassion the soul of the Polish Jew, molded by a civilization several thousand years old and filled with a nobility that never weakened, even during the times of supreme suffering. "Even the children understood that the Diaspora only repeated the story of Joseph. There were good Pharaohs, and there were bad ones. . . . God . . . while he does not prevent the appearance of evil, does not allow it to last. And in all things only endurance counts." This conviction of their endurance gives the humble victims a proud superiority over their tormentors.

However, this stoic wisdom that overcomes the partial pogroms with which the history of the Jews is paved, is liable this time to cause the irrevocable disappearance of the children of Israel. Manès Sperber's story would have been only an excellent piece of journalism had he not succeeded in dramatizing the almost metaphysical conflict of the Jewish community, faced by the dilemma of martyrdom or murder. The old rabbi, the "Zaddik" of Wolyna, and Edward Rubin, whose family has already been deported, are the protagonists of this conflict.

The rabbi is one of the innumerable "last of the Justs," preaching resignation to the will of God to their community, a collective calvary accepted as the fateful lot of the people of God: "For centuries the *auto-da-fés* have burned in Europe. Then it stopped for a while. . . . We have always waited and feared and that is how we live today. I am waiting for a sign that will tell me what the Almighty has in store for us" (p. 243).

But a few rebellious young Jews, temporarily saved from the massacre, refuse to listen to this talk any more, and Edward Rubin gives the rabbi his ultimatum: "Either the rabbi himself will urge the Jews capable of bearing arms to escape to the forest to die like men and not like sheep or else . . . he would stir up the population and go immediately into action." For Gentiles the answer is clear, unless they consider the Jew naturally predestined to the role of sacrificial lamb, as Schwartz-Bart maintains emphatically in his prize-winning novel. But, it is not out of cowardliness that the Just of Wolyna and the rabbis of numerous communities in Poland preached to their flock obedience to the S.S. up to the doors of the gas chambers. They were motivated by their conviction that they were not permitted to anticipate redemption before the appointed time, and that suffering was an act of purification for the chosen people: "The bloodthirsty enemy goes to his doom, his people will be humbled, but what concerns us is to know how we have deserved punishment in order to die with knowledge and expiation and not like our enemies in the blindness and darkness of the soul . . . we won't go to the woods, we will not die like murderers, but like martyrs."

The rabbi meets his chosen death, among his followers, but his young son Bynie joins the partisans, for his visionary spirit that will make him perform "miracles" shows him the advent of a new age that opens for his people: "I don't know the precise meaning of the arrival of the foreign Jew, nor why he asked us to defend ourselves. He is a gentle man, deep down, and yet with a toughness that I have not seen in any other human being. What does that prove? That proves that he is not acting according to his own will but to a superior will." This toughness grafted on innate goodness manifests itself soon afterward in the unparalleled struggle of the Warsaw Ghetto, and it characterizes the fighters who, not by arms, but with their soul, have brought about the resurrection of Israel. Is not this the sign of a superior will that the ghetto children waited for in vain on their useless calvary?

This is not said to accuse the millions of innocent victims, made gentle and peaceful by the prolonged influence of the Torah. Around them, in the Polish population, so many enemies and no support! Several sources confirm the episode reported by Sperber: "In Warsaw I saw a parade of children. A man was leading them, with a little girl in his arms. At the intersections trolleys stopped to make way for the parade of little Jews taken from the children's home to be led to the gas chambers. The leader, director of the home, did not look at the passersby. He expected no help, no word of pity. In the street, in the trolley, nothing but Poles." Even in the underground the Jews had to fight against the partisans as much as against the common enemy. In numerous situations, the only answer could consist only in this attitude of sublime dignity: "God is just, he makes us the victims and you the torturers." And even when the young rabbi Bynie chooses to resist, he suffers more in his soul at the prospect of killing than his father did in his body under the torture of the S.S. For "the act of killing makes no sense. . . . Try to describe a battle, you'll notice that the sum of all the exploits are more insignificant, more formless than a tear in the ocean."

It was perhaps the greatest, the supreme trial imposed on the Jewish soul, to resign itself to hastening its redemption by acts of violence. This trial, by causing the tears of the victims to overflow, was perhaps the decisive factor in the scale of the Providence that decides the fate of people.

By formulating these serious problems, "eliciting from the events alone the capital questions that they contain," *Qu'une larme dans l'océan* is, according to Malraux's expression, "one of the great tales of Israel."

24
Three Goncourt Prizes
Romain Gary, Roger Ikor, André
Schwarz-Bart

As if to give this book a sensational ending, the theme studied through the whole history of literature has just won an unexpected fame by the award of the highest distinction known in French literature to three successive Jewish authors, naturalized Frenchmen but Jewish not only by their background but also by the subjects of their novels. Jewish writing in the French language, which for centuries had led an honorable but not brilliant existence, has suddenly been raised to the rank of great literature.

This dazzling triumph does not exempt us, however, from a rigorously objective analysis of the prize-winning works, an analysis that will be critical, even severe, for the simple reason that their subjects are vitally significant today and reflect not only their authors but the world from which they come and represent before the French nation and the international public.

We shall proceed according to a logical rather than a chronological order and deal first with the two novels that belong more directly to Judeo-French literature: *Les Eaux mêlées* (*The Mingled Waters*) and *Le Dernier des Justes* (*The Last of the Justs*), beginning with the second, which is the latest to be published but which has caused one of the biggest stirs in the literary world.

André Schwarz-Bart

In *The Last of the Justs,* the author undertakes to tell the story of Jewish martyrdom under Nazi domination. It is a strange book, based on the abundant documentation that we possess on this period, but which aims at a metaphysical and theological explanation of the most atrocious tragedy in Jewish history. With that in mind, the author summarizes the series of bloody persecutions perpetrated from the times of the Crusades to the "Thousand Year Empire," through a chronicle of the Juste family, which gives each generation a sacrificial lamb, carrying the sufferings of his people. This "Juste" for each generation assures the unity of action to the innumerable aspects of anti-Semitic persecutions through the ages.

This device is not a simple invention on the part of the author. He draws on a Talmudic legend according to which mankind, in spite of its moral perversion, is saved from destruction thanks to thirty-six just men, the *Lamed-Vav,* unknown and humble, who redeem the evils of universal sin by their virtues. Their role is that of the ten just men whose existence might have saved Sodom and Gomorrah from destruction.

Schwarz-Bart, like Fleg writing a *Légende des siècles* of Jewish history, seriously studied or at least tried seriously to draw his philosophy of Jewish history, if not from official texts, at least from the Jewish folklore known to the child of a family of Polish Jews settled in Lorraine. But since as a young underground fighter he did not receive a systematic Jewish education, he gave the scattered elements of his childhood memories a completely erroneous interpretation to the point of falsifying the idea of the legend that is the leitmotiv of his novel.

The book is filled with distorted memories, and shocks any reader the least bit familiar with the subject. What is worse, the interpretation of the events conflicts with Jewish tradition. And, while crushed by the tragedy of which he, you, and I were the helpless witnesses and the last survivors, whether just or not, he wants to pay a grieving tribute to the six million victims, he betrays the nature of their martyrdom by interpreting it in contradiction with authentic Judaism.

Judaism has never adopted the thesis of a sacrificial lamb, individual or people, destined to assume the sins of mankind. The ceremony of the scapegoat during the Day of Atonement was a religious rite taking on the character of a symbol to express the innate redeeming power of contrition of the sinner himself. Never and nowhere in the Scriptures is the human holocaust considered an ideal.

Isaac's sacrifice is refused by God from the beginnings of Judaism, which, far from glorifying "a holy death," never stopped preaching respect for life in all circumstances, except when it can only be saved by mortal sin against God and man. The training for martyrdom, such as the last of the Justs practices with the help of his grandfather Mardochée, is thus nothing but the latest of errors written in good faith about Judaism. For the latter, life is not a systematic preparation for a noble death, but for a noble life with justice. The ideal of the *Tsadik,* the just, consists in the exemplary life of the pious man practicing goodness and equity. That is the whole secret of the *Lamed-Vav,* of the thirty-six just men who, by their noble example, uplift mankind and keep it from sinking into the neglect of the fundamental principles of morality and elementary social laws; no other secret password of initiates is learned from father to son in a so-called dynasty of just men, of which Ernie Levy would be the last. On that point in particular, the

author distorts the noble legend of the *Lamed-Vavs*,
when for example, the protagonists speak of themselves
in these terms: "I, who am a just man," like someone
who would say: "I who am modest." This basic error
is at the root of ridiculous scenes like this one, for instance: a delegation made up of the leading notables of
Zemyock goes to the bedside of the Just to tell him
about the widespread fear (for he has sired another
child besides the *Lamed-Vav,* who is a sufficient heir to
perpetuate the dynasty of the Justs) and they tell him
in substance: "Oh, venerable Just, what have you done?
Your ancestors produced a son, then died. Tell us, then,
if the child you are expecting is also a boy, who will
be your spiritual heir? Which of the two will be the
Lamed-Vav?" Whereupon the poor Just, bewildered by
the arguments of his followers grown skeptical, exclaims
in desperation: "Why do you harass me? . . . . It is not
up to me to decide these things. I haven't done anything
to delay my death" (p. 32).

The book is replete with scenes like this one, designed
to substantiate the absolutely paradoxical thesis that the
real Justs seek suffering and death and that they prepare
for it "according to the immemorial Jewish technique of
humiliation" (p. 278) and "that the Jewish heart must
break a thousand times for the greatest good of the
world, that is why we have been chosen" (p. 299). This
last idea is a false interpretation of the Spanish philosopher Juda Halevi, according to which the Jewish people
represents the heart in the universal organism that is
formed by the totality of nations. But if it is true that
mystically "the just man guesses all the evil that exists
in the world, and takes it in his heart" (p. 164), it is
not so that the people might offer a holocaust to God,
or to represent, according to François Mauriac, the agony
of Christ until the end of the world (*Express,* 8 October
1959). The Talmud recognizes a redeeming force guar-

anteeing the survival of mankind when it says: "The
world survives only thanks to the breath of little school
children," but that does not mean that it survives through
the murder of these innocent little schoolboys. When they
are sacrificed on the altar of human barbarism, they
certainly are not on the altar of God, who demands
"obedience, not sacrifice," life with justice, not death
with injustice.

The Christian interpretation of Jewish history found
followers among writers living on the fringe of authentic
Judaism, such as Margarette Sussmann with her book
Job and André Schwarz-Bart, whose grandfather was
still a practicing Jew, whose father was familiar with
Jewish traditions, but for whom Jewish traditions and
practices are sentimental and venerable reminiscences,
often misunderstood. He unconsciously adopts the viewpoint of his Christian environment, which perhaps was
not without importance in the verdict of the jury award-
ing the Goncourt Prize, just as the theme of total assimilation defended by Roger Ikor in *Les Eaux mêlées* could
not have displeased it. No doubt it was also motivated
by generous feelings, by an emotion akin to that gen-
erated by the Anne Frank case, and it wanted to express
its sympathy to the innumerable victims of a tragedy
without precedent, of an indescribable tragedy. For, after
all, the priests in the temple of literature can, at the
appropriate time, give precedence to the noble testimony
of a suffering heart over the qualities of an often clumsy
style.

And they are right, in spite of Gide, according to
whom "it is with noble emotions that bad literature is
made." For where Schwarz-Bart lets his heart speak,
nothing but his heart, and his personal experiences, free
of perfunctory theology, he draws from his harp such
heartbreaking accents that the reader is overwhelmed.
We are looking then, not at a book, but a face branded

with the calvary and the death of a people. And when as he starts the last chapter, the author exclaims "I am so weary that my pen cannot write any more," this sigh blends with the sobs of the reader, of the survivors weeping over the fate of their loved ones, deported and lost somewhere in Poland.

Schwarz-Bart does not have to defend himself, at least here, against those who accused him of extensive plagiarism, with the argument that he never was in a gas chamber and he had to use available documents. His agony is not any the less true than that of Anne Frank, literally killed; or, to remain in the literary field, his story is just as credible as Goethe's description of the suicide of young Werther or Romain Rolland's scene of the death of Jean-Christophe, the only difference being that Schwarz-Bart's hero dies six million times.

Thus, it is with two or three chapters that the author redeemed a book often too painful to read because of its dilletantish ignorance and especially because of its too-passive acceptance of persecution as a law of nature. For the real last chapter of the extermination, the one in which the survivors of the ghetto began to react against their fate, was also the first chapter of the national resurrection of Israel, when the helpless victims marked for martyrdom resolutely became fighters, conquerors of their country, not to die in it, but to live the life of the Just.

Roger Ikor

If Schwarz-Bart's novel is the work of a high-minded beginner who writes clumsily but with his heart's blood, Roger Ikor is an excellent writer who is thoroughly versed in the techniques of his craft and who very often is a remarkable psychologist. But his thesis developed in 616 pages is frankly "defeatist," harmful to a healthy concept of the Judeo-French symbiosis. In the novel *Les*

Fils d'Avrom (*The Sons of Avrom*),[1] Roger Ikor examines the process of assimilation of immigrants of Russian and Polish origin, their progressive adjustment to the mores of the host country, until they lose their originality completely, until they are totally recast in the crucible of the French nation. This thesis, extremely praiseworthy in the eyes of an earnest jury, no doubt earned the author the first prize awarded to Judeo-French literature.

The major thesis of the novel is stated at the very beginning of the section *Les Eaux Mêlées: Le Fleuve coulait vers la mer* (*The Mingled Waters: The River Flowed to the Sea*). All the currents mingle and dissolve in it to form a great homogeneous mass, and similarly the currents of immigration are fated to dissolve in the French crucible and all the foreign elements to be absorbed by the French race, homogeneous, pacifying, standardizing. This process is symbolized by the story of Avrom Mykhanowitski and his sons who flee pogrom-ridden Russia and seek asylum in France. The story revolves around the eldest son, Yankel, humble hatmaker, with little knowledge of things Jewish, but enamored of the great humanitarian ideas that since Napoleon's campaigns fascinated the poor craftsmen of Eastern Europe's ghettos. Yankel's great ambition is to identify himself with his new homeland, and he teaches love of France to his sons more than love for their hereditary religion.

The author himself seems to have only vague recollections of his ancestral religion, judging by the way he describes, for instance, the ceremony of the night of Passover, the *Seder,* although it is such a popular ceremony: "The next step is to sit down to eat and to laugh whole-heartedly. . . . At a certain point the father dips his little finger ten times in a glass of wine, then shakes

---

1. Novel in two parts: *La Greffe de printemps* (*The Graft of Spring*) and *Les Eaux mêlées* (*The Mingled Waters*).

it while he recalls in Hebrew the ten plagues of Egypt.
. . . And their eyes and their hearts are full of laughter,
for they must laugh . . . and by dint of laughing they
become truly filled with joy."

"Here they start laughing in earnest." Where did the
author gather his information to give so weird a description of Passover? When he reaches the part where laughter would be justified—that is, where the children are
"to steal" the piece of unleavened bread for the ritual
"dessert" and return it only in exchange for a modest
ransom, a custom introduced to keep the attention of the
children through the lengthy ceremony—he makes of this
folk rite a drama and a caricature: "The lucky thief had
the right to express any wish and the victim had to grant
it! But old man Avrom is suspicious. . . . Simon sneaked
stealthily behind him and, whoops, he had the matzoh.
. . . The grandfather took it very badly! 'Simon, give
it back to me immediately' . . . and worriedly: what if
the kid were to ask him for 100,000 francs! To pay his
debt the old man would have sold his store, even his shirt
without hesitation. But, of course, he preferred to avoid
it."

This story is simply ridiculous, but very useful to show
the author's complete lack of background in Jewish traditions. They are for him distant and bizarre memories
seen through the eyes of a thoroughly assimilated
Frenchman. He is closer to the French soul than to the
Jewish soul and the French types he portrays are far
more authentic than the clichés of the Jews in the fore-
ground of the novel. Only Simon Yankel's son, who is
successful in business and gains access to the French peasant class, where he finds a wife and is completely assimilated, gives a feeling of authenticity because he is
endowed with certain autobiographical traits. Bothered
by his origin as well as by the temptation to deny it, he
adopts the formula: "I, who am of Jewish background,"

and finally succeeds in being like everybody else. The author thus quietly marks the path to assimilation which is the thesis of his book, the progressive loosening of Jewish ties and the systematic integration into the new milieu. "His ties with the old Mykhanowitzkis had, of necessity, been loosened; they became more solid with Baptiste, without ever becoming too strong," for the author is too intelligent to underestimate the persistence of a difference developed over several thousand years of history.

This difference survives even after the calvary suffered in common under the yoke of German occupation and after the death of Yankel's grandson, the half-Jew Jean-Claude Mykhanowitzki "martyr of freedom and the fatherland, executed by the German barbarians at the age of eighteen, June 4, 1944." "All these crosses on all these tombs, how they looked at him! What is this Jew doing here?" they said. And Yankel hunched his back. A beautiful cemetery, yes. But not for Jews. For Christians, for the masters, for Aryans." The Catholic and Jewish grandfathers, Baptiste and Yankel, each claims the beloved tomb for himself: "Baptiste did not seem the least bit disposed to give up his place. It even seemed to Yankel that he stayed on purpose. For no reason, just to annoy him, Yankel, the Jewish grandfather! Did he think he had a priority because he was Aryan? Jean-Claude is my grandson as much as his, he told himself once more. More even, since it's on the male side!" (p. 50).[2]

He, Yankel, would gladly welcome all Aryan relations; he takes pride in these relations and studies with deep satisfaction the infinite combinations of blood and names: "How many other Mykhanowitzkis are hidden in the telephone books behind their trade names? And women

---

2. False arguments according to Jewish teachings, which recognize the rights of the mother.

behind their husbands' names? . . . Mykhanowitzki (René), pastor. . . . But I have to look up the Touquets too . . . and the Cheysans? Well! There is a General Cheysan? Hmm! Yankel didn't know that his granddaughter now belonged to the family of a general and he was very excited. . . . And the Saulniers? He never thought of looking up the Saulniers. After all, they were cousins too, weren't they? He finds a professor in the lot and there too he gargles with the word, pronounced with a Russian accent: rolled 'r' and accent on the last syllable. Then he goes back to the Paris telephone book and stands back frightened, for there are almost as many Saulniers as Levys. How can he recognize his relations in there? And he muses for a long time on the two telephone books. Ah! we are really mixed up, all together! he thinks vaguely" (p. 611).

Thus, toward the end of his life, Yankel finds his dreams fulfilled, his snobbishness satisfied: for we are snobs to the best of our abilities, with the means at our disposal, and Yankel's dream of acceptance by the Saulnier family is not less ambitious than Marcel Proust's to be welcomed by the Guermantes. And this Jewish graft of the French tree is bound to appeal to the jury of the Goncourt Prize, eager to reward the spokesman of such a democratic thesis, especially since it leads to the Cross.

The Jewish ancestor of the Mykha-Saulnier fusion is so delighted at the result of his ambition that he even contemplates attempting the gamble of a mixed marriage, belated, it is true, but a logical conclusion of a thesis developed with so much spirit.

This final temptation of the old man, central figure of the novel, betrays the weakness of his character and the fragility of his theory of assimilation, although the history of his family is typical of a great number of Jews who underwent the same experience. It is a modest artisan, for whom the whole spiritual tradition of Judaism is reduced to a few vague sentimental memories whom the author chooses as spokesman for his philosophy of assimilation, an assimilation from the bottom, for the author never considers in this voluminous work the loftier accomplishments of French thought, from whose association Jewish thought would benefit. Yankel grasps only the superficial aspects of the French mind, and he is not enchanted. "These Frenchmen were always in motion, they seized an idea, abandoned it for another, and mixed exasperatingly jokes and serious subjects. They were seen in one place, and immediately tchip, tchip, they were someplace else! Superficial minds! Impossible to talk with them!" (p. 55).

Nevertheless, Yankel, without understanding the true character of the France that attracts him, and without knowing the true wealth of the Judaism that he is abandoning more decisively than he fled pogrom-ridden Russia, is a gentle example of the tribe that through the mouth of the lawgiver of the Old Testament as well as by the preacher of the New Testament proclaimed the doctrine: "Love one another." And he retains, in spite of his social aspirations, a nostalgic attachment to his roots: "If I love the Jews, it is not because I am one of them. . . . But I know our Jews. They're not mean, that's why I love them. You can find thieves and crooks among us, all kinds of rotten characters, as anywhere else: men are all the same, aren't they? But murderers, no. There are no murderers among us. The Jew is too kind to kill, even animals. Do you see Jews who go hunting? No, right? There you are. The Jew knows the value of suffering. He knows that nothing makes up for it. Suffering experienced is suffering experienced. Irreparable. So what do you have against us? Why do you persecute us? We are the meekest of men!" (p. 25).

We can legitimately interpret Yankel's words, spoken on the tomb of his murdered grandson, as the author's

Jewish confession of faith, and perhaps, too, as a vague doubt about the legitimacy of his own thesis. For is it not worthwhile to conserve a human tribe that incarnates pacifism, and to preserve the purity of its waters?

Romain Gary

Romain Gary received the Goncourt Prize in 1956 for *Les Racines du ciel* (*The Roots of Heaven*).[3] His latest and most revealing work, *La Promesse de l'aube* (*The Promise of Dawn*), was published in 1960. This is the book that furnishes the key to an understanding of *Les Racines du ciel*.

This novel seems, at first sight, nothing but a slightly violent plea for the protection of nature. A "mad Frenchman," Morel, undertakes a campaign in Africa for the defense of the elephants threatened with extermination by the foreign and the native hunters. In view of the ineffectiveness of "legal methods" he goes underground and, attacked and ridiculed, wages at the risk of his own life a guerrilla fight for the respect of what he calls "human dignity" beyond doctrines and political and social ideologies.

It finally becomes clear that his defense of the elephants becomes more than the protection of a zoological species, although the story never loses its documentary quality. The book does indeed deal with the African fauna and it is full of magnificent images conveying the wild beauty of the black continent. But Morel's passion is more transcendental, and the fight he wages with his gun and his whip is not motivated merely by his concern for the threatened animal. The elephant becomes the symbol of the greatness, of the moral values that, in the face of technical progress and modern society, do not

---

3. Romain Gary is also the author of *L'Éducation européenne* (*A European Education*), a novel about the Resistance which contains a few poignant Jewish scenes.

seem to have any reason for surviving. Even in peacetime there is no truce in this existential struggle. "I believe in individual freedom, in tolerance, and in human rights. Maybe these too are outmoded and anachronistic elephants, embarrassing survivors of a bygone geological era, that of humanism," says the author in a brief introductory note referring to the sufferings that have preceded that confession. "The history of this century has proved in a bloody and conclusive manner, in my family six dead out of eight, and among my fellow pilots of 1940, five survivors out of two hundred, that the nationalistic alibi is always exploited by the gravediggers of freedom."

In the autobiographical work, *La Promesse de l'aube,* Romain Gary tells us more about the factors that have determined his personal position and his humanitarian philosophy. First of all, this book is a moving tribute to his Jewish mother, a Russian woman, eccentric and mad in the eyes of her new French compatriots, who molds her son in her fashion and prepares him for an extraordinary career. "Dirty little bourgeois cockroaches! You don't know whom you have the honor to speak to. My son will be ambassador of France, knight of the Legion of Honor, a great playwright, Ibsen, Gabriele D'Annunzio!" And the author adds: "It might be advisable to mention immediately, for the clearness of the story, that I am today general consul of France, Companion of the Liberation, Officer of the Legion of Honor, and if I have become neither Ibsen nor D'Annunzio, it is not for lack of trying" (p. 50).

And he has equally fulfilled the promise tacitly made to that mother to accomplish everything she expected from him in the sphere of heroism and self-realization. Rarely has filial piety expressed itself with greater affection, sensitivity, insight, gratitude. "If all my books are full of appeals to dignity, to justice, if my characters speak so often and so loftily of the honor of being a man, it is perhaps because I was supported until I was twenty-two, by the labor of an old woman, sick and overworked" (p. 185).

There is no reference to the father where "Tartar and Jewish ancestors" are mentioned without indicating whether they are on the father's or the mother's side. But without having known his father and without having felt his direct influence, Romain Gary feels that he has toward him an incalculable spiritual debt, an atavistic consanguinity, accentuated by the tragedy of six million of his fellow Jews. "I knew that he had died during the war in a gas chamber, executed as a Jew with his wife and two children. But it is only in 1956 that I learned a particularly revolting detail of his tragic end. He had not died in a gas chamber, as I had been told. He had died of fright on the way to his execution, a few steps from the entrance . . . he fell, literally frightened to death before entering. . . . The man who died this way had been a stranger to me, but that day he became my father, forever" (p. 105).

Thus, it is through the heritage of his parents that Gary recognizes himself always and instantly in all those who suffer, man or even beast. "An incredible number of people can attend a bullfight, look at the wounded and bleeding bull without shuddering. Not me. I am the bull." This recalls a comment of Heinrich Heine, who, under any circumstance, felt close not to the hunter, but to the hunted. It recalls especially the Talmudic doctrine according to which God is always on the side of the persecuted, whether guilty or not.

These atavistic or conscious influences have favored in Romain Gary the decision to struggle against backward forces, or even against the limitations that nature herself seems to impose on man, on what is known as the human condition. "I began to conceive man as a revolutionary experiment in conflict with his own biological, moral, and intellectual nature. The more I looked at my mother's aged, tired face, the more my sense of injustice and the desire to reform the world and to make it honorable grew in me" (p. 161). It is, however, dangerous not to respect the barriers set up by nature and an inert society, which is like an extension of our biological servitude. "I thoroughly understand those who had refused to follow DeGaulle. They were ensconced too comfortably in their furniture that they called the human condition. They were right from the point of view of cleverness, prudence, the rejection of risks, of the gamble, from the viewpoint that would have kept Jesus from dying on the Cross, Van Gogh from painting, my Morel from defending his elephants, the French from being shot, and would have united in the same void, cathedrals, museums, empires and civilizations, by preventing their birth" (p. 266).

While the author is identified as a disciple of Malraux by his idealism and his pursuit of an ethical heroism, by revealing the deeper sources of his spiritual training, he also elucidates the meaning of the rebellion of a Morel, who prefers the company of elephants to that of man, who would practically prefer to change species, transcend the natural state of man forgetful of his heavenly roots. This elephant story is really an indictment of the complacency of our time, of "the evils from which we have been suffering for such a long time, racism, absurd nationalism, dreams of domination, of power, of expansion," and it is a vibrant appeal to faith in something greater than ourselves, to true greatness that gives victims so great a superiority over their persecutors: "The idea that there was still in us something that they could not reach, a fiction, a myth that they could not take away from us, and that helped us to endure, drove them wild," says one of the prisoners of war (*Racines du ciel*, p. 49).

That is why in this story of elephants there is such a

constant preoccupation with atrocities committed by the worshipers of a false greatness. The author, unlike many colleagues who have returned to the pleasures of existence, is haunted by recollections that attack him all the time, by lampshades made of human skin, by bones transformed into gelatin and soap, by the fundamental indifference of the spectators, even their irritation, not against the persecutors, but the victims. "The irritation that we experience involuntarily when cripples strike our eyes a little too painfully. . . . They are unpleasant. We pity their sufferings, of course. But we resent a little the fact that they survived. It is partially in the name of this idea that the German theoretician of racism preached the extermination of the Jews: they had been made to suffer too much, and consequently they could henceforth only be enemies of mankind" (p. 103).

In passages like the following, expressed in a sarcastic and unequivocal symbolism, the author finally reveals the basic idea that preoccupies him throughout Morel's elephant adventure: "At the beginning, it is said, for instance, that elephants are too big, too cumbersome, that they knock over telephone poles, crush the crops, that they are an anachronism, and finally the same thing is said about freedom, freedom and man wind up being cumbersome" (p. 193).

Is it still necessary to explain why Romain Gary's book is used as a conclusion, not only to the three Goncourt Prizes won by Jewish writers, but also to the long and difficult attempt to trace the presence of Judaism in French literature. Here is a writer eminently successful in every aspect of his career, and whose services to his adopted country have been generously recognized and rewarded, but, who, at the pinnacle of fame, makes a proud confession of Jewish faith. Not a dogmatic confession, but in the form of a moving homage to the deepest roots of his person and his thinking. When a

French education, that is to say humanistic, has been grafted on traditions going back to the dawn of civilization, we have a modern knight wielding a sword and a pen, hungry for justice, for liberty, for love, "these roots of heaven so deeply sunk in his breast." Is there a better illustration of the stimulating influence of the Jewish element on French literature?

Epilogue

Malraux

A conclusion? We have drawn one at every turn of modern literature, at every new aspect that it presented. The definitive conclusion, the general impression, must be left to the reader, our closest collaborator, our faithful companion on a long and twisting road.

Yet this book must conclude with words that place the subject on a different plane from literature in the strict sense of the word. And these words can be spoken only by a man who is not only a brilliant representative of French letters but who, for a generation, has been at all the crossroads of contemporary history, who has fought with the pen and the sword on all the battlefields of Western civilization: André Malraux. His view on the concept of Israel is that of a visionary who, like Charles Péguy, prizes not its temporal, political value, but its mystical value, its roots of heaven that Malraux calls the roots of the soul, and through which the Jewish element vivifies the spirit of the nations of the world. "Israel[1] was perhaps the only Eastern people who took God completely seriously. Martyrdom was not absurd, because the martyr was God's witness; military courage was absurd, because ultimate victory depended only on God. Men were not born to conquer, destroy, or convert the infidels but to gather together to praise the Almighty.

---

1. In *Israël*, album d'Izis, preface by Malraux.

The sword of Islam will be covered with the same sand as the Macedonian spears and the Roman standards: God alone and God's teachings. Akiba, Israel's sage, joined the insurgents of Bar-Kocheba. But Rabbi Yochanan ben Zakkai, as wise and as famous, had accepted obedience to Rome on the condition that the Torah be respected. The teachings insured, more surely than rebellion, the survival of the indestructible people that grows only from the roots of the soul." We are inevitably reminded by these two figures, in which Malraux recognizes the two poles of the Jewish genius, of the dialogue in the novel by Manès Sperber[2] between the "Just" of Wolyna and Edward Rubin, about resistance through the underground or through martyrdom. The wars of Israel are waged on yet another plane: "The army of Israel seems like the revolutionary militia of an unknown revolution . . . these fighters are not wholly soldiers, this nation is not like the old nations of Europe, nor the nations of America created by uprooted energies. . . . Its people of city-dwellers does not want to forget metaphysics as it discovers the plow, its people ravaged by God and almost as much as by justice does not want to forget that when it discovers the reason of state. . . . Everything is tied to the invincible past from which the Almighty has not been expelled."

---

2. See above, chap. 23.

Bibliography

Ch. ADAM, *Vie et œuvres de Descartes*, Paris, 1910.

Jean ANOUILH, *L'Invitation au Château*.

Marquis d'ARGENS, *Lettres Juives*, Haag, 1736.

P. AUBERY, *Milieux juif dans la France contemporaine*. (Plon, 1957.)

BALZAC, *Œuvres*.

M. BARRÈS, *Scènes et doctrines du nationalisme* (Plon).

— *Les diverses familles spirituelles de la France*, Paris, 1917.

A.-J. BAUMGARTNER, *Calvin hébraïsant et interprète de l'Ancien Testament*, 1889.

BAZARD-ENFANTIN, *Doctrine de Saint-Simon*, Paris, 1829.

BÉDARRIDE, *Les Juifs en France, en Italie, en Espagne*, Paris, 1859.

Julien BENDA, *Jeunesse d'un clerc*.

— *Exercices d'un enterré vif*.

P. BENOIT, *Le Puits de Jacob*.

Henri BERNSTEIN, *Israël*.

E.-R. BEVAN-Ch. SINGER, *The Legacy of Israel*, Oxford, 1928.

H. BIEBER, *Heinrich Heines Confessio Judaica*, Berlin, 1925.

J.-R. BLOCH, — *Et Cie*.

J. BLOCH et E. LÉVY, *Histoire littéraire juive d'après G. Karpeles*, Paris, 1901.

M. BLOCH, *La femme juive dans le roman et au théâtre*, R. E. J., t. XXIV.

D.-S. BLONDHEIM, *Textes judéo-romains*, Romania XLIX.

— *Contributions à l'étude de la poésie judéo-française*, dans Mélanges offerts à M. J. Lévi, Durlacher, 1926.

R. DE BONNIÈRES, *Les Monach*.

P. BOURGET, *Cosmopolis*.

BOSSUET, *Discours sur l'histoire universelle*.

F. BRUNETIÈRE, *Etudes crit. s. l'hist. de la litt. fr.* Paris, 1903.

— *Nouveaux essais sur la litt. contemporaine*, Paris, 1897.

CARMOLY, *La France israélite*, Francfort, 1858.

Guy des CARS, *Le château de la juive*.

G. CATTAUI, *L'amitié de Proust*, Cahiers M. Proust, N° 8.

CHATEAUBRIAND, *Itinéraire*, dans Œuvres.

Joseph CHÉNIER, *Nathan le Sage*.

P. CLAUDEL, *Le pain dur*.

— *Le père humilié*.

G. COHEN, *Histoire de la mise en scène dans le théâtre religieux français du moyen âge*, Paris, 1926.

Albert COHEN, *Solal*.

— *Mangeclous*.

— *Paroles juives*.

— *Le livre de ma mère*.

A. COMBRIS, *La philosophie des races du comte de Gobineau et sa portée actuelle*, Thèse Clermont, 1937.

B. CRÉMIEUX, *XX⁴ siècle*, Paris, 1924 (Gallimard).

— *Du côté de Marcel Proust*, Lemarget, 1929.

E.-R. CURTIUS, *Marcel Proust*, éd. franc. : La Revue Nouvelle, 1928.

A. DARMSTETER, *Deux élégies du Vatican*, Romania III.

— *L'autodafé de Troyes de 1288*, R. E. J. II (1881).

Léon DAUDET, *Le Pays des parlementaires*, Paris, 1901.

S. DE BEAUVOIR, *La Force de l'âge*.

M. DEBRÉ, *Der Jude in der französischen Literatur von 1800 bis zur Gegenwart*, thèse, Wurzbourg, 1908.

C. DELHORBE, *L'affaire Dreyfus et les écrivains français*, thèse, Lausanne, 1932.

DIDEROT, *Œuvres*.

— *Encyclopédie*.

M. DONNAY, *Le Retour de Jérusalem*.

A. DREYFUS, *Les Juifs au Théâtre*, Conférence R. E. J., 1886.

E. DRUMONT, *La France juive*, Paris, 1886.

G. DUHAMEL, *Chronique des Pasquier*.

A. DUMAS, fils, *La femme de Claude*.

H. EMMRICH, *Die Juden bei Voltaire*, thèse, Breslau, 1930.

E. FAGUET, *La tragédie française au XVI⁴ siècle*, 1897.

E. FLEG, *Le Mur des pleurs*.

— *Œuvres poétiques et théâtrales*.

— *Anthologie juive*.

— *Jésus, raconté par le Juif Errant*.

— *Moïse, raconté par les sages*.

— *Salomon, raconté par les peuples*.

— *Vers le Monde qui vient*.

Ch. Fourrier, *Théorie de l'unité universelle*, Paris, 1843.

Anatole France, *L'Anneau d'améthyste*.

— *L'Ile des Pingouins*.

— *Le Procurateur de Judée*.

H. Franck, *La Danse devant l'Arche*, préface d'Anna de Noailles.

J. Frénel, *L'Ancien Testament et la langue française du moyen âge*, thèse, Paris, 1904.

R. Martin du Gard, *Jean Barois*.

— *Les Thibault*.

Robert Garnier, *Sédécie ou Les Juives*.

Romain Gary, *Les racines du ciel*.

— *Education européenne*.

— *La Promesse de l'aube*.

Gautier de Coincy, *Les Miracles de la Sainte Vierge*, éd. Abbé Poquet, 1857. Nouv. éd. Langfors, Helsinki, 1937.

André Gide, *Journal*.

Gobineau, *Essai sur l'inégalité des races humaines*, Paris, 1884.

E. et J. Goncourt, *Manette Salomon*.

A. Gorz, *Le traître*.

Abbé Grégoire, *Essai sur la régénération physique, morale et politique des Juifs*, Paris, 1788.

Abbé Guénée, *Lettres de quelques Juifs portugais et allemands, à M. de Voltaire*, Paris, 1769.

H. Heine, *Hebräische Melodien*.

H. Hertz, *Vers un monde volage*.

V. Hugo, *Œuvres*.

R. Ikor, *Les fils d'Avrom : La greffe du printemps ; Les eaux mêlées*.

J. Jacobs, *Jewish Contributions to civilization*, Philadelphia, 1919.

V. Jankélévitch, *Henri Bergson*, Paris, 1959.

J. Jéhouda, *La tragédie d'Israël*.

A. Jubinal, *Mystères inédits du XVe siècle*, Paris, 1837.

P. de Juleville, *Histoire de la langue et de la littérature françaises*.

Gustave Kahn, *Contes juifs*.

— *Vieil Orient, Orient neuf*.

— *Images bibliques*.

Zadoc Kahn, *Les Juifs à Paris depuis le VIe siècle*.

Kayserling, *Die jüdischen Frauen in der Geschichte, Literatur und Kunst*, Leipzig, 1879.

H. Kohn, *L'Humanisme juif*, Paris, Rieder.

B. KRAKOWSKI, *La Psychologie des peuples allemand et juif dans les romans de Romain Rolland*, Toulouse, 1931.

J. DE LACRETELLE, *Silbermann*.

— *Le Retour de Silbermann*.

LAMARTINE, *Voyage en Orient*.

DRIEU LA ROCHELLE, *Gilles*.

E. LAVISSE, *Histoire de France*.

B. LAZARE, *L'Antisémitisme, son histoire et ses causes*, Paris, 1894.

C. LEHRMANN, *Jüdische Geschichte und Weltgeschichte*, 1956.

— *Israels Auserwähltheit als ethische Verpflichtung*, 1958.

— *Juden in der Literatur, und jüdische Literatur*, 1961.

A. LEROY-BEAULIEU, *Les Juifs et l'antisémitisme*, 1893.

E. LE ROY, *Epoques de l'Histoire de France en rapport avec le Théâtre*.

J. LICHTENSTEIN, *Racine, poète biblique*, Neuchâtel, 1932.

M. LIFSCHUTZ-GOLDEN, *Les Juifs dans la littérature française du moyen âge*, thèse, Columbia, 1935.

Prince de LIGNE, *Mémoire pour la cause sioniste*.

J. LOEB, *La Controverse religieuse entre les Chrétiens et les Juifs au moyen âge*, Paris, 1888.

H. LÖWE, *Die Juden in der Marienlegende*, Berlin, 1912.

A. LONDRES, *Le Juif errant est arrivé*.

Armand LUNEL, *Esther à Carpentras*.

— *Nicolo Peccavi*.

G. DE MAUPASSANT, *Mademoiselle Fifi*.

— *Bel Ami*.

André MALRAUX, *Préface à Israël, album d'Izis*.

F. MAURIAC, *Thérèse Desqueroux*.

J. MILBAUER, *Poèmes juifs*.

MIRABEAU, *Sur Moses Mendelsohn, sur la réforme politique des Juifs...*, 1787.

A. DE MONTAIGLON, *Recueil de Fabliaux I*, Paris, 1872.

MONTESQUIEU, *Lettres persanes*.

— *Esprit des Lois*.

Mystère de la Passion d'Arnould Gréban, éd. G. Paris et Raymond, Paris, 1878.

Mystère de la Passion, éd. J.-M. Richard, Arras, 1891.

Mystère de la Passion et Résurrection de Jean Michel, éd. Kruse, thèse, Greifswald, 1907.

A. NÉHER, *Œuvres complètes*.

I. NÉMIROWSKI, *David Golder*.

P. NIZAN, *La Conspiration*.

J. Oesterreicher, *Beiträge zur Geschichte der Jüdisch-französischen Sprache und Literatur*, Czernowitz, 1896.

Pascal, *Pensées*, éd. par Léon Brunschvicg, Hachette, 1925.

G. Paris, *La Poésie du moyen âge, II*, Paris, 1903.

— *La parabole des trois anneaux*, R. E. J., XI, 1885.

Ch. Péguy, *Notre jeunesse*, Cahiers de la Quinzaine, cah. 12, Paris, 1910.

H. Pflaum, *Der alleg. Streit zwischen Synagoge und Kirche in der europ. Dichtung des Mittelalters*, Arch. rom., 1934.

— *Scènes des Juifs dans la litt. dramatique*, R. E. J., t. 89.

S. van Praag, *Marcel Proust*, R. J. G., mai, juin, juillet, 1937.

M. Proust, *A la recherche du temps perdu*.

Hommage à Marcel Proust, N. R. F., janvier 1923 (articles de Maurice Barrès, Léon Daudet, André Gide, Edmond Jaloux, André Maurois, Thibaudet, Valéry).

L.-P. Quint, *Marcel Proust, sa vie et son œuvre*, Paris, 1925.

Racine, *Esther*.

— *Athalie*.

J. Reinach, *Histoire de l'Affaire Dreyfus*, Paris, 1901-1908.

E. Renan, *Discours et Conférences*, Paris, 1887.

E. Renan-A. Neubauer, *Les Rabbins français du XIVe siècle*.

— *Les écrivains juifs français au XIVe siècle*, dans : *Histoire littérature de la France*, par les Bénédictins, t. XXVII, XXX.

A.-A. Roback, *Jewish Influence in modern Thought*, Cambridge (Massachusetts), 1929.

Romain Rolland, *Œuvres*.

C. Roth, *The jewish contribution to civilization*, Londres, 1938.

— *L'ascendance juive de Montaigne*, R. C. C., 30, XII, 1937.

J.-J. Rousseau, *Le contrat social*.

— *Emile*.

Saint-Exupéry, *Lettre à un otage*.

Saint-Simon, *Du système industriel*, Paris, 1820-21.

— *Nouveau Christianisme*, Paris, 1832.

L. Savitzky, *Gustave Kahn*, Mercure de France, sept., 1925.

Jean-Paul Sartre, *Les chemins de la Liberté*.

— *Réflexions sur la question juive*.

— *Les séquestrés d'Altona*.

P.-M. Schuhl, *L'œuvre poétique d'André Spire* (Cahiers de l'A.I.U., sept.-oct. 1959).

A. Schwarz-Bart, *Le Dernier des Justes*.

Ch. Sénéchal, *Les grands courants de la littérature française contemporaine*, Paris, 1934.

A. Sleumer, *Die Dramen Victor Hugos*, Berlin, 1911.

A. Spire, *Poèmes Juifs.*

— *Quelques Juifs et demi-Juifs.*

J. Schapira, *Edouard Drumont und seine Quellen*, thèse, Heidelberg, 1927.

E.-H. Schildener, *Jüdische Bestrebungen im Spiegel französischer Literatur der Gegenwart*, thèse, Bonn, 1935.

M. Sperber, *... Qu'une larme dans l'océan* (préface d'André Malraux).

M. Steinschneider, *Hebräische Übersetzungen des Mittelalters*, Berlin, 1893.

F. Strowski, *La jeunesse de Montaigne*, R. C. C., 30. III, 1938.

Jean de la Taille, *Saül furieux.*

J. et J. Tharaud, *L'Ombre de la Croix.*

— *Un Royaume de Dieu.*

— *L'An prochain à Jérusalem.*

— *Quand Israël n'est plus Roi.*

M. Vaublanc, *La France au temps des croisades*, Paris, 1834.

Vercors, *La Marche à l'Etoile.*

J. Vianey, *La Bible dans la poésie française depuis Marot*, dans R. C. C., 1922-23.

F. Vigouroux, *Les livres saints et la critique rationaliste*, Paris, 1890.

Voltaire, *Œuvres.*

O. Warschauer, *Zur Entwicklungsgeschichte des Sozialismus*, Berlin, 1909.

G. Weill, *Les Juifs et le Saint-Simonisme*, in R. E. J., t. XXXI.

I. Zangwill, *Chad Gadya*, dans « Les Rêveurs du Ghetto ».

Emile Zola, *Œuvres.*

PÉRIODIQUES

Revue des Etudes juives, Paris. (R. E. J.)

Revue des Cours et Conférences, Paris. (R. C. C.)

Revue juive de Genève. (R. J. G.)

Encyclopaedia Judaica.

Etudes de Lettres, Lausanne.

Evidences, Paris.

L'Arche, Paris.

Index